Sword of the Spirit

And take the helmet of salvation,
and the sword of the Spirit,
which is the word of God

EPHESIANS 6:17

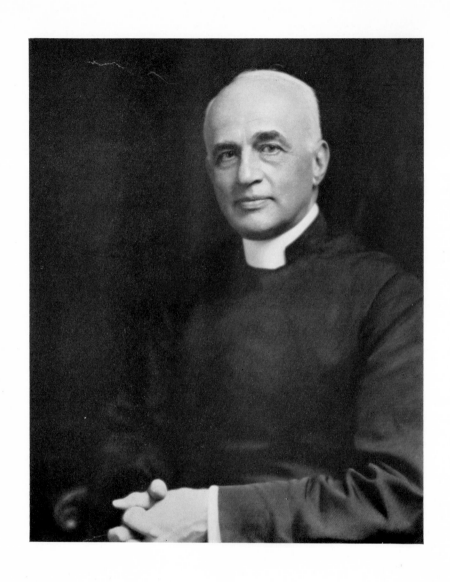

Samuel Tuxler

SWORD of the SPIRIT

A Biography of Samuel Trexler

By Edmund Devol

New York · DODD, MEAD & COMPANY · 1954

92
T7292

Copyright 1954
By The United Lutheran Synod
of New York and New England

All rights reserved

LIBRARY OF CONGRESS CATALOG CARD NUMBER: 54-7087

PRINTED IN THE UNITED STATES OF AMERICA
BY VAIL-BALLOU PRESS, INC., BINGHAMTON, N. Y.

To
believers
and to those
who want to believe
this book is dedicated

AUTHOR'S NOTE

Not without reason have I written this book. I was compelled so to do not only by the dictates of my own heart but by the persuasion of a great number of men and women who knew and loved Samuel Trexler.

I knew him well. I was his friend and comrade for fifty years. In a sense I shared his hopes and dreams, his disappointments and defeats, his struggles and achievements. Thus it was inevitable that I should assume the responsibility for writing his life story. This responsibility was emphasized by the fact that I became heir to his vast library of letters, manuscripts and sermons, as well as his diaries, in which he kept a day to day account of his activities from 1896 to 1949—a true record of all that had transpired.

Samuel Trexler's life was an open book. The pageantry of the years was before me. Yet, when I put my hand to the task of writing his biography I found it exceedingly difficult. The life of a man remarkable for Christian grace and humility, steadfastness of faith and serenity of spirit is not easy to delineate. The beauty of holiness is elusive, hard to grasp.

It is my hope that those who read *Sword of the Spirit* will find in this book inspiration and courage, a sense of the power and of the peace that faith confers.

PROLOGUE

THIS IS the story of a man who believed in God. Fortune smiled on him. Fame followed him. But he sought neither fame nor fortune. A faithful servant of the Church he loved, he devoted his life to the fulfillment of his ministry, reposing his trust in the God of his fathers, confident in all things in His goodness and grace.

He was a man of the simplest virtues, serene and steadfast of faith, genuinely humble, loving and speaking the truth as he perceived it. Through his exceptional ability to impart to others a measure of his own glorious faith and hope, Samuel Trexler met a deep need of the human heart.

High honors deservedly came to him for his able and far-sighted leadership as president of the United Lutheran Synod of New York and New England. Eminence did not change him. He remained kind, loving and selfless to the end.

The golden years of his happy, purposeful life were crowded, colorful, eventful. The world was his home. His friends were legion. Among them were many of the outstanding church leaders and statesmen of his time as well as men and women prominent in the world of arts and letters.

In the sunset of his years he founded the Samuel Trexler Fellowship through which young men in the ministry could have opportunities for advanced study and for travel which would not otherwise be at their command. His life, girded by the sword of the Spirit, transcended death.

Samuel Trexler will be remembered for the significant contribution he made to the Lutheran Church in America and to the advancement of Lutheran world unity. Above all he will be remembered for his goodness. Once, of course, this man was a little boy . . .

CONTENTS

Sword of the Spirit

THE HILLS OF HOME

But as for me and my house,
we will serve the Lord

JOSHUA 24:15

THE MOST vivid recollection of his boyhood was a song. He was sitting between his father's knees on a small box in a shining black buggy behind a willing mare. The man and the boy were traveling along a winding road between green fields under a bright blue sky. The sun was rising in glory, and his father was singing a song, *Hallelujah Schöner Morgen!* It was a song of salutation to the beautiful morning, a hymn of welcome to a new day. The boy delighted in the fields of rippling grain, the silvery streams, the rising sun and the exultant song.

Sometimes his father drove to Rehrersburg, again to Millersburg. In these and other villages in the Pennsylvania hills were Lutheran congregations to which the Reverend Daniel Dietrich Trexler ministered as pastor and spiritual mentor. In making the pastoral rounds with his father Samuel Trexler gained early insight into some of the hardships as well as the joys of a country preacher. Many miles they drove together, and on the anvil of

· 1 ·

the days an enduring comradeship was forged between the man and the boy who was to follow him in the ministry.

The Trexler homestead was in Bernville, a little village in Berks County, Pennsylvania, about twelve miles across the hills from Reading. The substantial old brick house, framed by flowers, full of light and life, and widely known for its warm-hearted Christian hospitality was a focal point for visiting pastors and missionaries from near and far. It was a house that welcomed guests and the stranger within the gates, and like all houses that are *lived* in, it bore the stamp of those whose lives it sheltered. To encounter its indwelling spirit of serenity and peace was a marvelous experience. In this home of simple refinements, mutual consideration and lofty purpose, Samuel Trexler was born, October 19, 1877, and in surroundings at once beautiful and austere, he spent his boyhood.

His ancestry was deeply rooted in Berks County, his fore-fathers having come to this country from Würtemberg in the Palatinate in the first decade of the eighteenth century. In the *Minutes and Proceedings of the First Reunion of the Trexler Family* (attended by some five hundred members) in Kutz-town, Pennsylvania, 1907) it is recorded that a Peter Trexler came to America some time prior to 1720, settling in Berks County and removing shortly thereafter to Upper Macungie township in Lehigh County. It is to this emigré ancestor, "the first white settler in the Macungies," that Samuel Trexler's line of descent is traced.

From the standpoint of heritage it is interesting to note certain characteristics of the Trexler family as presented in these *Minutes and Proceedings* because they were strongly evident in Samuel's own personality. "The Trexler family (it is stated) is an industrious family. At the rising of the sun they are up and at their work. It is a very ambitious family and their ambition urges them to be the head of anything they may undertake. The family is a very musical one and has a great veneration for the old church hymns and the songs of long ago. The Trexlers always were and are to this day fond of horses and also good horsemen. They are a law-abiding and patriotic people, very fond of their own, their native land, loving 'its rocks and rills, its woods and templed hills' and fighting nobly in their country's cause . . ."

For generations the sons and daughters of this family, whether engaged in industry, farming, government, law, medicine, teaching or preaching, have contributed importantly to the life of the communities in which they lived. One branch of the family was notable in industrial enterprise and philanthropic minded, as exemplified by General Harry Clay Trexler of Allentown, Pennsylvania. Another branch brought forth sons intent upon making a spiritual contribution to their generation, and these dedicated their lives to the Church.

Samuel's father, Daniel Dietrich Trexler, was born in Greenwich township, Berks County in 1842. As a lad he worked on his parents' farm during the summer, attending nearby public schools in wintertime. At seventeen he was confirmed in Grimsville and so deep was the impression made upon him by the catechetical lectures and the confirmation vow that from that day his goal was clear. He determined to enter the ministry so that he himself might instruct and confirm catechumens. And although it was not easily come by, as he had little money and few to advise him, he succeeded in reaching his goal.

Freeland Seminary at Collegeville, Pennsylvania was the first stepping stone and in 1868, at the age of twenty-six, he was graduated from the Lutheran Theological Seminary in Philadelphia and was ordained in the ministry. A month later he was called to the pastorate of the Lutheran congregation at Rehrersburg. Included in his charge as time passed were Bernville (Northkill), Little Tulpehocken, North Heidelberg, Shartlesville and Lenhartsville. When he died at seventy-two, Daniel Trexler had become one of the best known Lutheran ministers in eastern Pennsylvania, having served his congregations, scattered over a wide area, for forty-six years. Hundreds of parishioners "held him almost as a father," and many traveled "great distances to hear him preach." Both the example of his life and the eloquence of his sermons made a deep impression on his people and he was lamented as one loved as well as respected.

Agnes Amanda Geiss, whose family had also for generations been identified with Berks County, was nineteen when Daniel Trexler made her his bride. Ten years younger than he, she was among the first catechumens whom he confirmed during his early ministry in Bernville. Their marriage was a happy one. She was a sweet and modest young woman who brought to her handsome young husband loving devotion and a gaiety of spirit that offset the seriousness of his nature. She was to be his one love and an understanding companion to the end of his days. Gentle and sensitive, she endeared herself to everyone she met. It was not in Mrs. Trexler to say an unkind word.

Three sons were born to her of whom Samuel, christened Samuel Geiss after his maternal grandfather, was the second. His elder brother was named Martin Luther and his younger brother, Charles Daniel. Though her heart and hands were full rearing three boys and managing a busy household, Mrs. Trexler accompanied her husband to services of worship and to many weddings, baptisms and funerals as well. Her life, too, made a lasting impression upon the parishioners and the Church she loved and served for sixty years.

Idleness was unknown in the Trexler household. Father and mother rose with the sun and sometimes before. The pastor's days were filled with preaching, teaching, solemnizing weddings, baptizing children, comforting the sick, burying the dead and tending his acres. His wife devoted her energies, which seemed inexhaustible, to the maintenance of an immaculate home and to the well-being of her loved ones. Not, however, to the exclusion of Sunday School picnics, church dinners, strawberry festivals and quilting bees where her cheerful laughter and sparkling spirits enlivened the gatherings for young and old.

She was a great hand for visiting and loved to entertain and in the midst of all the comings and goings she remained serene, unruffled. The family board was memorable for its home-cured hams, home-made sausage, home-baked bread, succulent young turkeys, fat roosters, garden-fresh vegetables, apples, peaches and pears from the sunny orchards. There was peace and plenty at this hospitable table and grace was said at meals. How Samuel and I looked forward to holidays in Bernville! "Mother is preparing the feast of the turkey . . . Mother is boiling apple-butter . . . Mother is baking the Christmas cookies . . ." he would write me. "She hopes you can come . . ."

The home was bound together by strong ties of love, trust and common purpose. Father and mother devoted themselves to the upbringing of their children, striving constantly to make possible for them a larger, more abundant life than they themselves had known. Day in, day out, these parents patiently taught their sons love and respect for the word of God, trained them in cogent moral and religious truths, guided and helped them to greatness. It was a happy home in which the family Bible and the Sabbath were sacred adornments. The beauty and holiness of the Sabbath were woven into the web of childhood experience. Samuel once told me that he could not remember when he did not love God.

Evenings were spent by the family together, the head of the house pondering his sermons or his farm accounts, the mother busy with her sewing and her thoughts, the boys studying or reading. Samuel early enjoyed the comradeship of books, for books there were in plenty and magazines too—*The Lutheran, Harper's,* and *Harper's Round Table, The Atlantic Monthly,* the *Ladies Home Journal,* the *Review of Reviews.* The boys grew up in an intellectually stimulating atmosphere, enlivened by the eloquent company and learned discussions of innumerable Lutheran preachers. "At home I assisted in entertaining," Samuel recorded in 1898, "and had the pleasure of speaking with all the ministers. I felt very honored to be in the presence of such a galaxy of notables."

Problems there were of course, and the inevitable differences between older and younger generations. But there were no cruel rocks beneath the surface, no bitterness and estrangement; parental authority was as unquestioned as parental love. It was not difficult for me to understand why this home, with its intensity of family feeling and integrated family life was dear to Samuel. Nor is it surprising that in later years when he found an hour's release from the multiplicity of tasks that had fallen upon him he went home and that he reiterated with conviction that the regeneration of the world would be brought about by the influence of Christian homes—each family a fellowship of believers.

As the boys grew older they had their appointed tasks in the stable, the fields, the garden and the home. There were horses to tend, harnesses to grease, mud-encased buggies to wash. There was hay to cut, corn to husk, harvests to store. There were seeds to plant, potatoes to dig, beans to pick, rows to weed and hoe.

Yet their childhood was by no means all work and no play. They tramped the hills, explored the forests, fished the streams and swam in the creeks in the way of boys. They visited relatives and friends, galloped over the hills on their father's horses, attended country fairs and carnivals and went calling on the girls.

Their father, however, saw to it that his sons shirked no responsibilities. He impressed upon them the "sacredness of time," the necessity for "improving each passing moment—not knowing what a day might bring forth." He taught them that life is a trust and that they were in this world for a purpose —to serve God and humanity. He admonished them that their lives must be useful. "I seek nothing but the glory of God, your happiness and your *usefulness*," he wrote Samuel when he was a student at the theological seminary in Philadelphia. "Continue to prepare your sermons well; watch and pray that you enter not into temptation and you may then expect the blessings of God." "Watch and pray . . . Learn to labor and to wait!" These were household words, never to be forgotten.

He taught his sons the virtue of thrift—to regard money neither as an end in itself nor as a means toward the gratification of personal desires. "Never spend it wilfully," he admonished them when he sent money for expenses at school. When Samuel was earning fifty dollars a month as a young mission pastor his father counseled him:

"Try to put by something for a rainy day. Mama and I worked and saved when we were young and now if it pleases us to do so we would neither have to work nor save. Mama can live in our same house in the same manner when I die as she does when I live. She would not be in the position of some of our widows who have to sew all day long to support themselves or work in a factory or clean other people's houses . . ."

Nor did his father's lessons in thrift go unheeded. In the back of his diaries Samuel kept carefully itemized accounts of receipts and disbursements. During his young years these were reckoned largely in pennies: haircut 15 cents, shoes soled 20 cents, carfare and church 26 cents, Emerson's Essays 12 cents, laundry 24 cents, board (3 meals) 38 cents, dictionary 90 cents, three shirt studs 10 cents, India Missions 35 cents, Plutarch's Lives (3 volumes) 85 cents, Orphans' Home 50 cents. In later years he accounted no less carefully for dollars earned and spent.

When weighing alternatives on the eve of graduation from the seminary, Samuel sought his father's advice. "When all is said," the Reverend Mr. Trexler wrote, "you have as much money as you *need* and can let the merits of the situation determine your decision—just remember that money and happiness are not synonymous."

The family livelihood depended more upon farming than it did upon preaching. Both depended upon the grace of God. When the elements were favorable the acres yielded their harvests and the congregations convened to listen to the word of God. But there were seasons when the crops failed and impassable roads led to empty churches. Small wonder that there was scarcely a letter from Daniel Trexler that did not refer to prevailing winds and weather.

"The oldest citizen does not remember such cold . . . ten degrees below zero and falling . . . I was overturned in my sleigh yesterday crossing the snow-covered fields . . . We had such a hailstorm in the past half hour as I have never seen the like of in Bernville—the stones flew against the windowpanes as large as hickory nuts and cracked like pistols . . . It rains and the wind is never weary—the roads are full of water, mostly frozen over, and the mud deep below. A howling wind has been blowing down trees, even houses—the left cupola of the church was blown away."

The congregations to which Daniel Trexler ministered were not rich in worldly goods and the salvation of souls was not counted in gold coin. Income from his labors in the Lord's vineyard never exceeded five hundred dollars a year. With three sons to educate he was compelled to look to his acres to provide the wherewithal. His acres—and his horses. A skilled trainer, his pure-bred horses were famous throughout the county. The boys shared his fondness for horses. When he had a mishap, Samuel never blamed the horse. Horses knew what they were about, he said, while the same compliment could not always be paid to their riders.

Letters from his father who had great pride in his grain fields and grass lands seldom failed to mention crops during the growing season: "The grain and grass fields look well and no better field of grass from here to Reading than mine . . . Our grain looks as well as any in this vicinity, if not considerably better

. . . I have three acres of grass in the water field and no better to be found in this section—the clover is two inches above my knees . . ."

Nearly a century ago Daniel Trexler was practicing crop rotation and soil conservation. He called it by a different name. He spoke of observing "the Sabbath of the land": *Six years thou shalt sow thy land and shalt gather the increase thereof, but the seventh year thou shalt let it rest and lie fallow.* News of the livestock market, grain and produce prices, yields per acre, troubles with tenant farmers, the love he had for the land, the anxiety and care the land exacted—all his problems, satisfactions and disappointments are set forth in letters to Samuel.

"This morning I arose at four and went out on the farm. The hay is made, the wheat is being reaped, our potatoes are in splendid condition—free of grass and bugs. We have two hundred and twenty bushels and potatoes are bringing fifty cents a bushel in Reading. The late corn is good and the Baldwin apples are excellent. We have much work on hand with butchering— yesterday we killed a steer which weighed when dressed 691 pounds. Sausages are next . . ."

There were times, however, when responsibilities outweighed his satisfaction in farming. In 1898 he wrote: "Oh how glad I am that I have no more farms! I went out on one of my farms today. My tenant farmer was making the second crop of hay. He was edgy. If I had said one word against him he would have cracked like a match—the roof leaks, the wheat crop is poor, the straw has given out, etc., etc. I am only too glad I have not yet more land to worry about. The farms are sometimes quite a problem what with my services, lectures and other duties. I have more duties sometimes than I desire to have. Work makes life sweet, but too much of it is tiresome . . ."

And a few weeks later: "This afternoon our tenant farmer came in great excitement reporting that our farm was being visited by ghosts which called on the horses, the cows and the family, treating them badly. He was very much agitated. I finally succeeded in calming him somewhat . . . and persuading him to go home."

The silent hills did not ensure the serenity of the human beings they encircled. Daniel Trexler contended with treachery, murder, suicide and many lesser evils and iniquities including poverty, ignorance and superstition. Regarding these things he wrote sadly from time to time:

"I suppose you saw in the papers that a family by the name of ―― committed a double suicide on one and the same rope . . . The family had six children, the oldest eleven, the youngest three months . . . The children found the parents hanging in the attic . . ."

"Last Sunday John ―― went out to the field and did not return. When his sister sought him she found that he had blown out his brains with a shotgun. Of what good was the inheritance he had from rich parents . . . ! Why do such men not have the common sense to watch and pray in time . . ."

"When I was told Sunday morning that Henry ―― had committed suicide by hanging himself in his barn it shocked me so severely that I could hardly gather my thoughts . . . I am almost certain that I had not my thoughts from the terrible deed for half a minute during the services . . ."

"On New Year's day huckster ―― went to Reading with a load of goods. He was ill when he left. His wife tried to persuade him to stay at home but he said he had to go. He went, and Wednesday died at the home of his concubine—as Scripture has it. The language of today would be different . . ."

Within the boundaries of his parishes he was confronted by the hopes and fears, the aspirations and despair, the bitterness and strife of men the world over. Against the forces that undermine and debase he waged unremitting war, and there is little doubt that the impact of his ministry was felt to the betterment of many souls in Berks County. There was dauntless courage in Daniel Trexler's strong, bearded face.

When injustice and wrongdoing was brought to his attention he made no sacrifice to uneasy compromises, and there were those who disliked, even feared him. Close to reality, he was direct and plain spoken and he could be brusque. "People do not like to be told disagreeable facts," he said dryly when informed that his censure had stung. But to widows and orphans, to all who were weak and helpless, he was the soul of kindness and a tower of strength.

An eloquent and fiery preacher, he strove to "give satisfaction" in his sermons. A man of giant frame and stern countenance he was an impressive figure in the pulpit. All his sermons were committed to memory (he never read a sermon) and delivered with passionate conviction. "The report in the *Reading Eagle*" (in which his colorful discourses so frequently appeared in print), Martin wrote Samuel in 1896 "is that the Reverend Daniel D. Trexler held his audience spellbound. I hope his eloquence will be a heritage to his sons."

Samuel's father was equal to the heavy burdens he carried and to the hardships of a ministry that demanded fortitude as well as faith. In blistering heat and freezing cold he traveled the hazardous mountain roads by buggy and sleigh, lodging where he could, many times uncertain of reaching his destination.

"On Saturday night (he wrote Samuel in the winter of 1899) snow fell. This morning even the Blue Mountain was white. The roads are difficult to travel by foot or wagon. Still, the Gospel must be preached . . . I am only afraid that I shall not be able to reach Lenhartsville by nightfall as it is impossible to make any distance because of the drifted snow—and still falling. But I will try . . ."

The close family ties were not broken when the three boys left home for college. "The Parents" (as letters were often signed) wrote weekly in reply to letters expected and received from their sons. Samuel, whose sense of filial duty was lively and lasting, carried on a voluminous correspondence with his father and mother. He was an indefatigable letter-writer, nor could he bring himself to destroy a single letter from home. His father's letters are instructive and entertaining. Would that I could share them all with you. Thus he wrote:

Bernville
August 8, 1899

Dear Son:

We received your letter on Friday as we desired. It gave me a good illustration for my Sunday sermon when I preached on the many reasons why men and women should go to church. Among other reasons, I said that we should go to church to hear about Christ our Saviour. I remarked how anxious we are for news from our sons, as are all parents, and how even more eager we should be to hear of our Saviour . . .

· 13 ·

I left here on Saturday morning, stopped under the shade trees and studied my sermon, ate my dinner on the way as I drove along and arrived in Lenhartsville a little before one . . . We had quite a respectable audience. Almost everyone congratulated me on my sermon, some as a matter of course, others sincerely.

After services I went to Sister Mary Anne whose seven sons I found at home, all engaged to teach school next winter at some place or other. In all I traveled the greater part of a hundred miles—had no expenses and no income, but enjoyed the journey from beginning to end.

Yours etc.

D. D. Trexler

Bernville
January 18, 1900

Dear Son:

We received your letter and were glad to read that you are getting along as well as you think you are. We take it for granted that you are getting along as well as you report.

Things have moved along in the even tenor of the way since you left home. On Monday I started for the County Home where I was to visit one of my members. The steward received me kindly, had my horse unhitched and fed, took me to his office and there got the whiskey out to treat me. I refused politely. He urged me but I was as immovable as the everlasting hills. Whether his estimation grew I do not know, but I myself prefer the reputation that I refused. You know how much is sometimes made of little. I always rejoice that I have never been confronted by reports of conduct not befitting a Christian minister. The worst that could be said, as you know, is that I took a little rooster away from a chicken hawk and gave it to a poor family.

Your Father

And as the years sped swiftly by:

Bernville
September 20, 1911

Dear Son:

We received your letter and read it with pleasure. We can say with David: "Lord we have loved the habitation of thine house and the place where thine honor dwelleth." It is therefore your letters are so welcome to us. . . .

If your letters contained news of some sort in which your team was victorious or news of your election to some high political office, we would not welcome them so much. But when they bring news of God's kingdom in which you are taking an active part, they are welcome indeed. You need not trouble to write us about anything other than news about your church and the part you are taking therein.

We also received a letter from Charles Daniel this morning. He expressed a good opinion of your work and was pleased with your sermon. He said that you spoke favorably of his congregation. Well, it pleases your parents very much that you think and speak well of each other. You are the sons of more prayers and more heart's desire than almost any other sons can be.

The Parents

Bernville
December 12, 1912

Dear Son:

The sun shines nicely in my face as I write. Tomorrow is a sacred day to me. It is then forty-one years ago that mama and I were married. It seems but a short time ago. Still when we think of the many things that have happened in these years, we realize that it was long, long ago, especially when we realize that we have sons who have built churches and established congregations and who themselves are growing old in the service of the Lord. While I did not have the opportunities open to me that you and Charles Daniel have, I nevertheless would not change places with any of my 60 cousins. The principal reason I am satisfied with my accomplishments is that both my sons seem to be accomplishing good work and I hope and pray you may continue to prosper. I cannot see how you could enjoy any work more than the work you are doing.

The Parents

In only one respect did Samuel disappoint his father. He never married. More than once his father with growing concern urged him to take a wife. Samuel was thirty-four when his father wrote:

Bernville
October 19, 1911

Dear Son:

On this day of your birth, sacred to you and to us, I say again to you that before another birthday passes you find yourself a wife. Select a fine, respectable Christian lady, marry her, and have children while you are yet young.

As Martin Luther has observed "earth has nothing more tender than a pious woman's heart." The world has next to God's word no greater treasure than a God-fearing, home-loving wife with whom you can live in peace and to whom you can entrust all your possessions, even your life. It is not good that man should live alone, and I do not appreciate your arguments to the contrary. Now you know what your parents wish you to do. Let that be enough of the subject.

Your Father

In Daniel Trexler's countenance there was nothing unfulfilled. In sowing and reaping, in his wife and sons, in making full proof of his ministry he had given and found himself. Samuel climbed to heights his father never dreamed of. But it was his father who taught Samuel to walk before he could run, lifted him over stone walls before he could climb.

His mother did not relax her vigilance for the welfare of her sons' souls when they were no longer under the parental roof. Letters, hastily penned, crowded with details of her busy days, are full of tender concern for their health, contentment and spiritual well-being. They were not intended for publication— these letters from a mother to loved sons. But I am sure she would forgive my disclosing these few lines to Samuel, so revealing of her solicitude:

Bernville
October 10, 1913

Dear Son,

We saw in *The Lutheran* that your work as Students' Pastor is bearing fruit for which we are thankful. We always thought that our Samuel was a good boy, but did not realize how high up the ladder he would climb—and higher yet you may climb. Be careful that you do not fall. Just remember the old saying: "Fly only with the birds willing to fly with you." You always speak of having such happy times. I hope it will continue so to the end. Good health and contentment is my prayer for you.

Mother

Bernville
May 2, 1926

Dear Son,

I know your heart is in your work, but one should have some time for himself so that he may *think*. Too much crowded life cannot give satisfaction . . . As for sleeping in the rooms prepared for President Hoover, just remember that you too have the title "President," with many people under your care though of course not as many as President Hoover . . . It must be a delight to preach to such large audiences. In this respect you are greatly privileged. Take care or you will overdo again.

Your Mother

Dear Son,

We received your letter and could not but feel happy because you felt so happy when you wrote it. You seem to be happy all the time. What a blessing! The service one can render—that is what makes life worth while. You are so fortunate in many respects, especially in the good you can do and the help you can give . . . I am glad you are visiting churches in your Synod that have never before been visited. Well done . . . After tomorrow you will feel released for a time from your obligations to Synod and so just be a good boy and then you can come home and we can rest together . . . May God's blessing rest on your labors is the prayer of

Your Mother

Letters. Letters reminding Samuel that he was remembered and loved. Letters that recalled faces and places and experiences of a happy childhood. Letters that kept the memory of home vital as the flame on the hearth, bright as the sun on the doorstep, sweet as the lilacs at the gate.

It was to his mother that Samuel confided his inmost thoughts, "all the things that happened since I waved you good-by." His devotion to her was beautiful to see, and in her lifetime he brought her no grief. She alone had access to the sanctuary of his heart. In many respects he was his mother's son. He had her gentleness of manner and voice, her kindly disposition, her radiant smile, her felicity; and his life was marked by the same intense activity that was dominant in her being.

These two were constantly pleading with each to "go slower," neither heeding the other's advice. "I am afraid you are again undertaking too much and will again overdo . . . Hold back a little . . . You must go slower . . ." she urged. And she was in her eighties when Samuel wrote her resignedly: "It is too much for you to undertake, Mother, but it is useless for me to say more. When you determine to do things you do them as you please. How I wish you had cultivated the habit in your youth of going more slowly . . ."

By nature self-effacing and unassuming, she nevertheless had a will of her own. Her stalwart husband and sturdy sons were no match for her in a contest of wills. "I wanted by all means to get extra help for your Mother's housecleaning," his father wrote Samuel in the spring of 1912, "but she refused and went at it with all her might from four in the morning till nine at night. I am astonished that she can endure it. I could not endure such effort even half a day . . ."

The passing years did not change the familiar loved pattern of Samuel's days at home. As long as his parents lived he remained a child at heart in his father's house, doing the same things in the same way, with the same eagerness and willingness he had as a boy. Deep was the love he had for his father and mother and for all the beauty and serenity that surrounded him in childhood—the pageantry of sunsets, the flowers of the fields, the flight of swallows, the nearness of the stars, trees laden with snow . . .

It was never moonlight to Samuel. It was *brilliant* moonlight. Never a sunset, always a *radiant* sunset. Never a rose, always an *exquisite* rose. Not a bird singing, but a bird singing *gloriously*. Seventy years did not dim for him the brightness of morning heralded by song. He never lost the sense of miracle and mystery, the humility and expectancy of the child in the hills of home.

CHAPTER TWO

SUN AND SHADOW

Now then we are ambassadors
for Christ

2 CORINTHIANS 5:20

AMONG SAMUEL TREXLER's manuscripts filed long ago, I came across a faded photograph of the Class of 1896, Muhlenberg College, Allentown, Pennsylvania. Twenty-five young men, all serious of mien, returned my meditative gaze. None more serious than Samuel, whose earnest young face is a study in solemnity.

Higher education was not taken for granted in those days. Nor taken lightly either. Muhlenberg College, founded in 1867 and named in honor of Henry Melchior Muhlenberg, the first pastor sent from Germany to labor among the Lutherans of Pennsylvania, demanded high moral and spiritual standards as well as proficiency in scholarship.

Youngest member of the class, Samuel had qualified for entrance at fourteen, and his diaries for the next four years indicate that he was well aware of the importance as well as the opportunities and responsibilities of a college education. "My entry into a larger life came when I enrolled at Muhlenberg College," he recorded when bidding farewell to its classic halls.

Among those under whose watchful eyes he was disciplined and trained and to whom he acknowledged a debt of gratitude were President Theodore L. Seip "who in all his comings and goings was a Christian gentleman," the Reverend Doctors Davis Garber, Matthias H. Richards, William Wackernagle, George F. Spieker and Stephen A. Repass, pastor of the College Church. "It is a testimony to the personalities with whom I came in contact at Muhlenberg College," he later wrote, "that the freedom I enjoyed at the age of fourteen was not abused."

The academic curriculum made heavy inroads on time and energy but it is apparent that Samuel did not spend all his time in the library. He was an active member of numerous social and literary organizations including the Phi Gamma Delta fraternity, the Missionary Society, the Franklin Literary Association and the Euterpean Society. The goal of the latter is thus described: True to her motto *Watch and Advance,* her work is to discipline the powers of the mind and soul of each of her members so that they may be able to engage manfully in life's stern conflict.

The records show also that Samuel was a member of the Press Association at Muhlenberg, assistant editor of the Ciarla—the college year book, and a member of the Banjo, Mandolin and Guitar Club. He went in wholeheartedly for sports and athletics too, describing with enthusiasm the pleasures of swimming, baseball, bicycling, lawn tennis, sleighing and ice skating. "The ice was rough but it was exhilarating skimming along in the cold air and I enjoyed it immensely . . . The sleighing was excellent and we spent a truly enjoyable afternoon." A ringleader in serenading professors at unwelcome hours, notations like the following are not infrequent in the diaries of those years.

At eleven-thirty P.M. our string quartet went out serenading. At first it went quite well but toward the last the cold benumbed our fingers so much that we sounded far from sweet—it certainly did not increase our popularity with the faculty.

At eleven P.M. a goodly number of the boys banded together to serenade Dr. Fry (Jacob Fry) on his sixty-fourth birthday. Sang about six songs until finally the Doctor appeared and made an appropriate address.

Campus "demonstrations" held special appeal and the Spanish American War provided extenuating circumstances for students to engage in them. The bonfire in March 1896 is typical of many a campus conflagration.

In the evening we formed a plot to burn Captain Weyler of the Spanish forces in effigy. Collecting a large pile of boxes on the campus and making a Spanish flag and an image of Weyler we burned them at ten-thirty with great ceremony, speech-making, parades and yelling . . .

Samuel loved a parade, delighted in spectacles, pageantry, festivals and fireworks, and not less at sixty than when he was sixteen. These things were part of his love of life . . . his interest in people. There was never enough time for him to do everything he wanted to do, to see all the things he wanted to see, to go everywhere he wanted to go, to read all the books he wanted to read.

At Muhlenberg the days were filled with Latin and Greek, theology and astronomy, calculus and the classics, recitations and examinations. His diaries show that he kept a strict accounting of time from the hour he arose, early, to the time he retired, late, but he was not always satisfied that he had invested time profitably:

Read and studied the entire afternoon although not as profitably as I should have done—I resolved hereafter not to idle away so much of my time at college.

So far this day was put to very little account—but such waste makes one more resolute not to allow a repetition.

The foundations of his greatness were evident in these early years. A sense of purpose, of a mission in life that called for the development and full use of his talents was apparent in his anxiety to make the most of his education, his eagerness to excel in his studies. Samuel Trexler wanted to make his life count and this, his father had charged him, called for exacting preparation. He consistently aimed high. A proficient scholar, he had little difficulty in making good marks. But he was not satisfied with good marks. "Not pleased with my classwork this day . . . Not up to standard in recitations today . . . Did not do myself credit in Hebrew . . ." So runs the thread of self appraisal through his diaries. Less than perfect in recitations or less than a hundred percent in examinations was not to Samuel's liking.

Defeated once in a Bernville spelling bee (to his dismay by a young lady) he never forgot the word which was his undoing. What the word was I cannot now remember (vignette?) although Samuel mentioned it many times, and for many years afterward. He was an excellent speller, and as I am probably the worst speller that ever graduated from medical college his proficiency stood me in good stead. "How many p's in 'apartment'?"

I would call out, interrupting him in the midst of paper work. Or, "How do you spell redundancy?" "Try it," Samuel would reply, without much hope.

He was a prodigious reader. Wherever he went he had a book in his hand. Spare moments at college, between matins and lectures, vespers and supper, time spent on trains and in waiting rooms at railway stations (especially in waiting rooms at railway stations) Samuel devoted to reading. It would never have occurred to him to visit a city without visiting its libraries. He probably held membership cards in more libraries than any man in the States.

The books he read were almost invariably geared to his studies and work. He seldom read purely for entertainment and he often read for hours at a stretch. "Became so enamored of it (Schaff's *Apostolic Church*) that I read continuously from six to twelve . . . Spent the entire afternoon and evening reading *Germany —Its Universities, Theology and Religion* . . . Read *Richard Carvel* without interruption from one to seven-thirty—so much was I enjoying it . . ."

In the back of his diaries are listed books read each year. When Samuel was a student these numbered between fifty and sixty. What books did he read? Selected at random from those listed in 1899 are: *Lectures on Preaching* by Phillips Brooks, *Gospel for a World of Sin* by Van Dyke, *The Young Preacher* by Cuyler, Carlyle's *French Revolution, Addresses* by Henry Drummond, Boswell's *Johnson*, Kipling's *Jungle Books*, Van Dyke's *Sermons to Young Men*, Kent's *History of the Hebrew People*, *What a Young Boy Ought to Know, Conflict of Christianity and Heathenism, Biography of a Grizzly, Animal Symbolism in Ecclesiastical Architecture*, Asa May's *Natural Science and*

Religion, The Workers by Wyckoff, *David Harum, The Little Minister, Essays in Literary Interpretation,* Elbert Hubbard's *Little Journeys to the Homes of Great Men and Good,* Ford's *The Manysided Franklin* and Fairbairn's *Christ in Modern Theology.*

Men collect a variety of treasures—trophies of the hunt, rods and reels, stamps, coins, Rembrandts. One man I know collects armour. Samuel collected books. Many of his volumes are rare; many out of print. Some of the books in his library (presented in accord with his desire to the Lutheran Theological Seminary of Mt. Airy) were handed down to him by his parents and grandparents who had them from their parents. The one he cherished most was Arndt's *Wahres Christenthum.* This volume was published in 1862. Five inches thick and ornamented with heavy brass clasps it bears the name of his maternal grandfather, *Samuel Geiss* in gold on its carved leather binding. The treatise was a gift to young Samuel from his grandmother on his twenty-first birthday.

It was impossible for him to pass a bookstore without going in, and once in, it was difficult to get him out. I never knew anyone who so much enjoyed browsing in bookstores. During his student years he frequently lacked the funds to indulge his desire for books. In his senior year at Muhlenberg College he ordered Scribner's *New Bible Dictionary.* Costing $24, he arranged to pay for it in installments. Through error the bill was sent to Bernville where it was opened by his father, who wrote Samuel a letter of reprimand, pointing out that he was "paying more than the true worth of the book" warning him that installment buying was "both unwise and uneconomic" and admonishing him to "shun such unsound practice in the future." Dutiful son though he was, Samuel continued to acquire coveted books by this "unwise and uneconomic" procedure. He could not resist the temptation books held out.

Many the hour he spent dusting and arranging the volumes that tiered his walls. Not that Hattie or Susie, who kept our house neat as a pin, could not be entrusted with this task. Samuel just *liked* doing it. Many of his books he read many times. "It is like revisiting an old friend," he said. "There is always new delight, new inspiration, in rereading a good book." I do not know how many times he read Alexander V. G. Allen's *Life of Phillips Brooks*. It was almost always on his desk or night table. It has been said that no man can study the life of another whom he reveres and admires without being influenced by it. If this be true, among those who influenced Samuel Trexler's life, a prominent place must be given to this great preacher whose *Life* and *Letters* were a never failing source of inspiration to him.

Like most young people, Samuel clipped newspaper and magazine articles of interest to him. Neatly filed in envelopes were cherished fragments of prose and poetry and columns of newsprint—faded, falling to pieces, time-stained the color of raw umber.

It did not astonish me to discover that he had saved many articles relating to time. Young people today could well afford to ponder them. For example:

The right use of time is one of the serious problems of life and one on which many other problems depend for solution . . . Our use of time means of course our use of life . . . So the young person is wise who carefully apportions his time among life's duties—resolutely adhering to the purpose to be systematic in his use of time . . .

In the gift of time are comprehended all other gifts . . . Our life is not measured by the number of our years, but by our use of them. A full life is one which best fills the hours and years with noble living . . . he who freights each moment with worthy deeds and thoughts attains truest success . . .

How revealing of his inmost spirit are the words a man treasures in youth, I thought, reading these homilies that had appealed to Samuel more than half a century ago. In one envelope were articles pertaining to hymns, recalling to my mind how emotionally stirred Samuel always had been by the great hymns of praise and thanksgiving. In another were paeans to the beauties of nature. Words of joy and praise like these:

And purple ironweed of matchless hue and goldenrod that seems each year to be brighter than before and scarlet lobelia, the torch that lights the footsteps of departing summer, a retrospective bloom, not like April violets, a prophetic flower . . .

I thought of the many times Samuel Trexler had called my attention to the miracle of spring and the glory of the heavens— the wheeling stars, the floating brightness of the moon, a dark cloud rimmed with blazing gold. I remembered his pleasure in the first flowers of spring . . . how he delighted in fireflies flashing their lanterns in the misty valleys of June . . . how he loved all seasons—the whole beautiful, mysterious world around him.

In another envelope I found sermons preached by outstanding men of his day, among them Dwight L. Moody, Doctors Howard Duffield, Henry Eyster Jacobs, Charles H. Parkhurst . . . and in still others editorials from *The Philadelphia Ledger and Daily Transcript*. Earnest and lofty in text and tone, they include discourses on truth and tact, industry and thrift, discipline, temperance, forgiveness, honesty, charity, happiness, freedom, self-sacrifice and other subjects related to principles of human conduct, moral, social and religious standards.

As I weighed in my mind the content of these old clippings —the sermons and the editorials, the poems and the anthems seemed to compose themselves into a design. In this design I clearly perceived the motifs, the bright strands, the high purpose which Samuel had woven into his life and ministry. The traits of mind indigenous to his character, the qualities of spirit that made his ministry unique were manifest in his youthful years. In returning the brittle fragments to their frail wrappings I withheld one. It was my wish to share with you the confidence and trust in God the message conveys.

"Your external circumstances may change, toil take the place of rest, sickness of health; trials may thicken within and without. Externally you are the prey of such circumstances; but if your heart is stayed on God no changes or chances can touch it, and all that may befall you will but draw you closer to Him. Whatever the present moment may bring, your knowledge that it is His will, and that your future heavenly life will be influenced by it, will make all not only tolerable but welcome to you, while no vicissitudes can affect you greatly, knowing that He who holds you in His powerful hand cannot change, but abideth forever."—Jean Nicholas Grou

Few men have so serene a faith. Samuel Trexler was one of these. . . .

Samuel and his brother Martin were close companions. Martin was a gentle, cheerful boy, thoughtful, considerate of others and looking forward with joy to entering the ministry. Like Samuel, he loved books. But even more than books he loved flowers. It was Martin who taught Samuel how to trim the honeysuckle and the roses, how to tend the lilies of the valley and the peonies, how to cut back the dahlias in their mother's garden. He it was who knew where the trailing arbutus bloomed under the lingering snow.

Unhappily illness had interrupted Martin's studies in the theological seminary at Mt. Airy and he had been compelled, despite pleadings, to return home. The brothers kept in touch with each other by letter. On the eve of his graduation from Muhlenberg College Samuel wrote:

Allentown, Pa.
May 6, 1896

Dear Brother Martin,

The whole class arrived in New York at 9 A.M. We immediately went to the Central Park Museum and examined the fossils which were interesting—nit. After taking in the Metropolitan Art Galleries— also in the Park—we went downtown and procured seats in the upper gallery of Abbey's Theatre to see Irving and Terry in Macbeth. Excellent performance. By five o'clock we were out and went downtown to register at the Hotel Continental, Broadway at 20th Street. Rates $1.00 a day.

After supper my friend Hotty (Marcus Stephen Hottenstein) and I went to the Eden Musee, observing your precaution to speak to nobody for fear of taking the living for the statues, or vice versa. The great Electrical Exposition next claimed our attention. Imagine our excitement at hearing the Niagara roar over Long Distance Telephone!

Sunday morning Hotty and I arose at 5:30 and walked up Fifth Avenue, viewing the palatial residences in which their millionaire occupants dream of Eldorados—I saw the homes of the Goulds, the Vanderbilts, Russell Sage and many others. (Little did Samuel dream that he would one day be an honored guest in these same palatial residences.)

We attended Low Mass at St. Patrick's Cathedral, of which Corrigan is Archbishop, and at 9 A.M. we took a boat up the lordly Hudson. The scenery and points of interest were splendid. We visited West Point and Newburgh where we saw Washington's headquarters and numerous Revolutionary relics. The next morning we visited Staten Island, saw the Statue of Liberty, Castle Garden, the Battery, the Stock Exchange, and the whole southern part of the city . . .

We next went to Trinity Church and stood at Alexander Hamilton's grave—also visited St. Thomas' Church and the Park where we saw the famous baby hippopotamus. Thus ended Gotham.

Arrived back at school at 7 P.M. tired but elated by the idea that we had seen New York. The whole trip cost me about $10.

Yours dearly,

Samuel

Commencement Day concluded four years of hard work and happy camaraderie. "Delivered my second Honor Latin Salutatory to my satisfaction," Samuel wrote in his diary, "and gave farewell to Muhlenberg." During the flurry of final examinations, professors' farewell teas and receptions, student parties and picnics—all the sadness and gladness of college leave-taking—Samuel from day to day noted in his diary: "Worked on the preparation of my sermons."

When honors were announced Samuel sent a postcard to Martin on which is revealed more than percentages:

Allentown 6 P.M.
Wednesday, May 20, 1896

Dear Brother:

The standing is as follows:

Hottenstein	—98.23
Trexler	—98.19
Cooper	—97.98

Yours in disappointment

Samuel

Nevertheless sermon-writing continued: "Worked at my sermons . . . Tried to work at my sermons . . . Worked at arranging one of papa's sermons which I was to preach in case he should need me which he thought he might . . ." For he was in receipt of a letter from his father:

Bernville
June 2, 1896

Dear Son:

If you have a sermon prepared by the time you come home you shall have a chance to deliver it. You shall have all the chances in my power to prove yourself . . . I have an idea that you will enjoy your vacation more by doing something rather than just being idle.

I might make an appointment at Rehrersburg for morning and evening services the first Sunday you are home. The second Sunday you could fill my place at Lenhartsville, preaching in the evening at Hamburg. These arrangements would of course make no money for you, but would give you employment and more enjoyment than idleness. Think about these things . . .

Yours etc.,

D. D. Trexler

The sun was hot; the days long. Samuel and Martin, sometimes taking one horse and sometimes hitching up the team, made the rounds of grandparents, aunts, uncles, cousins and friends. They drove to the Overlook for apples, to the Waterfield for peaches, to Moses Reber for cucumbers. They gathered cherries ("ate a great many"), delivered surplus cats to Jared Miller ("received pears, cake and wine in return for cats"), helped with the haymaking ("the yield was very abundant"). Samuel ran errands, cleaned the stables, groomed the horses, mowed the lawn, dug weeds, and "assisted mama about the house." Between times he read the New Testament in Greek and rehearsed his sermons in the apple orchard.

With his father he drove to Rehrersburg:

July 5, 1896

With papa went to Rehrersburg where I preached my first sermon —Matthew 6:24—*No man can serve two masters* . . . Considering the weather which was very uncertain I had a nice audience. I succeeded very nicely.

With his mother he drove to Shartlesville:

July 26, 1896

Mama and I went to Shartlesville where I preached for papa who had a funeral at Millersburg. The church was full and I was well pleased with my effort.

With his brother Martin he conducted services of worship in Strausstown, Millersburg, Hamburg, Shumakersville, Lenhartsville and other villages, Martin reading the service and Samuel preaching, both in English and German:

August 16, 1896

Started away at 5:30 A.M. for Lenhartsville. Had a very pleasant drive in the clear morning light. Arrived there at 9:30 where we found a large congregation. Preached more to my own satisfaction than ever before. Collection $3.06. Enjoyed the whole excursion immensely as also did Martin. Enjoyed the preaching as well as the excellent entertainment we received.

Everywhere the congregations received the young men kindly. Driving leisurely home from the little churches, the brothers paused to feed the horse, to gather wild strawberries, to listen to a songbird, to watch the setting sun paint the blue sky rose and gold and deep purple. The fabric of the days was interwoven with innocence and peace—the faithful discharge of duties, the pursuit of simple pleasures, knowledge of love and security, serenity of soul, nearness to God. They knew fields of golden grain, drowsy lanes fringed with wild flax, ponds in which yellow water lilies grew, and a home where welcome awaited them. In recalling these days and this way of life, the heart is saddened by the knowledge of irreparable loss.

How quickly the days sped by! Summer was a golden chalice brimming with sparkling hours. Little by little the cup was drained. Soon it was September and then October and November . . . His father wrote Samuel:

Bernville,
November 6, 1896

Dear Son,

You will want to know how Martin is getting along. I cannot say that he has improved since you left for the seminary, nor would I say that he has lost ground. But he must do a great deal better before he can return to the seminary to study. Whether his new medicine will live up to our hopes time alone will show. I hardly think you need wait expectations of rooming with him this year before Christmas, and maybe never.

Your Father

In the spring of 1897 the two boys went to Washington where they were the guests of their cousin, Mr. Charles C. Wagner (who served as aide to Presidents William Howard Taft and Woodrow Wilson and later as chief of Presidential correspondence at the White House). Samuel and Martin left no stone unturned in an intensive and extensive sightseeing tour of the capital. For Samuel, no experience was entirely unrewarding, no disappointment without compensation:

Then we passed up G Street to the White House where we expected to see the President, but he was not receiving that day. However, we rested for some time in the beautiful East Room with its magnificent yellow furnishings . . .

After a two hour wait, so great were the crowds, succeeded in squeezing into an elevator which took us to the top of Washington Monument. The view was very much obscured by the heavy fogs. Nevertheless it was a satisfaction to have been up 500 feet . . .

Returning from the new Corcoran Art Building which is grand in all its proportions, we stood in line in the rain for at least one and a half hours in hope of being received by the President, but in vain. However we saw Secretary of War Alger . . .

The climax of their excursion to Washington was the Inauguration Day parade:

March 4, 1897

Contrary to all precedent Inauguration Day turned in very pleasantly though somewhat windy. At 10 A.M. Charles Wagner, Martin and I went up on the roof of the building adjoining the Southern Railway Company from where we saw the Escort of the President to the Capitol. The parade was 30 minutes long and very colorful. A mounted Band and the Cleveland Militia on black horses were a special feature. Saw President Cleveland and President-elect McKinley in their carriages.

Resumed our places at one P.M. and watched the large and cosmopolitan crowd congregating in the streets and stands. Not until three o'clock when McKinley and Cleveland returned with their escorts did the great parade begin. The sight was really grand—grand uniforms, grand maneuvers, grand men. The Ohioans were beautifully uniformed. The parade moved continuously and had passed at 5:30 when we returned to Monument lot to where Pain of New York discharged a brilliant pyrotechnic display. A flag attached to a balloon was the feature. The city was illuminated very brilliantly. Searchlights swept the skies . . .

In July ground was broken for a new Lutheran church in Bernville. Scarcely a day the young Trexlers did not appear on the scene of activity, observing the progress, assisting in the staking out and excavating. "The congregation which is building this church is one of the oldest in America," wrote the *Philadelphia Public Ledger* when the cornerstone was laid, "its history replete with some of the most stirring events of provincial Pennsylvania. Reverend John Casper Stover, an early pioneer preacher of the Lutheran denomination organized it in 1730. The records show that in 1747 the Reverend Henry Melchior Muhlenberg administered communion in this church when members worshiped in a log building near the site of the cornerstone laid today, a structure which often served as a place of refuge for the early inhabitants during their encounters with the Indians in the Blue Mountain region. In the graveyard adjoining lie some of the first settlers of Berks County . . ."

During the summer the brothers again conducted services of worship, Samuel receiving his first press notice. "Samuel Trexler, a theological student at Mount Airy occupied the pulpit on Sunday morning at the Lutheran church," reported the *Reading Eagle*. "He is a forcible speaker. A large congregation was present which greatly appreciated the sermon. His brother Martin assisted in the service." The happy weeks sped by. But there was a lengthening shadow across their sunlit path.

Returning to his room at the seminary one evening in November, Samuel was startled to find his father there. "Father informed me that he had thought best to bring Martin to the German Hospital (Lankenau) for examination," his diary relates. Leaving Martin comfortable and cheerful the Reverend Trexler returned to Bernville. The following afternoon when

Samuel arrived at the hospital he was informed that his brother was critically ill and sinking rapidly. In his diary he recorded the hours and days that followed.

November 7, 1897

I telegraphed home that papa and mama should come immediately. Then came trying moments for me. Was I to tell Martin of his serious condition or not? Would I do wrong to tell him that the end was near? He had been rallying until this afternoon and was hopeful. Should I crush his hopes? Yet I wanted him to die at peace with his God . . .

Not knowing when papa might come, I asked Pastor Goedel to give Martin spiritual ministration. After the pastor left, I read Martin suitable Scripture passages and psalms and prayers which he desired. He seemed resigned to his fate and content and was peaceful as to his soul. He had nothing to trouble him—but he wished that papa and mama would come . . .

I tried to console him. At seven he wished me to place some flowers that were standing behind him where he might see them. After that he became irrational. The nurse and the doctor came in frequently but only to tell me that the end was near.

It was a trying time for me to be all alone at Martin's dying bed. He grew weaker and weaker. His breath became more and more labored and at 10:58 P.M. after a few gasps, his soul went back to its Maker.

November 8, 1897

At 7:30 the long wait for papa ended. He had not received my message until late the evening before. He came prepared for the result. He made preparations for the funeral, Doctors Fry and Spieker to deliver the addresses. I returned to the seminary while papa accompanied the body home. After packing together a few belongings

I went to Philadelphia. I bought a black cutaway suit at Wana-
maker's with the twenty-dollar goldpiece I received from mama at
Commencement in '96. Arrived home at 7. Everybody was very much
broken up.

November 12, 1897

Arose at 6 A.M. Helped around the house wherever I could be used
until 8:30 when I changed my attire. The house was all torn up by
the cooks and waiters when yet quite early. Soon after 9 the people
began to pour in and when 10:15 came the house was crowded with
people.

Martin's remains rested in a broadcloth-covered casket with silver
plates on the lid giving the name and age of the deceased. Martin
was dressed in his own suit. He looked very peaceful. Rev. J. J.
Cressman offered prayer and delivered a short address at the house
in German, after which the funeral procession went up to the cemetery.

At the house, the Sunday School, of which Martin was Acting Superintendent and Bible Class teacher, sang "I would not live always."
The singing was beautiful and sweet all through the service. At the
grave where for the last time did I behold that dear form here on
earth, Rev. Cressman pronounced the "dust to dust and ashes to
ashes," and the Sunday School sang "Asleep in Jesus."

Returning to the church Rev. A. J. Long read the Scripture lessons
in German after which Rev. Z. H. Spieker preached in German, holding forth the glorious hope of resurrection. Dr. Jacob Fry preached
in English, opening with a brilliant eulogy for Martin. Every body was
very much taken with Dr. Fry's address. The Sunday School sang
"I heard the Voice of Jesus say."

Dr. F. J. F. Shantz then delivered an animated address in German
after which Dr. Mahlon C. Horine delivered a substantial talk on
the Providence of God and its comfort. Rev. C. J. Cooper closed with

testimony from Allentown and Muhlenberg College which was of the most eulogistic. The Sunday School sang "Nearer my God to Thee." Biography was delivered by Rev. Cressman, prayer by L. D. Stambaugh, and the benediction by Rev. T. C. Leinbach. The Sunday School sang "O Paradise, O Paradise," one of Martin's favorite hymns.

Thus ended Martin's Funeral Services, which could he himself have been there, would certainly have pleased him greatly. Everybody could not but speak good of him.

Sorrowing hands placed a sheaf of wheat on the grave, banked the mounded earth with roses, chrysanthemums and smilax, and soon snow fell. "The flowers had faded," Samuel wrote when he visited the grave at Christmastime, "but the sheaf of wheat remained—emblem of how though the body may die, the fruit of toil remains."

The following summer Samuel's father arranged for him to visit New England and Northfield, Massachusetts. "Papa decided I was to attend the Conference at Northfield and provided me with a purse of $50," his diary states. "Very pretty spot," he records. "Arrived by stagecoach and at 7:30 the great Moody spoke in the auditorium. Enthusiasm great and spirituality also. Influence of place very wholesome. Addresses effective and inciting to better life. The singing is inspiring— beyond all I have yet heard."

Samuel was in his element in Northfield, plunging into a series of lectures, seminars and classroom work as strenuous as the schedule at the seminary. It was a "vacation" pleasing both to father and son, from early morning devotions to late conferences on "Life Work." When the ten-day conference drew to a close Samuel noted that he was "rather tired." "At four Mr.

Moody called a meeting of those wishing to receive the Holy Spirit. It was a very impressive service at which he asked us to kill sin and receive the Holy Spirit. At the Platform Meeting in the evening the speakers impressed on us the Christian life. Robert Speer, the young missionary, spoke on his recent trip around the world. Was rather tired with so hard a week's work—though very beneficial."

Leaving Northfield "thankful for the inspiration given" he proceeded to tour nearby New England—Concord, Plymouth, Newport, Cambridge, Charlestown, Boston . . . Churches, universities, libraries, museums, bookstores, historic and literary shrines beckoned. He visited many and in the evenings in Boston sat on the Common "watching the masses of people" and "studying the faces in the crowds."

His twenty-first birthday found him again in New York City, this time a delegate to the Third Annual Convention of the Luther League of America. "Today I attained my majority," he recorded soberly. "I pray that in the grace of God I may acquit myself as a man."

"This past year," he wrote, "has brought much pleasure, and I hope by the help of God much benefit. My trips, especially to New England, and the New York trip where I attained my majority, were events of more than ordinary interest—and all through father's and mother's generosity." With these words of gratitude he closed his diary for 1898.

The first class (eight men) to receive three years' instruction at the Lutheran Theological Seminary at Mount Airy (founded, as had been Muhlenberg College, by the patriarch Muhlenberg) was graduated in 1867. Samuel's father was one of eleven graduates in 1868. His three sons and a grandson all attended the seminary—Martin in the class of 1897, Samuel 1899, Charles Daniel 1906 and Charles Daniel, Jr., 1949.

"There seemed to be a special drive that sought to get me into active life at an early age," Samuel wrote thirty years after his ordination. "With this my father was thoroughly in sympathy and I rather enjoyed the exhilaration. My youthful mind lapped up everything within reach. The opportunities brought by my residence in Philadelphia were eagerly seized. What a richness was spread out before the theological students in the City of Brotherly Love!

"In the pulpits of Philadelphia were strong, consecrated men. At the Second Presbyterian Church in Germantown was the Rev. Dr. Charles Wood, with whom twenty-five years later I was to visit the Holy Land. At St. Mark's Church there was the Rev. Dr. Samuel Laird, who as president of the Ministerium of Pennsylvania, ordained me to the ministry." Dr. Francis Landey Patton, then president of Princeton University, frequently preached in Philadelphia and his sermons were eagerly listened to by the students.

"In the pulpit of Trinity Church in Reading was the Rev. Dr. Jacob Fry with whom I studied homiletics at the seminary. And at the head of the seminary faculty was Dr. Henry Eyster Jacobs, a master in many departments of theology and a constant source of inspiration to his students." With what affection and gratitude Samuel spoke of these men, and others—Doctors Adolf Spaeth, George Frederick Spieker, Joseph A. Seiss . . .

Samuel Trexler worshiped true greatness in men, and far from resenting their criticism, he welcomed it as his diaries of seminary years reveal: "In the morning I delivered a German sermon skeleton to Dr. Spaeth. He criticized it honestly but severely and I was decidedly the gainer by it . . . Also Dr. Jacobs gave me some valuable advice—his criticism was just and constructive—it is a great privilege to have the benefit of his counsel . . . I preached my examination sermon on Mark 5:17 before Dr. Fry. He praised the sermon and the delivery, finding fault only with the rapidity of presentation. He desired me to speak more slowly—in order not to telescope my words— which I shall strive to do."

When there was work to be done from painting a floor to preaching a sermon, Samuel could be counted on as a volunteer. "Offered my services . . . assisted wherever I could be used." His willingness to assume responsibilities did not go unnoted. When he was a student he served as president of the Father Heyer Missionary Society, executive officer of the West Philadelphia Mission Committee, chairman of the Chapel Committee, head of the Boarding Club and president of the Reading Room Association. His qualifications for leadership were early apparent and he was singled out not only for his cheerfulness in shouldering responsibility but for his dependability in meeting obligations.

He enjoyed the practical phase of his training at the seminary—preaching assignments and home mission work—recording his experiences in the field with enthusiasm. For instance:

Went out to canvass for the Sunday School that is to be built on Sixteenth and Susquehanna Avenue. My territory was between York and Morris Streets. I took cards and presented them at each house and at some places I even did some proselytizing in which I met with some success. Enjoyed the work very much—profitable experience . . .

I attended a special meeting of the Missionary Society at which it was decided to start a new Lutheran Mission in East Philadelphia. The next day, immediately after lunch, I went down with eight of the boys to canvass for the mission. My territory was Fifty-second Street, although I overleaped the bounds. My experience was very varied, but pleasant and successful. I was compelled to argue with one lady as to future punishment, but could not convince her.

Traveling from place to place was not easy in those days. Preaching assignments took Samuel to Albany, Elizabeth, Royers Ford, Minersville, Wayne Junction, Rockville Center, Mt. Joy and numerous other cities and towns to which he journeyed by stage, trolley, train, ferry and foot.

On Christmas Day 1898, he was scheduled to preach at Mt. Joy, Pennsylvania. The journey from the seminary, a distance of less than a hundred miles, consumed eight hours. After a restless night at the Red Lion Inn ("the bell snickels were quite loud and noisy and I feared lest my sore throat should not serve me in the morning") he delivered the Christmas message to an audience of thirty-five.

"The day did not seem like Christmas to me, being away from home," he recorded in melancholy mood. "I hardly enjoyed it and was not sorry at returning to school. Rather while meditating did it make me sad to think that I could no longer enjoy Christmas vacation as I used to do."

The winter of 1898–99 was severe, with below freezing temperatures and heavy snowfall. "Snow fell briskly and in good earnest," the diary tells us. "In the evening it began to snow and snowed continuously for at least fifty hours . . . The drifting snow blocked roads and made progress slow . . ."

In February he again journeyed to Mt. Joy and after preaching to an audience of 22 at the morning service and 34 in the evening noted after dinner at Pyle's Boarding House: "Though we had small audiences, the Presbyterian Reverend Conway and the Methodist Reverend Bozorth could only report half as many. Spent the evening reading, conversing and playing the piano." The next morning:

February 13, 1899

Arose at 6:45. Went to the station for the 7:37 train but on account of the severe wind and snowstorm no trains could be run. Waited at the station until noon. Then returned to Pyle's and reconciled myself to the fate of being snowbound. There were no trains the entire day. Read considerable of Hubbard's "Little Journeys to the Homes of Great Men and Good."

February 14, 1899

Arose at 6:30. After breakfast shovelled snow at Pyle's. Went to the station. No trains were running in the a.m.—perhaps after dinner, I was informed. Finished "Little Journeys." Enjoyed it very much. A new light on great men. Spent the afternoon visiting and reading. This blizzard is the worst I ever experienced. Almost three feet of snow fell within eight days.

February 15, 1899

Arose at 7 in order to make the first train to Philadelphia which is the only one the Pennsylvania Railroad promised to get through today. Left Mt. Joy at 8:15. The ride was necessarily slow—with two engines and three cars—we were compelled to stop quite often. The entire country is snowbound—pretty sight. The trees look beautiful all laden with snow. Soon after we left the clouds broke and a very pretty scene presented itself. From beneath the clouds on the horizon the sun shone on the cloud fragments in the zenith—a very impressive manifestation of Nature. I was in one of those contented, happy moods that at times come to one spontaneously and without apparent cause.

A number of congregations to whom Samuel preached approached him regarding his attitude toward a call to serve as their pastor. He had come to no decision when he made the following entry in his diary:

March 10, 1899

Today is notable for a new idea entering my being and taking firm hold. Reverends A. Steimle and H. S. Knabenschuh from Brooklyn called at the seminary and asked me to consider missionary work in Brooklyn. This seemed like the hand of Providence . . . I was very much taken with the idea and later meditation confirmed that I would do more good there and enjoy a greater satisfaction than by taking one of the small congregations in this vicinity.

("Well do I remember," Doctor Henry Eyster Jacobs wrote Samuel twenty-five years later, "the visit of Pastors Steimle and Knabenschuh in behalf of the Brooklyn Missionary Society to our Seminary in 1899 and the pleasure that I took in having the precise man literally in sight when they asked for aid . . .")

His father, apprised by Samuel of the opportunity to consider missionary work in Brooklyn, wrote:

Bernville
April 27, 1899

Dear Son,

I will say that you seem not to be in want of preaching places and I hope finally not in want of a regular call. You are fortunate to have so many opportunities. Very few of my classmates had calls before ordination . . . You used to be afraid that you might not have any call by the time you were ordained. Now it seems that you have so many that it is difficult to decide which to accept.

Of the two you are weighing in your heart and mind, it is true that they have a fine church at the latter and none at the former, and more work at the former than at the latter . . . However, you are a man who likes to put his shoulder to the wheel . . .

Yours etc.

D. D. Trexler

In May Samuel accepted an invitation to visit Brooklyn. After a walk with Pastor Knabenschuh for the purpose of seeing some of Brooklyn's immense Lutheran resources and preaching "in the basement of the pastor's pretty new church just now in building," he made this entry in his diary: "Pastors Steimle and Knabenschuh told me they were very much in favor of me and hoped that I would be called to the Brooklyn mission field."

At historic Trinity Lutheran Church in Reading—the metropolis of his boyhood—the candidates for ordination were examined before the Synod committee. "Papa had come to Reading by this time and appeared in the examining room," the diary notes. "He later told me that Dr. Fry had informed him that I was one of seven of the seniors to receive 'D' as distinguished for my work—also that Dr. Jacobs had praised me highly. So conclude my school days, which go back before my memory well nigh. I hope however that my school days will never end."

On the twenty-ninth of May he was ordained in the ministry.

May 29, 1899

Arose at 6 and left directly for New York and thence to Reading. At 2 P.M. the candidates for ordination were presented to the President of Synod.

At 7:45 our ordination took place. The thunderstorm during the service interfered not at all. The church was crowded to witness the solemn service. We—the 25 candidates—marched in, in procession. The officers of Synod conducted the service. Dr. Harkey preached an excellent sermon on 2 Corinthians 5:20: *Now then we are ambassadors for Christ.* There at the altar we made those solemn vows "with my whole heart" and were set apart by the "laying on of hands." It was the most solemn act of my life and I pray for grace to live up to my vows.

So ended the years of academic preparation. The doors of the seminary closed behind him. New doors opened. Without hesitating, Samuel entered.

CHAPTER THREE

A CHURCH IS PLANTED

But watch thou in all things,
endure afflictions, do the work
of an evangelist, make full proof
of thy ministry

2 TIMOTHY 4:5

THREE DAYS after he was ordained Samuel Trexler received a call from the Brooklyn Missionary Society to serve as city missionary in Brooklyn, New York. He was in Bernville when the letter of call reached him, and immediately prepared to depart for the City of Churches. "I feel the call to be Providential," his diary recounts, "and that I could be satisfied no other place."

Gathering his effects together, he embraced his mother, received his father's blessing, bade farewell to his friends and said good-by to Mary Miller, the girl with whom he walked in the moonlight. "I said good-by to everyone at home—gently," he records. It was a different leavetaking from any he had known before. This time he was entraining to make his way in the world and it was not easy for him to say good-by to the hills of home.

In the early sunshine of a perfect June morning he crossed Brooklyn Bridge, standing on the running board of an open trolley car, a small suitcase in one hand, his guitar in the other. But he had with him more than the belongings he carried in his hands. Not yet twenty-two years of age, he brought with him the hopeful buoyancy of youth and indomitable faith.

In the Greenpoint section which was his destination Samuel did not know a soul. "Until the spring of 1899, Greenpoint was to me an utterly unknown land," he said in retrospect. "I had but a vague impression of Brooklyn and was familiar only with the historic Brooklyn of Beecher, Storrs and Cuyler—a city dominated by New England culture and Puritan tradition. What a contrast to the city of multiplying peoples which was to become my home for a decade!"

At the turn of the century Greenpoint was a sprawling, densely populated community of some 70,000 souls most of whom were workers in her humming factories and roaring shipyards. The verdure which had occasioned New Yorkers, looking across the East River, to name the area *Greenpoint* had long since surrendered to men and machines. The city was in the early 1900's a rapidly growing, polyglot community in which the Lutheran church was represented by large numbers of immigrants from Germany, Sweden, Finland and other European countries.

In this thickly settled industrial area, so different from any community he had known, Samuel was charged with planting a church which would minister to the children of foreign-born parents—in the English language. It was a pioneering job that involved breaking with old-world traditions and conflict with old-world theologians, who held that a service of worship to be valid, must be conducted in the mother tongue. The establishment of English Lutheran churches for English-speaking Lutherans was to meet with resistance, particularly on the part of old guard German Lutherans.

This epoch in the history of American Lutheranism, in which Samuel Trexler was destined to play a signal role, was marked by clash and conflict of wills between the conservatives and the more liberal-minded among the clergy. Samuel was in full accord with those men who recognized the strategic importance of establishing churches in which English-speaking Lutherans would feel at home. From the beginning his ministry was forward looking. He entered upon his tasks in Greenpoint with the zest of youthful hopefulness. Weekly letters from home reassured and encouraged him:

> *Bernville*
> June 20, 1899

Dear Son,

For the first time I address you as *Reverend*. I have addressed many letters to you at Allentown and Mount Airy in your student days there. I intentionally postponed writing you until this evening because I hoped that by now you would be so full of your first days in Brooklyn that you would be unable to refrain from writing fully in reply at your earliest possible moment.

Your second letter has arrived in the meantime. Mama and I both rejoice with you and everyone asks about you—a pastor, now, in a big city. We are so much interested in you and your mission task. Only do your duty faithfully and success will come in the end.

> Your Father

I have often wondered whether the three pastors who counseled Samuel during his early ministry realized how grateful he was for their confidence and advice when the going was rough. In his diaries Samuel again and again noted words of kindness or prudence from the Reverends A. Steimle (Holy Trinity Church), S. G. Weiskotten (Church of the Redeemer) and H. S. Knabenschuh (Christ Church). Perhaps these men discerned the bright promise of his ministry or perceived in the hard-working young pastor the unique gifts of the spirit which the years affirmed. At any rate, they stood by him, and in times when he sorely needed support. So also did the Honorable Charles A. Schieren, treasurer of the Brooklyn Missionary Society and a former mayor of Brooklyn. "There was no man whose counsel and support so helped me during that trying period," Samuel said in looking back to these early days. "My heart never fails to warm at the remembrance of his effort in my behalf." "I hope you will meet with good success in your work," he wrote me a few weeks after my arrival in Greenpoint, "and may the Lord bless you in your work."

In the beginning, the day by day canvass to enlist Lutherans in the projected mission church met with little encouragement or success. But Pastor Steimle, whose pulpit Samuel had supplied for a few weeks wrote him:

Albany, New York
June 15, 1899

My dear Brother Trexler:

My hearty thanks for your services in the pulpit of Holy Trinity during my absence. I hope your future field will yield more abundant results than the first canvass of which you wrote. There are Lutherans in that section, and they must be found! With God's grace, you will find them.

Very faithfully,

A. Steimle

Finding living quarters at a price the young mission pastor could afford proved as difficult as finding "unattached" Lutherans. "Was disappointed to find desirable locations far beyond my ability in price . . ." his diary states. "Left to hunt a room and saw quite a number but the desirability of the locality is shown by the price of the rooms which are far beyond my purse . . ." It was the middle of September when he recorded: "After long hunting found a second-story, front room for two dollars-fifty cents per week at 206 Halsey Street—Mrs. Horton. During the evening I tinkered at various matters—unpacked my books, read the second *Jungle Book* and enjoyed the pleasure of seeing myself settled."

The problem of locating quarters in which to house the projected mission church was even more disheartening. "In the P.M. scoured through my mission district looking for a hall— was not successful . . . In the afternoon took an extended walk looking for a hall—was not successful . . . Resumed my search for a hall and spent a great part of the evening going about in the pouring rain attempting to find one—was unsuccessful . . ."

Months of unrewarding pavement pounding had dimmed Samuel's usually bright outlook when he recorded dejectedly: "Prepared to write a sermon but the mail brought me a letter from Pastor Weiskotten urging me by all means to *find* a hall for services. This seeming the more imperative duty, I put aside the sermon I was working on and spent almost four hours scouring about my district. In the P.M. I again made desperate attempts to find rooms for services—found several places— but how they will suit the Committee, I do not know."

Evidently they did not suit the Committee because two weeks later he noted: "Spent the whole morning on my feet and returned with a rather heavy heart because Pastor Weiskotten told me the authorities were somewhat displeased at my not pushing matters more—which to me is impossible. I despaired so much that I even doubted whether I was really called to this field."

At this point Pastor Knabenschuh, from whose pulpit Samuel for several Sundays had been preaching, informed him of general complaint by his parishioners that he spoke "too indecisively in preaching." Samuel's comment (diary): "This of course made me rather downhearted—yet I hope by the grace of God to overcome it." The following day he engaged a voice teacher, Miss Martha Hicks Dye, an attractive and capable young woman under whose tutelage he found voice culture no burden at all. With this exception—that Martha Dye insisted upon the broad "A."

One Sunday morning (with Miss Dye sitting well up in the front of the church) Samuel found himself confronted by three "A's" in one sentence. "There will be a meeting of the Ladies' Aid Society Wednesday *a*fternoon at h*a*lf p*a*st two." He made the first self-conscious leap safely, and then seeing two more "A's" to be hurdled, refused the jumps. Transposing ha-a-l-f p-a-a-s-t two to a muffled "two thirty," he hastened on with the

Lesson for the Day. Miss Dye looked at him reproachfully. After the service she made no reference to his defection.

(One morning, years later, Samuel and I were in the Louvre absorbed in contemplation of one of Rubens' voluptuous masterpieces. A sweet voice shattered our musings. "Come, come," said the sweet voice, "come along now. It's never been explained." Behind us stood Martha. Again she gave Samuel a reproachful look. She was married then to Mr. William Herbert Appleton and in her London home we spent happy hours recalling the days when she was coaching Samuel in diction and he was paying for his lessons with money earned by tutoring students in German and Latin.)

Not the least of Samuel's woes during his early days in Greenpoint was homesickness. For this he took himself to task.

September 17, 1899

Today is a day of anniversaries and dedications at home and I long to be there. Spent the entire day in my room reading Spaeth's "Life of Charles Porterfield Krauth." Interesting to me both on account of Dr. Krauth's biography and the interesting period of our Lutheran Church which it covers. Showed Dr. Krauth's struggles when in about the same position in which I now am—at the very beginning.

In the evening a sense of the absence of all my old friends came upon me quite forcibly. Saturday evening during the summer was always a period of relaxation but now there is nothing for me to do other than return to my room and work. But it goes without saying that sometime in my life I must break away from the traditions of youth and lay on the duties of a man.

It was about this time that I came to know Samuel. I had seen him on several occasions during the summer months hurrying along the hot streets, intent upon his errands—a slender, preoccupied young man with dark observant eyes and a ready smile for his neighbors. Usually he was wearing a solemn suit of indifferent cut and always he had a book under his arm. Perched on his head was a straw sailor several sizes too small for him. ("Bought at a close-out," was his casual explanation when out of curiosity I remarked its misfit.)

One evening as I was leaving the Bradbury Richardsons' home on Milton Street, Samuel passed by their garden gate. In his book *Crusaders of the Twentieth Century* he describes the circumstance of our meeting:

My life in Greenpoint had not yet run the course of a year and the future progress of Messiah Church still weighed heavily on my mind when late one summer night I went to post a letter to my mother. On the way I met one of my neighbors whom I had often observed, but to whom I had never spoken.

He was a young physician—reputed to be a man of some consequence. There were many stories of his sympathetic willingness to help in cases of distress. He stopped. "Have you seen Mr. Brown?" he inquired. Everyone in the neighborhood knew Mr. Brown almost as well as they knew his master. Mr. Brown was the doctor's dog.

Neither Samuel Trexler nor I dreamed that this chance meeting (or was it by chance?) was the beginning of a friendship which was to endure and deepen for fifty years to come, that henceforth we would be companions on a lifelong journey. But so it was to be.

I myself had been living in Greenpoint only a few months, having previously been House Physician at "Interpines," a sanitarium for mental and nervous diseases in Goshen, New York.

Glancing through the newspaper one morning I noted the avail-
ability of a doctor's practice in Brooklyn, he having been
"drowned in the sea." I had gone immediately to his office at 114
Nassau Avenue where I was informed by his widow that her
husband had had a large practice with many patients coming in
daily—fifty cents at the office, seventy-five cents for outside
calls and ten dollars for confinement cases—including all visits
before and after. Then and there, acting on impulse as always, I
decided to establish my practice in Brooklyn.

The neighborhood was not attractive, nor was my outlook on
Nassau Avenue inspiring. As I recall it, there was a saloon on
one corner and a small grocery store on another flanked by
dreary houses. My facilities for practice consisted of a narrow
railroad flat divided into a waiting room, office and small sleeping cubicle. (Today the flat is a barroom.) At the suggestion of
Dr. and Mrs. Richardson I shortly transferred my residence to
Milton Street where I was happy to discover an attractive house
(once the boyhood home of the Honorable Charles Evans
Hughes) for rent—Number 127.

The rank and file of the twentieth century had not yet in-
vaded Milton Street when Samuel and I were young. Bordered
by pleasant homes set back of lawns and gardens, it still retained the serenity of a vanishing era. The rising industrial tide
lapped but had not yet engulfed this little street. Our outlook
was enhanced by glittering carriages, high-stepping horses, liv-
eried coachmen, gracious ladies in rustling silks. Across from
Number 127 was the mansion of Elihu Dwight Church, graced
by priceless paintings and one of the finest private libraries in
the world. Living on Milton Street at the time, also, were the
Walter Howes, the Noel Clarks, the Robert D. Browns, the Rob-

ert Whittemores, the famous landscape painter Blakelock, the G. H. Gerards, and the Thomas C. Smiths whose vivacious golden-haired granddaughter Isabel, Samuel tutored for a time in German—an undertaking in which he was not notably successful.

Well pleased with my house on Milton Street, I lost no time in persuading my beloved sister Charlotte, then living in the south, to come north and transform the house into a home. She was an exquisite young woman and was with me only a few weeks when Dr. William Artemis Boies, a classmate of mine, won her heart and hand and took her with him to Knoxville, Tennessee. Her blithe spirit, rippling laughter and flower-laden hats had filled the rooms with brightness and gaiety. After her departure I found the house unbearably lonely and dull.

Samuel had moved to 145 Milton Street, where he was well content with board and lodging at six dollars a week. We had developed many interests in common and had become good companions. The thought occurred to me that it would be pleasant if he would share my bachelor quarters. I discussed this with him. He hesitated on the grounds that he would be unable to assume a proper share of the household expenses. But when I had convinced him that he would have better facilities for pastoral work at Number 127 he agreed to my suggestion.

"Dr. Devol invited me to take up residence with him in his house," his diary records. "I demurred owing to my inability to take proper part in the household expenses as a young pastor receiving fifty dollars a month. Pay as much as you choose, was his warmhearted reply. So I accepted the invitation."

Deeply absorbed in our work, eager and ambitious, the days were filled with interest and excitement. As the scope of our work widened and larger quarters were indicated we moved to Number 133 Milton Street. Here for ten happy, hardworking years our home was referred to as the "House of Friendship" where anyone in trouble could count on help.

As I look back upon those years, I marvel how we found the time and energy to do all the things we did. Our telephone rang incessantly, the doorbell tinkled from morning till midnight. The wrought-iron gate swung open to Samuel's parishioners beleaguered by problems, all urgent. Through the same gate came my patients beset by physical infirmities, also urgent.

The house was in a state of constant crisis and confusion. Through it all, Samuel retained his composure. His self-possession amazed me. No matter how trying the circumstances he never lost his temper, never raised his voice. I strove to emulate him, but not with any degree of success.

We soon discovered that in many instances we could be of greater service through combining our skills. Although psychiatrists were not in vogue and the word "psychosomatic" had not yet been coined, we were aware, working together as pastor and physician, of the interpenetration of body and soul. We had not traveled far on the road of knowledge nor did we have the wisdom which the years alone can give. But we strove mightily in behalf of those who came to us with broken hearts or broken bones. We learned many things in those ten years not taught in seminaries or medical colleges. There were times when we were overwhelmed by the paralyzing fears of men, and times when we reflected in wonder at the invincibility of the human heart.

"I frequently tell Greenpointers when I meet them," Samuel wrote our old friend Mrs. Charles Bierschenk long after we had left Brooklyn, "that there I spent the happiest days of my life.

They were hard as you say, but no end of satisfaction and while they now seem golden, when we were in the midst of them there were sufficient tragedies oftentimes to engulf us." He held no brief for the way things used to be.

It is true, they were hard as well as happy years. Especially were they trying from a financial standpoint. At the outset of our careers neither of us earned much money and it was touch and go to make ends meet. Fortunately, our requirements were modest.

One morning while we were gloomily contemplating our bank balances the postman delivered a letter. It was from the gas company. "Bills! Bills!" I remarked impatiently. "I was hoping it might be a check from a delinquent patient!" and threw the letter on the table. There it remained until evening when Samuel opened it. "Did you ever *hear* of anything so delightful!" he exclaimed. "It's a *check*—from the gas company!" "A *check?*" I interjected. "From the *gas* company? What for? How much?" "A dollar and sixty-three cents," Samuel said complacently. "A refund for an overcharge . . ." Absurdly delighted we spent it for balcony seats at the Academy of Music.

Our experiences were many and varied, sometimes startling. There were no dull moments. I shall never forget the first New Year's Eve we spent together. Long afterward a reporter asked Samuel what had been his most disconcerting experience in the ministry. "Well now, let's see," Samuel replied. "I would say the whizzing of a bullet through my hair while I was preaching at a Watch Night service in Greenpoint. In 1900 . . . I think it was." The reporter leaned forward. "A bullet?" "I ended my sermon rather abruptly," Samuel continued in a matter-of-fact tone. "We found the bullet later in a Christmas tree . . . someone welcoming the new century with a loaded gun, was our guess. We also found the hole in a stained glass window through which the bullet had flown." "That I would say," observed the reporter, stuffing his notes into his pocket, "was a hair-raising experience."

Samuel appeared mildly amused. He had long since lost his hair. "Another disconcerting incident of my early ministry," he said, walking to the door with the reporter, "or perhaps chastening is a better word, occurred on a bright Sunday morning. I was standing at the foot of the steps leading up to the church, observing with pleasure the men and women coming to the service. A pert little old lady, leaning on a cane, approached. "Young man," she said, "would you kindly assist me up the steps?" I gave her my arm and when we had made the ascent, she thanked me and then, before entering (I can still hear her silvery voice) asked whether I knew who was preaching that morning. "Yes," I replied smiling. "I am." She looked at me, sighed briefly, and then said in the friendliest way, "Young man, would you kindly assist me *down* the steps?"

The reporter laughed. "Wonderful!" he said. "Did you ever see her again?" Samuel shook his head. "I am sorry to say," he answered, laughing himself, "I never saw her again."

Samuel's harassed explorations in search of a hall in which to hold services finally led him to a vacant grocery store on Kingsland Avenue in a section known to residents as "battle row." This storeroom was procured at a rental of eight dollars per month and here, surrounded by dilapidated houses, he began his ministry. "The neighborhood is very disorderly," he noted with misgivings, "so as to cause worry . . ."

"We rejoice exceedingly that your expectations were realized," his father wrote him when the storeroom had been acquired. "If Mama and I were able to help you in increasing your audience, we would be among the faithful in attendance. If you go at your work with the self-consecration I believe you do and with the active sympathy as well as the cooperation of so many good men, God will bless your labors. Do your duty and God will do His duty by you."

The opening service was scheduled for October first. Samuel obtained an improvised platform placing on it a simple altar. In the store window he displayed a card announcing AN ENGLISH LUTHERAN SERVICE IN THIS BUILDING, SUNDAY, OCTOBER FIRST AT TEN THIRTY AM. EVERYONE IS WELCOME! With youthful temerity he invited a distinguished churchman, the Rev. Dr. W. J. Miller of Rochester who was in the city at the time, to preach at the opening of this new venture in Christian missions. "I have considerable hopes for the service," his diary confides.

Long before the appointed time Samuel was at the "church" prepared to welcome the congregation. "I anxiously wondered whether forty-five chairs would be enough," he wrote in retrospect. "For a month I had been climbing the stairs of neighboring tenements, becoming acquainted with the residents and inviting them to the service. As the time of the service approached and no one turned up, I consoled myself that everyone was late in rising because the entire city had for two days been given over to the reception of Admiral Dewey, just returned from the Philippines.

"The time of the service arrived, and still no one there to participate. A young medical student, J. Daniel Freitag, was at the organ. My guest preacher, Dr. Miller, vested, was ready to begin. Again and again I went to the door, but there was no sign of life save for some goats browsing among tin cans in the vacant lots of Kingsland Avenue. Finally, fifteen minutes late, timidly there came a young woman with her sister and then a mother with her boy and girl . . .

"I announced the hymn and when that diminutive congregation lifted up its voice, the neighborhood which had ignored us before, began to take notice. The sound of singing went out through the open doors and summoned men and boys—curious to know what new thing had come among them. With hope for a congregation risen anew, I went to the door and invited them in. They did not come in, but neither did they disturb the service which consisted of a brief address by Dr. Miller and the lesson and prayers for the day."

"We have at least started," he recorded, with the optimism of youth. But the experience of this first service of worship very clearly indicated that the search for a "suitable place of worship" must be renewed. Revisiting those who had disappointed him and as many new families as time allowed, Samuel obtained permission to use the near-by Universalist chapel the following Sunday morning. The second service, however, showed little advance in numbers attending. Seven were present. "It certainly requires patience," he noted ruefully.

Samuel Trexler was not easily disheartened but that week the cloud of discouragement hung low. "It is not easy to go on," he wrote dispiritedly. Nor was his morale improved by receiving word at this point from the Brooklyn Missionary Society that "after November further salary will depend upon reports of work accomplished."

The third Sunday he again held services in the Universalist chapel recording that "a kindly Providence brought seventeen to the service." He consulted the *Greenpoint Star* and advertised the services. By the end of October, confident that his mission could succeed, he called a meeting of the faithful:

October 30, 1899

In the evening we had quite a gathering of Lutherans in the Universalist Church. Thirty were present. Reverends Weiskotten and Knabenschuh conducted the meeting and after the devotional exercises we proceeded to organize the congregation. The name chosen was "The English Evangelical Lutheran Church of the Messiah." A constitution was adopted and signed by fifteen of those present. Thus it was given to me in my short pastoral work to organize a congregation—which never falls to the lot of some men.

Now that he had brought into being a congregation, it was necessary for him to cradle it. The limited hours available in the Universalist chapel made a new church-home imperative. Another vacant storeroom (this one an abandoned saloon) was rented on Norman and Humboldt Streets. Samuel pitched in with brooms, mops and scrubbing brushes in a heroic effort (not wholly successful) to eradicate the dark stains and heavy odors that identified the dingy quarters with other days and other gatherings. An altar, pulpit and lectern replaced barroom décor. "The whole prospect is extremely bright," he recorded happily after viewing the results of his labors.

November 12, 1899

At 10:45 we had the first service in our new home. It was beautifully decorated with flowers. I was glad to see that my people thought thus. We had an audience of thirty. At 2:30 we had Sunday School with forty children present—very encouraging. At 7:30 the evening service—audience of forty-five. Thus ended my first full day as pastor. Though tired out I enjoyed it thoroughly. All the world seemed bright to me.

Somehow when the struggle is not in vain, the hardships are forgotten. As the weeks passed, reports of work accomplished were well received by the Missionary Society. Membership steadily increased and the Sunday School grew by leaps and bounds. Though working under severe disadvantages Samuel was somehow able to rise above his surroundings. To the north of the church-home were the city dumps, particularly disagreeable in the heat of summer. In the wintertime it was not uncommon for wayfarers, mistaking the church room for the former saloon, to wander in, look uncertainly about, settle down beside the warm barrel stove and snore their way through the service. "We became so accustomed to this experience," Samuel records, "that it did not disturb us."

It was soon necessary to rent the floor above the church room to accommodate the expanding religious and social activities of the congregation and not long before the congregation overflowed these larger quarters. When a Norwegian Lutheran church in the vicinity kindly invited him to use the basement of their building for services, Samuel accepted gratefully. "Unfortunately it is necessary to hold services at the same time as those of the Norwegian congregation," he noted a few weeks later, "and despite every effort at neighborliness the strong Norwegian chorales oftentimes drown out my effort to preach to our congregation below . . ."

It was now that the Honorable Charles A. Schieren took a hand in the affairs of the young congregation. As treasurer of the

Brooklyn Missionary Society, he had his hand in many matters of public welfare in the borough, and the young mission pastor's winning fight against heavy odds had not gone unnoted by him.

Mr. Schieren had come to this country from Germany at the age of twelve. It had been his ambition to become a pastor but his parents had lacked the means to enable him to study for the ministry. It is possible that he enjoyed in some measure, through Samuel, a vicarious realization of his own youthful ambitions. At any rate he became and remained one of his staunchest supporters.

In the heart of the community which the Church of the Messiah was to serve there was an area of six acres called Winthrop Park. On the Russell Street side of this park there were some vacant lots. Mr. Schieren suggested to Samuel that he "look into these lots" as a possible site for a permanent church home. Overjoyed, Samuel lost no time in doing so and there was great rejoicing when Mr. Schieren made a substantial contribution toward purchase of the property. "It was a great day for us and a proud moment for me" Samuel recorded.

It became apparent immediately, however, that funds for a house of worship would have to be obtained outside the congregation. Samuel found that only one of his members was in a position to pledge as much as twenty-five dollars and as it turned out this pledge was never redeemed. There was but one thing to do—solicit financial support outside the membership and there was but one person to do it—Samuel. That it was extremely difficult for a young mission pastor to interest men of affairs in a struggling mission church he soon discovered.

In those days it was not customary to telephone for appointments. It was necessary therefore for Samuel to go to the houses or offices of the men he wished to see, hoping to find them in, hoping against hope that if he did find them in, they would be willing to see him. Many men he visited eight, ten, a dozen times. To convince industrial leaders that the Church of the Messiah was and would be an asset to them and to the community proved much more difficult than he had anticipated. His most eloquent arguments met with refusals, rebuffs, even, I am sorry to say, insults.

Many were indifferent. Some were skeptical, others contemptuous. Even those more kindly disposed regarded the venture at best as visionary. Samuel held his peace. He knew that he *must* convince business and industrial leaders of the significance of the projected church if the proposed house of worship was to be taken from the architect's drawing board to the vacant lots opposite Winthrop Park. And convince them he did. But it was a long uphill fight as his diary of those days reveals:

Continued calls on moneyed men of town but found them very tenacious of their money. I was disappointed in not seeing a more generous response. In the afternoon I met with some success in soliciting money from the brewers. In the evening again went to Brooklyn, but met with no success. Felt indisposed and spent a miserable night . . .

Left here early in the morning and solicited subscriptions in New York. Was rebuffed by Cornelius Bliss. In the P.M. went to New York again, but did not see my people. In the evening visited some people in Brooklyn for money—no direct results. Was very tired after my exertions.

In the afternoon went to New York, but after running about the whole P.M. could not find the people I sought. After dinner went to see Mr. J. A. Geissenhainer. Overheard him saying to the servant who announced me, "Such persistence! The man doesn't know when he isn't wanted!" Came home, thought and planned . . . ("This shows what persistence will accomplish," he noted in his diary several months later, when Mr. Geissenhainer finally made a contribution to the building fund.)

Made many calls. All pled adversity. Saw Mr. Pope on Bushwick Avenue, but was told to come to his office. In the afternoon covered parts of New York in quest of money—no direct results. Left for Timothy Woodruff's home to solicit his aid. Ran after him for some time, but could not in the end find him. In the evening went to Williamsburg to see ex-Mayor Wurster. Had a direct but polite refusal. Made further financial calls but was unsuccessful. Consulted Dr. Laidlaw about my heavy cold. He exhorted me to be careful of my constitution as I had 50 years of usefulness before me . . .

Went to New York quite early to see various parties. Saw them, but they were not prepared just then to help. Went uptown to see Andrew Carnegie but to no avail. Had brutish treatment from his secretary. In the afternoon, made further bootless calls and unsuccessful attempts at procuring money. Went to Columbia University to see Seth Low—too busy. In the evening saw a number of parties financially—could obtain no satisfaction. I was glad when the day's work was at an end. Felt very tired from yesterday's incessant running . . .

Solicited for the building fund in New York and Brooklyn. It seems that I cannot at all get into the ways of money any more. In the afternoon did more running about. At the first place—Wohlers—I received a sound berating. Spent the entire afternoon in making calls —beat the record by making forty. Finally ended at Pastor Steimle's where I always receive consolation. Came home thoroughly worn out —stayed awake for some time.

Day after day, week after week, month after month of "incessant running," of coming home "thoroughly worn out." Usually he went directly to bed, too weary for conversation. Once in a while he would relate some incident in the day's work that had pleased or amused him. One of the men he had been calling upon hopefully was a sugar magnate. "As you know, Mr. — sometimes proffers a five-dollar bill," he said one evening, with a wry smile. "Well, today he was about to hand me a bill when he noticed that it was not one, but two bills stuck together. He was quite flustered, but finally succeeded in separating them."

People often remarked that "money came easily to Dr. Trexler." So it did—after he had achieved success. But it was not always so. The men who came to his aid in the early days of his ministry when his sole working capital was a capacity for hard work, persistence and a pleasing personality did not know how enormously their dollars loomed in the light of his hopes and dreams.

One by one as the years went by, he enlisted the business leaders, the public-spirited citizens, the heads of industrial concerns of Brooklyn—The Hecla Iron Works, the Standard Oil Company, Continental Iron Works, American Manufacturing Company, Eberhard Faber Pencil Company, and many others. "As long as you stand by the work in Greenpoint, Pastor Trexler, I shall stand by you," Mr. Frederic Pratt of Pratt Institute assured him. Men like Elihu Dwight Church, Seth Low, Nils Poulson, president of Hecla Iron Works, Thomas Fitch Rowland, builder of the Monitor, and his nephews, George and Samuel Tibbals became not only his loyal supporters but his devoted friends. As they gained insight into the work he was doing and some understanding of what the Church of the Messiah could mean as a force for good in the community, business and industrial leaders began to see things in a different light. Long before the beautiful Gothic church graced Russell Street, Samuel had impressed upon the minds and hearts of these men the message of its lighted cross.

But how many young pastors would have continued the struggle in the face of the discouragement and difficulties Samuel Trexler encountered? I do not believe it ever occurred to him to concede defeat. The tenacity and endurance he displayed were amazing. In addition to raising money there were all the details relating to the life of a congregation, the cares and responsibilities of everyday life—consoling the sick, encouraging the despondent and the lonely, untangling problems, attending meetings of the Ladies Aid, the Luther League, the Brotherhood, the Confirmation class, the Sunday School Institute, the YMCA, teaching and preaching. Many times distractedly working on sermons the message of the text eluded him. "Worked on my sermon but was unable to concentrate properly . . . Worked on my sermon but got nowhere. Attempted to write a sermon for Sunday but could not seem to organize my thoughts," the diary reiterates. Emotionally tired and physically exhausted, Samuel did the thing at hand and kept going, despite troubles within and vexations outside the fold.

He had been elated when a committee met with him "to transfer a large number of German Reformed" to the Church of the Messiah. The factional dispute that resulted became so bitter that it threatened to founder the flock. All Samuel's efforts to restore the peace were fruitless. "I do not know what new trouble our renegade members may be prospecting," he sighed on the way to a meeting of the church council. "It certainly does try one's faith."

After eight months of friction, he was forced to the reluctant conclusion that the quarrel could not be resolved peaceably. He requested the unruly minority to resign. To his dismay they refused. "The matter is very unfortunate for me, being my first attempt in life," he wrote sadly, "and very discouraging—except for the words of Pastors Steimle and Weiskotten who sympathized with me and commended me for my stand."

In the end the Brooklyn Missionary Society was compelled to resort to legal measures. The newcomers were suspended and expelled. "Thus ended a very unpleasant matter," his diary states. "The prospects now are that we may proceed in peace—trusting in Providence."

No sooner was this trouble resolved than a new problem presented itself. Samuel was accused by the Reverend F. W. Oswald, pastor of St. John's (German) Lutheran Church on Milton Street, of having solicited funds—without authorization so to do —from members and former members of St. John's Church; further, of having received a former member of St. John's Church without said member having obtained his proper letter of dismissal. "My German colleague, Pastor Oswald, is up in arms against me," wrote Samuel. "He is very much opposed to our efforts and today told me that he would prefer charges against me before Synod."

Aware of the embarrassment this would cause the whole English Lutheran movement in Brooklyn, Samuel was greatly disturbed. How to meet this unforeseen arraignment? "I am in a strait," he noted in his diary. "There is no denying it—the affair is lamentable." Though Samuel may have "overleaped his bounds" as he had done during seminary days (he was making more than 200 calls a month) the German pastor's grievance was grounded in deeper emotions than personal disaffection for the younger man. The English Lutheran movement was making rapid strides in Greenpoint. English Lutheran mission churches in Brooklyn were making headway and the breach between German and English Lutheran congregations was widening. A clash between conflicting loyalties was inevitable.

When the argument was at white heat, Samuel's father wrote him imperturbably: "Do nothing unbrotherly to brother. Treat your opponent with all due respect, but if the field is open do not hesitate to enter. It is fortunate you have friends in meeting opposition."

Tempers flared. The Reverend Mr. Oswald's indignation reached such proportions that Samuel's presence on Milton Street affronted him. He demanded in a letter (November 20, 1900) to the Reverend George C. F. Haas, president of the New York Ministerium, that "the younger brother change his place of residence on or before December 20th so that it shall be *at least one inch* nearer the property which his people are said to have bought on Russell Street than our church on Milton Street." Up to this point, Samuel had adopted a conciliatory attitude. Now he took a stand. Throwing caution to the winds, he refused to move "one inch." He would not, perhaps I should say he could not, yield a moral surrender.

Precious time was consumed in airing grievances. The upshot of the affair is disclosed in a letter (January 10, 1901) from the Federation of Churches and Christian Workers. In it are listed thirty-three names whose connection with St. John's Church on Milton Street had been in question. At the request of the presi-

dent of the Federation, Pastor Oswald had checked fifteen of these names. Appended is a note from Walter Laidlaw: "Dear Mr. Trexler: Mr. Oswald says that these are his sheep and begs me to request that you regard them as his care."

Despite growing pains, the Church of the Messiah flourished. The congregation was vigorous and strong. Attendance at services of worship continued to increase. ("Always some new faces.") The Sunday School burgeoned ("There were so many children in the community that it was but necessary to open the doors for them to tumble in"). Samuel founded a church paper, christened it *The Chronicle* and for a masthead decided upon "The Faith of the Fathers in the Language of the Children."

The work that the church was engaged in was out of all proportion to its financial strength. Fairs, church concerts and church suppers afforded pleasant times but negligible monetary returns. We were jubilant when a musicale staged at our home netted the church two hundred and fifty dollars. "The concert was a success all through," Samuel recorded happily. "Everybody was highly pleased. Came home and read *Biography of a Grizzly* to allay my excitement." But such events were necessarily too few and far between to count—financially speaking.

Many plans for the projected house of worship were drafted only to be set aside as far beyond the congregation's limited means ("The estimate on our new church is $18,650—far more than expected"). The first thousand dollars toward the building fund was laboriously gathered in bills of small denomination. "This last donation of $10," Samuel recorded in March, 1900, "completes the first thousand dollars."

"You may have heard me say, and if not, I have often said from the pulpit," his father wrote a week later, "that the two hardest things I had to do was to collect money and to bury people who had not led a Christian life. Beyond a doubt you have already experienced the same. I do not want to discourage you but the second thousand will require more of an effort than the first. Still I say as we used to sing 'O do not be discouraged, for Jesus is your friend,' and wish you Godspeed as ever."

Called by unanimous vote of the congregation, Samuel was installed as pastor of the Church of the Messiah in the fall of 1900:

October 31, 1900

At 8:15 the service began. The church was filled with people—three to four hundred. All the English churches in Brooklyn were well represented and so was St. John's German Church. The entire service was very impressive. It certainly was a great occasion for me. Pastor Knabenschuh preached the sermon to the congregation. Pastor Steimle gave a fine charge to me. *But watch thou in all things, endure afflictions, do the work of an evangelist, make full proof of thy ministry.*

Hindrances notwithstanding, the work went steadily on to success. "When I came out and saw the immense audience," Samuel recorded the following Easter Sunday, "a thrill of joy passed through me. The day was most highly encouraging to all —a token of good things to come. I was happy in living this morning . . ."

Ground was broken for the new edifice in March 1902. It was a wintry day. The bare-limbed trees in Winthrop Park shivered beneath a chill gray sky as Samuel nervously awaited the arrival of the "crowds."

March 16, 1902

I was in a great tension in regard to the service. As the hour for ground breaking approached, I was somewhat discouraged by the weather and by no crowds appearing. The latter however, sprung up as by magic. As we were ready to go up to the ground a heavy drizzle set in. We crowded as many as possible into the Norwegian church. Many, however, could not get in.

The program passed off nicely. At the close we all adjourned to the lots and had the formal Ground Breaking. There the crowds were immense. Wherever one looked there was a sea of faces . . .

The cornerstone was laid in the spring. "A great crowd assembled at the site," the *Greenpoint Star* reported, "and filled the sidewalks and even overflowed into the park across the street. Distinguished Lutheran clergymen and prominent public men were present. Many were content to stand through the entire service. The exercises incident to the laying of the big, glistening block of marble commenced at about four o'clock . . . The Honorable Charles A. Schieren, a sort of patron-saint of this new church, who has agreed to loan money without interest for the new building, gave a bright and happy talk in which he emphasized the importance of gathering the young people into the fellowship of the church, and urged the people to stand by the Reverend Mr. Trexler and assist him in making the church a success. 'I claim,' stated Mr. Schieren, 'that this Evangelical English Lutheran Church has a great future before it, that this church will be a power in the neighborhood!' "

"Arose at 7," Samuel's diary records, "although I had been awake since 4:30 watching the weather, which finally became settled. At 4 we had the Cornerstone Laying. There were between 1,000 and 1,500 present. The service went on beautifully without any trouble. Mr. Schieren's address was especially good. I laid the stone . . ."

Autumn had painted Winthrop Park in gold-leaf when the Service of Dedication for the partially completed church was held in September, 1902. Messiah's congregation was in a festive mood, decked with bright expectations, looking forward joyously to the day. A pity it rained . . .

September 28, 1902

The day started in unfortunately as to weather. I was at the church the entire morning with father and mother who had come to witness the dedication. Instead of the day improving it began to rain.

The keys were given to me and I entered speaking the words *Peace be to this house* . . . The auditorium which accommodates 450 people was crowded long before the service. With the regular service I dedicated the church, the Reverend C. Armand Miller preaching the sermon. At the Vesper Service father delivered the sermon.

Vividly do I recall the proud look with which Daniel Trexler regarded his son, the satisfaction with which the old warrior's eyes surveyed the scene, and how the uplifted voices of father and son mingled with the voices of the congregation in their triumphant hymns of faith. "For the first time," wrote Samuel, "I came into the joy of my ministry." It had been for him and the congregation of Messiah Church a year of hopes and the realization of hopes. "Thus the year 1902 comes to a close," he noted after the service New Year's Eve, "memorable in my life for having built our church."

Five years later a new drive for funds to complete the building was made. It was no longer difficult to gain access to those in a position to help, and money with which to complete the church building was readily forthcoming. The Church of the Messiah, emerging from the chrysalis of its humble beginnings, lifted a golden cross heavenward. The sun shone on granite walls, sparkled on high windows stained the color of sapphires, emeralds, amethysts and garnets. In April 1908 the massive doors were opened wide. The people entered joyously. Samuel thus describes the day of Consecration:

April 5, 1908

The beautiful morning was the crowning climax to this—one of the greatest days of my life. The new church was opened at 10 and the crowds soon poured in. At 10:45 the solemn procession came to the front, and according to the complete service, the church was solemnly consecrated.

Everyone was most highly pleased with the entire building. It exceeded all expectations. At three the Sunday School marched into the church—five hundred children—and Mr. Schieren addressed us, expressing his extreme satisfaction.

The days were full to overflowing. On Sundays Samuel held two services prior to the eleven o'clock service for those unable to attend at eleven. In the afternoon he conducted the Sunday School. Gentle and understanding with children, they were devoted to him. He knew each child in the Sunday School by name. Running along beside him in the street they would catch at his hands, eager to walk with him. "Spell *Bible*," they would coax. "Spell it again," they would urge. And he would smile down at them, his two hands full of little hands. "B—buy it," he would say gravely. "I—investigate it. B—believe it. L—love it. E—enjoy it." They would listen delighted, repeating the letters and the words after him. "The duty of children is to bring sunshine into life," he would tell them. And they would smile knowingly up at him.

On the occasion of the tenth anniversary of Messiah's founding in 1909, the *Brooklyn Standard Union* stated:

The Reverend Mr. Trexler is the man who has fought the battle of the Church of the Messiah, and when the din and the turmoil was greatest and the vision of all obscured by the haze of discouragement which seemed to overshadow the whole enterprise, his eye was clear and he guided the church and the congregation out of the many difficulties into which they had fallen. The career of the church has been his career. The making of the institution of which he is the spiritual adviser has been his making.

When he relinquished his pastorate at the Church of the Messiah the membership was upward of 500, and more than 700 children were enrolled in the Sunday School. During his ministry in Greenpoint he was approached more than once by other churches. Always his reply was in the negative. There are recorded in his diary repeated invitations from the Church of the Holy Communion in Philadelphia to preach there. "As they implied my candidacy," he wrote, "I was compelled to decline." It was an old and powerful congregation and their overtures were naturally flattering to a young pastor. In February 1907 he noted the receipt of a very urgent letter from Judge Staake in regard to the Church of the Holy Communion, and on a Sunday morning when the Judge telephoned asking him to reconsider the matter of a call to Philadelphia. Samuel replied,

"I cannot leave my work here. My responsibility to my people will not permit it. It is impossible."

Although Samuel loved the Church of the Messiah with his whole heart and had no thought of leaving her, it was destined otherwise. In 1912 he was called by his Synod to another field of labor, assigned to another pioneering job. But this church which he had planted in Greenpoint, this church which had spread its roots wide and deep and put out great branches was ever dear to him. Through the years he made it a point to be with her on festival and anniversary occasions.

The golden anniversary of the founding of Messiah Church and the golden anniversary of Samuel's ordination were celebrated in 1949. It was granted to him to be present at the golden anniversary of his ordination in May but he did not live to attend Messiah's fiftieth birthday in October. It was my sad necessity to bring to the congregation Samuel's greeting and farewell. As best I could, I said the things needful to be said.

Ah, dear God, it was a hard thing for me to speak to the people in his stead. And how inadequate were the words spoken . . .

It has been my cherished privilege to share with you these fifty golden years. Through the first years of your life I was closely associated with Samuel Trexler, your beloved founder and first pastor and witnessed his unceasing labors, his struggles—at times desperate —and his final great accomplishment.

Too, I well remember when he was called by the Synod to another field of labor, how reluctantly he left Messiah Church—his first love, and one which he cherished during the entire fifty years of his great ministry. With what eagerness he was looking forward to this Golden Anniversary Service!

It is with deep humility that I have the honor to bring to you his greetings, and to tell you that he believed Messiah Church, under the leadership of your new pastor, the Rev. Herbert D. Dichsen, has a real future of usefulness to the people of his beloved Greenpoint. He also was grateful for the consecrated pastors who served Messiah in her fifty years. He knew and co-operated with each and all of them —Pastors Trabert, Worth, Deitz, Jaxheimer, Buller, Schaertel, Klahn, and your present pastor.

Building a church requires more than engineering skill and architectural genius. A church transcends steel and stone. A church is invisible. It is the Kingdom of God in the hearts of men. A church is a fellowship of human beings. It is a revelation of the love of God in Christ. A church is a sanctuary dedicated and devoted to the service of Almighty God.

Planting a church exacts the pain and travail of bringing life into being. A church is a living thing nurtured by the spiritual convictions and sacrificial labor of many hands and hearts. With what faith, hope and love Samuel Trexler planted the Church of the Messiah!

"Enter into the House of God humbly . . . Walk quietly . . ." he told the children who crowded the open doors like sunbright flowers at a garden gate.

CHAPTER FOUR

THE SOARING BRIDGE

Behold I will do a new thing

ISAIAH 43:19

No ONE knew better than Samuel Trexler the importance of youth to the Church. If not from the ranks of youth, where then were reinforcements to be drawn for the army of the Church of God? And who would serve as shield bearers? As armor bearers? Who, if not the young men? The young men—having everything in readiness and equal to the challenge. The young men prepared for the command, eager for the march. The young men waiting the call to serve—as he had waited. Samuel knew these men well. He had been one of them.

He also realized, and full well, the importance of the Church to youth. If not to the Church, where were young men to seek spiritual counsel and strength? Where were they to be invested with the moral courage and spiritual valor essential to victory? Where, if not in the Lord's House was youth to be armed with the Sword of the Spirit?

Contacts with old-world scholars and church statesmen during summers spent in Europe had enhanced Samuel's appreciation of the magnitude of the task confronting the Church in a changing world, impressed upon him the vital role that effective leadership had played in the march of the Church from the shores of Galilee westward. A decade in the ministry had brought issues into sharper focus and to his mind, when he returned from Europe in 1911, no issue was of greater import to the Church than that of leadership.

The problem of enlisting young men of talent and ability in the Christian ministry was of growing concern to Lutheran leaders at the time. The number of students graduating from the theological seminaries was insufficient to fill the ranks. Many also lacked the essential qualities for successful leadership. Where were the men whom the Church desired to enlist in the ministry? For the most part in colleges and universities intent upon careers that had little or no bearing upon the Church. They were preparing to serve industry, law, medicine, journalism, music, architecture, the sciences. But not religion. They were seeking degrees in arts or sciences. They were interested in becoming doctors of philosophy. But not doctors of divinity. Thoughtful churchmen realized that some way must be found to present the cause of the Church to youth.

In May 1910, delegates of the Lutheran Synod of New York and New England convened in the Church of the Redeemer, Binghamton, New York. "The President (Dr. Samuel G. Weiskotten) in his report called for a new impetus to bring men into the ministry," Samuel's diary records. "He appointed a committee on *More Men for the Ministry* to study the problem and present its findings at the convention next year. I was appointed chairman. The other two committee members are the Reverends William M. Horn and F. B. Clausen."

When the Synod met the following year in Christ Church, Brooklyn, New York, the committee was ready with its findings. Said Chairman Trexler: "Potential leaders are being lost to the church because no attempt is being made to reach our young people in nonchurch institutions of learning, a rich field, properly cultivated, in which to recruit men for the ministry." The Committee was then instructed to investigate the practicability of calling a pastor whose sole duty it would be to minister to students in colleges and universities.

Happy in his pastorate at the Church of the Messiah, Samuel recorded glowing accounts of the congregation's collective flowering "Larger attendances from week to week . . . Record numbers in the Sunday School Parade, the Easter Service more glorious . . . the Christmas Service more sweetly impressive than ever before."

Sitting at his desk, deep in study and thought, only half listening when I would ask a trivial question (Isn't Margaret a darling?) or make some immaterial comment (Brooks sent the ties) he would look up and smile—courteous but inattentive. He seemed always to be working against time. "Time!" he said one afternoon, getting up from his desk and pacing the floor. "There is so much to be done and so little time." Full of plans for the Church and the congregation he loved, he did not know at all that the pattern of life he had been weaving for twelve years was running off the loom; that he would soon be called upon to weave an entirely new and different pattern.

Nothing had changed nor were any changes in plans indicated when Samuel boarded a train for Boston in May 1912 to attend the convention of Synod in St. Mark's Church. The committee of

More Men for the Ministry reported that of Lutheran young people in eastern universities a survey showed that at least eight hundred were entirely out of touch with their own church, and recommended that a Students' Pastor be called by the Synod to take up work among the Lutheran students in Columbia, Cornell, Syracuse, Yale and Harvard universities, for the purpose of enlisting men in behalf of the ministry and strengthening the spiritual fabric of student life. As a result of their recommendations, the committee was charged with nominating a man "eminently qualified" to serve as the first Lutheran Students' Pastor.

Thus far the committee had discharged its obligations creditably. Now the members found themselves at a loss. What man was thus eminently qualified? Also able and willing to serve? Whom would they nominate? Months passed. Searching their minds inconclusively the three men could not seem to arrive at any solution to the problem. Time was running out and they were far from an answer to the predicament.

One afternoon as the Reverend Mr. Horn was walking home from a committee meeting which had produced no constructive plans, a brilliant idea flashed in his mind. The man was their own chairman! Highly elated he hastened to Pastor Clausen's home to disclose his happy thought. "Of course!" exclaimed Clausen, delighted. "Why didn't we think of it before! Trexler is the *perfect* choice!"

The two men then looked at each other somewhat uncertainly. The same thought had occurred to both. Could they gain Samuel's consent? Both were aware of his deep allegiance to the Church of the Messiah. Would he be amenable to their proposal? They did not know. Could they prevail upon him to accept the nomination? That was the question.

They put their heads together, marshaled the excellent reasons why Samuel should accept the nomination—his engaging personality, his initiative, energy, enterprise, courage, his enthusiasm for the project, his ability as an organizer and leader, and above all his confidence in youth and his understanding of young people. All these qualifications they rehearsed carefully before calling on Samuel to inform him of their decision.

When they met with him, however, they used none of these convincing arguments. Instead, after exchanging pleasantries, Pastor Horn turned to Samuel and said simply: "As to the man eminently qualified to serve as Students' Pastor—*you* are the one to undertake this thing, Trexler. You are the *only* one!" Samuel was startled. Taken off guard, he could find no words either of assent or dissent. He was perturbed as well as startled. He would have to *think*, he told his colleagues in parting.

Their insistence that he was the man best qualified to serve was gratifying. But it was also disconcerting. "My fellow committeemen today spoke to me of taking up the student pastorate work," he noted in his diary. "It set me thinking . . ."

Where did his responsibility rest? To self-advancement Samuel gave no thought then or later. To his own pleasure in the matter he gave no thought, either. The questions he asked himself were: In fairness to his congregation, would it be wise or just to transfer his responsibilities to another at this time? Who would carry on at Messiah Church in his stead? And, in any event, *was* he the man to assume leadership in this pioneer work? Were there not others, perhaps better qualified?

These and other uncertainties and anxieties were in his mind as he pondered the unexpected turn of events and discussed with me the changes that his decision, if favorable, would inevitably bring about. I said nothing to influence him one way or another. It was a decision he would have to make alone. That I knew. And I also knew that when all was said and done, the final decision would depend on his answer to the question, How^ and where can I best serve my church?

In his unsettled state of mind he wrote his father and from him received an immediate reply:

Bernville
October 5, 1912

Dear Son:

Were I in your place I would not like to leave the congregation you now have. It is a great honor to have started your congregation in such a humble way and built it into such a flourishing body. You are in a great metropolis and have won the respect of the whole city. Your success has been astonishing. People speak in highest terms of you and your work—which pleases us. You certainly have God's blessings on your labors and I cannot see how you can enjoy any work more than the work you are doing . . .

Yours etc.

D. D. Trexler

As the decisive moment neared, Samuel's uncertainty deepened. He determined to go to Bernville and talk the problem over more fully with his parents. "Found father and mother well," his diary tells us. "Disclosed to them further my ideas as to the Student Pastorate and at first found no sympathy. Later they changed . . ."

Returning to New York he conferred with his revered friend, the Reverend Doctor George U. Wenner, founder and for sixty-six years pastor of Christ Lutheran Church, New York City. This beloved clergyman (never too busy to receive young pastors) listened attentively to all Samuel had to say, promising to give the problem prayerful thought. That same evening he dispatched a letter to Samuel:

New York City
October 8, 1912

Dear Brother Trexler:

It is with fear and trembling that I venture to advise in a case involving an eventful life decision. For that reason I hesitated on Saturday evening to give a decisive opinion. But you are not helped by such an attitude. Anyway, the real decision rests with yourself—in prayerful submission to the guidance of God. Two things I assume: That you will have the support and backing of your brethren, and that the preliminary vesting is such as to afford you exact information in regard to the field—the number and character of the students in the various institutions.

That settled satisfactorily, after careful thought on the subject, I would say that it is a field into which you might enter with the greatest enthusiasm. It is large enough and important enough to demand the energies of a lifetime. And nothing less than this should be your purpose—to give it the best effort of a life-long service. It is an untrodden field, unique and vast in its possibilities.

Fraternally yours,

G. U. Wenner

This letter set Samuel's mind at rest. "After luncheon the Executive Committee of Synod met," he recorded in his diary October 14th. "All there but one—and elected me their Students' Pastor. May God in His wisdom and strength guide me aright."

Though the good people of Messiah Church were reluctant to accept his resignation, they had no desire to stand in the way of Samuel's wider ministry as pastor to university students. They tempered their sighs and regrets with smiles and good wishes. "The Church Council held a special meeting to receive my resignation," the diary states, "and their attitude to it was finer even than I had expected."

The *Greenpoint Star* (October 15, 1912) was more explicit:

"Then the resignation was read. Rarely has the request of a minister in Greenpoint to have severed his pastoral relations with the congregation created so tense a situation. Halfway through the reading of his letter, Rev. Mr. Trexler was nearly forced to silence by his emotion. The councilmen sat speechless . . ."

Imprinted with the seal of the Evangelical Lutheran Synod of New York and New England, the Call to the Student Pastorate was inscribed on parchment with illumination in crimson, blue and gold. When Samuel showed the document to me he was standing at his study window. A shaft of sunlight slanted across his hand and lighted up the gemlike letters. (How beautiful is the call to serve! I thought.) I looked at Samuel. His face was composed. It was not possible to read his thoughts as he stood there contemplating the call which was to have such far-reaching significance in the annals of American Lutheranism.

"This day my pastorate of the Church of the Messiah quietly but relentlessly ran out," he wrote after preaching his farewell sermon—"My love be with you in Christ Jesus—Amen." He was installed as Students' Pastor December 11, 1912, President of Synod Edwin F. Keever officiating and the Reverend William M. Horn preaching the sermon. From his parents he received a heart-warming letter.

> *Bernville*
> December 11, 1912

Dear Son:

We have been wishing for a fine evening for your sake. We are sure if the weather continues as this afternoon you will have a crowded church tonight for your installation as the first Students' Pastor to be called by the Lutheran Church. If it were not for the distance we would be among the audience.

We hope and pray that you will do well in your new work, that you will enjoy it and that you will do a great deal of good. It was a hard choice. However, your people have shown how much they appreciated your ministry to them which is a great consolation. We read all the newspaper articles. They were very flattering even though what they say is true.

May God's blessing rest abundantly on your new work as it did on your work in Brooklyn. You will encounter new difficulties, but these you will overcome. God's grace has been sufficient to you heretofore and will suffice you in the future.

> The Parents

One snowy evening, many winters later, Samuel and I were sitting before an open fire recalling bygone days. "I do not think we ever fully realize the crises of our lives while we are living through them," said Samuel, prodding the logs so the sparks flew upward. (How true, I thought, seeing again in the golden flames the illuminated parchment on which had been inscribed his call to the Student Pastorate.) "It may be," he added, "that we are too preoccupied with details at such times, too involved in practical things to be done . . ." (Yes, yes, that is the way of it, I mused, remembering how our attention had been divided between packing cases and the amenities of farewell as we prepared to leave Greenpoint.) With Samuel's departure for Manhattan, it had seemed propitious that I also make my residence in New York City where some months before I had opened an office. So together we had closed the house on Milton Street—the house of friendship, with all its experiences, sad and glad, all the memories of the young years.

We crossed the East River by ferry as we had done so many, many times. Ferryboats were in their glory in those days. During the crossings we enjoyed skylines and sunsets, friendly conversation with fellow passengers and exchanged greetings with the captains. "Remember Captain Adams?" I asked Samuel.

"I shall never forget crossing the river the day we left Greenpoint," he replied, gazing out of the window at the falling snow, "and Captain Adams blowing three blasts of the whistle in parting salute as we crossed the gangplank and were lost in the crowds on Twenty-Third Street . . ."

The ministry to students was one into which Samuel could throw himself heart and soul. He liked everything about the assignment. University life was agreeable and stimulating to him. He enjoyed the company of young people and was accepted by the students as one of them. He had pleasure in the companionship of cultivated men and women and was a welcome caller in

the homes of college presidents and professors. His Synod probably could not have called a man better qualified to present the
challenge of the ministry to university men.

"I congratulate you with my whole heart and also the young
people to whose spiritual needs you are to minister," Lady Brues
wrote him. "In you the Church has made a wise choice—earnest,
efficient, able and steadfast as you are." Her letter was one of
many expressing gratification regarding his appointment.

Losing not a day (the decorators were still at work in our
apartment at 438 West 116th Street) Samuel made an excursion
into the heart of Columbia University. In less than a week he had
completed working arrangements, met most of the department
heads, discussed his plans with Chaplain Knox (The Reverend
Dr. Raymond C. Knox), spoken to an audience of students in
St. Paul's Chapel on Optimism (Psalms 45:7) and made "gratifying calls on undergraduates."

Samuel properly defined his university ministry as "peripatetic." The work called for initiative, resourcefulness and imagination. It also involved long-range commuting. However, he did
not seem to find trains a hardship. As a matter of fact, he liked
trains and did much of his planning and writing in Pullman cars.
With Columbia University as the hub of the wheel, he traveled
back and forth to the colleges and universities committed to his
care, making the circuit over and over with growing pleasure and
enthusiasm. He did not disregard Lutheran woman-power,
either. It was not long before Barnard, Vassar, Smith, Wellesley,
Mount Holyoke, Sage and Radcliffe appeared on his train schedules; and he recorded "delightful dinners—the tables filled with
Lutheran girls."

In planning the student pastorate work Samuel considered it

important to gain not only the approval but the active co-operation of university authorities. In this he was highly success-ful. Officials commended the Lutheran Church for effectively meeting a need which the universities were not in a position to meet. President Lawrence Lowell of Harvard immediately put the resources of the university at Samuel's disposal and to facili-tate what he called "shepherding the students" made available to the young Students' Pastor the academic records of the stu-dents.

Professor Edward Caldwell Moore, chairman of the Board of Preachers at Harvard, gave unqualified approval to the work. Professor Anson Phelps Stokes and President A. T. Hadley cleared the way for him at Yale. Chancellor Day of Syracuse University volunteered to do "everything in my power to help." Acting president T. F. Crane of Cornell extended a cordial hand and Andrew D. White, Cornell's first president, discussed the objectives of the student ministry at length with Samuel both at the university and in his home.

Phillips Brooks House provided a center for meetings at Har-vard. At Cornell and Syracuse Samuel made his headquarters at his own fraternity house (Phi Gamma Delta) from which he wrote happily of "reliving student days" and "rallying Lutheran forces." He did not wait for students to call on him, but sought them out day after day: "Made student calls . . . Spent the afternoon and evening making student calls . . . Made happy student calls . . ."

He organized Lutheran Clubs and invited Lutheran leaders of note to the meetings so that students could come to know per-sonally their church leaders. Whenever possible he brought stu-dents of the various synodical bodies together thus implanting in their minds the desirability of more unified Lutheran forces. It was characteristic of him to tackle the difficult thing first. Satisfied that he had "effected a closer touch with the fundamental aspects of the work" at Columbia University, he went to Cornell where he anticipated hard going as there was no Lutheran church at or even near the university. At the outset of his work only a handful of men called on him during his consultation hours. Shortly after he arrived at Cornell he wrote me, "This morning three students came to see me—the largest number I have thus far had—tell it not in Gath." Small beginnings, however, were not discouraging to Samuel. He did not expect to sow in the morning and reap in the evening of that day.

Ways and means, the organization and administration of his student pastorate responsibilities are recorded in his reports to Synod. But there are intangibles equally important to the success of the new venture—the spirit in which Samuel Trexler carried out his mission, the enthusiasm with which he hailed the day's work, his indestructible faith. Letters he wrote from the universities reveal more clearly than could any words of mine the fervency with which he entered what Dr. Wenner had envisioned as "an untrodden field, unique and vast in its possibilities."

> *Ithaca*
> January 21, 1913

Dear Edmund:

Today has again been busy—as all the days are. Had my two hours for consultation at Barnes Hall with good results. Had an appointment with Acting President Crane, a very gracious gentleman who took me to the School of Agriculture and presented me to Dean

Bailey. Spent the afternoon very profitably calling on students.

Life here is almost as gay as in Manhattan. On Saturday evening we had a very interesting party at the Doctor Covilles. One of the nicest accidents to befall me was calling on Professor Sill—where I was presented to Professor Burr, one of the choicest spirits I have ever met. He asked me to go with him to The Town and Gown where he presented me to a large number of important men of the faculty. We sat about the Round Table with the deans of at least three colleges, and had a convivial time.

I am frankly surprised to see how much of a stir my being here has created. As I am introduced, I am usually a known figure beforehand. This seems to hold with the faculty more than with the students. I have some strenuous days before me. I was delighted to hear of the many calls for your professional skill. One is happiest when he finds demand for himself in his life's work. Other honors then are but secondary.

S. G. T.

Ithaca
February 18, 1913

Dear Ed:

Last night we organized our Lutheran Club with 26 present—very gratifying and good spirit shown. Yesterday afternoon I had rare good sport in tobogganing with the men. It is the most exhilarating thing I have done for some time and would repeat it today except for meeting President Schurman at a faculty reception. Tomorrow evening I dine with 300 girls at Sage College. I do not think I shall go to the Masquerade Dance. It is altogether too worldly . . . Be good and happy.

Trexler

New Haven
February 28, 1913

Dear Devol:

I was whizzed to New Haven in scarcely any time—satisfied my luncheon hunger with a sandwich and a cup of coffee at the station— and then made straight for the Acting President's office.

There is a charm about the mellow softness of Eli's campus as over against Cornell, though the campus at Cornell is certainly very beautiful. In the absence of President Hadley I called on Secretary Stokes. He was very cordial—had a committee meeting staring him in the face and asked me to come to see him at three. All this happened before two. He introduced me to YMCA secretaries Wheeler, Ballou and Vreeland from whom I obtained lists of the students. At three Mr. Stokes received me and showed genuine interest in my work. He invited me to dine with him at 6:30. I have the names of 25 Lutherans thus far.

Yale is overflowing religiously this week. Dr. Parkhurst is giving the Lyman Beecher Lecture Series on preaching and Newman Smythe, the National Taylor Lectures.

The cordial welcome of the Yale men was not anticipated. My impressions are so many that I seem to have been here much beyond a half day. Keep well and happy.

S. G. T.

Syracuse
March 10, 1913

Dear Edmund:

I happily had a five-minute margin in making the train last night and after that there was nothing nerve-wracking. My time is occupied solely with work. Chancellor Day has volunteered to do everything in his power to help me. He invited me to speak to the students in the chapel on Wednesday morning.

I have seen the register and secured the names of our Lutheran men—more than I anticipated—upward of 100. Also visited the YMCA and planned my consultation hours.

Called on one student—a fine-looking young man of whom everybody speaks well. I am hoping to land him in the Lutheran ministry. This evening I heard Bishop Henderson at an evangelistic meeting and afterwards called on Dr. Jeremiah Zimmerman, dean of our Lutheran clergy in Syracuse. The simplicity of things here is very interesting . . .

Yours

Trexler

Cambridge
April 12, 1913

Dear Doc,

This in my room at the Colonial Club. Time 10 A.M. Frame of mind happy. Wish you were here to share with me the glorious spring morning. For the former I pay but $1.25—for the latter nothing.

Real people rarely if ever disappoint. Aristocratic Harvard gave me a warm welcome. Was cordially greeted by President Lowell. He is delightfully simple with a delicious sense of humor. Met Josiah Royce and then had a consultation with Dean Hurlburt who heartily commended the work. Afterwards called on Professor E. C. Moore, a splendid young man who immediately pledged himself to my service. This afternoon student consultations and tea at the "Fly."

Yours

S. G. T.

Cambridge
May 11, 1913

Dear Edmund:

Harvard had its first Lutheran meeting last week. There were 17 present—all splendid men—and with earnest spirit we organized a club. There was no difficulty in securing an able man for the presidency—anyone would have qualified. This is the first meeting of Lutherans that Harvard, during its well-nigh three centuries of existence, has witnessed.

My days have been crowded with work. Went to St. Mark's Evangelical Lutheran Church this morning where I made a communion address. The following appeared in St. Mark's Calendar of today:

"The student pastorate work at Harvard, although in its humble beginnings, is an indication of what can be done in the future. There are thirty-five young men at Harvard who have been reared and confirmed in our Church, and therefore look to her for spiritual guidance and sustenance. The Church seeks so to minister to these men during their student days that they may go out into life with a faith strong enough to meet its problems. This the Church owes her sons. On the other hand, these exceptionally gifted and trained men will bring the Church a leadership and a vision which she greatly needs."

I am very busy and happy. Between work and play I am scarcely catching my breath. Hope everything is going well with you . . .

Trexler

During brief intervals in New York, Samuel was light-hearted and carefree. Evenings with old friends were occasions of festive reunions. He looked forward eagerly to these visits, enjoying immensely the gay dinner and theater parties, the marvelous music at Carnegie Hall and the glittering spectacles at the Metropolitan. Richard Wagner was his favorite composer, *Die Meister-singer* his favorite opera.

We also spent frequent week ends at the White House calling on Miss Margaret Wilson, the President's eldest daughter, attending embassy teas and receptions and generally enjoying ourselves in high government circles in Washington.

To the casual observer our social life was impressive; to some it seemed "glamorous" not to say worldly. "What's wrong with dining with princes?" I retorted crossly one day when one of our friends remarked that we seemed overly inclined toward "high society." No one was less impressed by a man's title, position or financial status than Samuel Trexler. His interest was solely in the individual and whether prince or bellhop was not of moment to him. He had friends in every walk of life, many among the great of this earth, many more who could not be so designated. "I like people for what they are," he said, "not for what they pretend to be. It is better for us to be what we are."

He was at ease with people he met because he knew and accepted them on equal terms. "Sam even put sinners at ease," one of our friends wrote me, "and I ought to know." He did not regard himself as a "brilliant thinker" or intellectually superior to his fellowmen. On the contrary. "Put it down to my plodding Pennsylvania-German mind," he said when criticized for coming to decisions slowly. By and large he did come to decisions slowly, but once he had made up his mind on fundamental things he remained as had his father "immovable as the everlasting hills."

At a dinner at the Lotus Club in New York in the spring of 1913 in honor of Rudolf Eucken, well-known professor of Jena University, Eucken extended an invitation to Samuel to visit him in Jena. "I accepted Professor Eucken's invitation with pleasure," he noted, "and immediately made plans to spend the summer in attendance at continental universities."

June fifth he sailed for Europe, eager for wider knowledge of student life abroad. While attending lectures at the University of Jena, Samuel lived at the Black Bear Inn, where in 1522, Martin Luther "disguised as a knight in a red bonnet, trunk hose and doublet, and with a sword by his side," had conversed with Swiss students on his journey from Wartburg to Wittenberg. Beyond the four-centuries-old university stretched the field where Napoleon had defeated the Prussian army in 1806. Not far away was the famous castle of Goethe.

"All this is indeed stimulating," he wrote, "and it is even more stimulating to sit at the feet of men like Leitzmann, Meinel, Wendt and Eucken. In the continental universities the science of theology is taught on an equality with all other sciences—by men of Protestant training in Luther's spirit."

Because of its association with Muhlenberg and the early history of the Lutheran Church in America, he was equally enthusiastic about the University of Halle. Here he came to know Professor von Dobschutz who was to visit the United States the following winter as the Harvard exchange professor. In Leipzig he was a guest in the hospitable homes of Wilhelm Wundt ("untiring in his investigations of truth"), Ludwig Ihmels (later Bishop of the Church in Saxony) and Nathan Soderblom (later Archbishop of Upsala and Primate of Sweden). "These men," he wrote, "and others—Franz Rentdorff, authority in the field of liturgics, Albert Hauck, master church historian, Rudolf Sohm, unequalled authority on Luther's conception of the church, and Reinhold Seeburg ("there is nothing in the English language comparable to his history of dogma") are the real giants of German thought and it is a great privilege to listen to them."

In the company of fellow students in Leipzig and Berlin, Samuel tramped the countryside, climbed mountains, explored battlefields, museums and music halls, exchanged ideas and opinions on social, political, economic, philosophical and theological subjects. "The religious life of students is not much in evidence," he wrote from Berlin, "but there is much intellectual swordplay in the fetid fumes of public halls where beer mugs are filled and refilled."

Before leaving Germany, Samuel visited Homburg, then gay with the presence of the German court. He later recounted this incident: "One August evening, while I was walking along Tannenbaum Aller, through a deep forest of pines, I heard singing in the distance. The song approached, receded, died away— as a regiment of soldiers neared, passed and disappeared into the forest. Walking on, I came to an opening in the trees. As I stood there resting for a moment, three men stepped out of the woodland opposite. One I recognized as the German Emperor . . ."

"Aha," I interrupted, "what happened?" "Nothing," he replied. "An aide strode across the clearing and said politely: *Haben sie die freundlichkeit zu warten.* In a few moments the Imperial motor car arrived and the men stepped in and roared off." I was about to ask the point of his story when Samuel added morosely, "I have wondered ever since why I did not present myself to his Royal Highness—as one Lutheran to another." Just like him, I thought, to describe an encounter with the Kaiser from a Lutheran viewpoint. But I kept silent.

On his return to the States, Samuel went immediately to Bernville to share his experiences abroad with his parents. "In the bracing autumnal morning, walked about town reviving many childhood memories," his diary relates. "Then drove to Rehrersburg where Father's resignation from his parish after forty-five years of service produced sincere sorrow. Met a number of old friends and rejoiced to be among them once more." The memory of friends warmed his heart till the day he died.

Berlin, Jena, Halle, Leipzig—all the cities and rivers and castles and universities of the old world faded in the sparkling sun that made everything so clear in the hills he loved. But the voices of the men he had listened to in the historic lecture halls of Germany did not fade. There is no question that Samuel's thinking was profoundly influenced by old world scholars with whom he explored new worlds of the mind and spirit that summer in Germany. He resumed his work as Students' Pastor with wider knowledge and deeper understanding both of the problems and the opportunities of his university ministry.

How little we know the minds even of those with whom we are closely associated! I did not think of Samuel during those years as a teacher. But having studied his addresses to students and talked with men whom he counseled in those years, I realize now that he was a gifted teacher.

"It is a very difficult thing," he once said to me (after struggling all day with a manuscript which he finally tore up) "to interpret eternal truths in such a way that young people can grasp them." There was a note of despair in his voice. "Sometimes," he said frowning, "I feel totally inadequate to the task." "What are you trying to interpret?" I asked hesitantly. "Salvation by faith through grace," he replied. "But I have not succeeded in making it clear—not to my satisfaction at any rate."

Perhaps he succeeded better than he knew. Many of the students whom he contacted during his student pastorate years continued to correspond with him long after they had said farewell to ivy-covered halls. Whether they understood the meaning of salvation by faith through grace I do not know. But they had gleaned some knowledge, gained some understanding of spiritual truths. Their letters testify to this and to the fact that their lives were influenced for good by his teachings. There is for example this excerpt from a letter from Robert Vander Hoof Ackerman (Columbia University): "It has ever been the case when I was with you that I wished to express certain subjects with a deeper sense of purpose and feeling than at any other time or with any other person, and I am sure that if I have been able to broaden my life and viewpoint, your kindly inspiration has been a very productive catalytic agent." And this statement in a letter from a young man who later entered the ministry: "I somehow always feel after meeting you that I would like to be a better man—and happier."

Above all Samuel Trexler was genuine. One thing he never acquired was the professional touch, the stage smile, the studied sympathy. He had no use for the trappings of inadequate piety. Youth, quick to sense sincerity and consistency in those who preach it, followed his leadership widely and gladly. There was no vagueness of belief in the religion he preached. And he exemplified by word and deed in his own humble, happy, self-forgetful life the Christian precepts he taught.

No student who came under Samuel Trexler's discerning ministry was uninformed regarding the life and work of Martin Luther, unfamiliar with the principles of the Reformation as championed by Luther, or lacking in instruction in the heritage, history and tenets of the Lutheran Church. It is interesting how like

Luther, in many traits of character, Samuel was—in his hunger for knowledge, his reverence for his teachers, his great love of music, his tireless zeal and energy, his consciousness of the "awful responsibility of preaching—of speaking to the people in God's stead."

In the manuscripts written during his student pastorate— manuscripts in which words, phrases and sentences are so frequently crossed out, rewritten, crossed out again—are many references to Luther. Again and again Samuel drove his point home by quoting from the writings of the great reformer. For example, in an address to the Lutheran Club at Columbia University in which he stressed the importance of being true to self, "sensitive to the voice of conscience," he asked his listeners to ponder Luther's deathless words before the Diet of the Emperor at the moment when his enemies fancied him overawed at last and about to retract or at least temporize: "Unless I be convicted of error by the holy Scriptures or by cogent and evident reasons, I neither can nor dare retract anything; for my conscience is held by God's Word and it is neither safe nor right to go against conscience. Here I take my stand. I can do no otherwise. God help me." . . . "It is not always easy to be true to one's self," Samuel pointed out. "It was not easy for Luther. But it is essential to happiness as well as to courage. It is a dangerous thing to temporize with conscience."

He made men feel accountable for their beliefs and actions, reminding them that the cultivation of a true sense of values and delineation of a clear picture of the goals toward which they were striving is not less important than intellectual prowess and scientific achievement. Samuel Trexler had the greatest respect for the human intellect and the "miracles" of science. But his province was the world of the spirit and it was the windows to this world he opened for young people.

He taught them that "more important than man's conquering his environment was the conquering of himself." He urged them to be always on guard, to distinguish between "what is pleasing to the senses and what is profitable to the soul," and to remember that "heights gained by trampling others prove treacherous and lonely summits." He told them that obstacles could be stepping-stones, difficulties an incentive as had been demonstrated time and again in the lives of great men. He pleaded with them to think for themselves instead of taking refuge in the minds of critics, commentators, columnists. "The church and the world need men who can think independently," he declared. "If you lack opportunity to form your own opinions on a particular subject, create the opportunity so to do."

He pointed out that a man gets out of this world what he puts into it, that society owes a man just what he pays society and that "to whom much is given, of him much will be required." He told them to be faithful in small things, to cherish love and friendship, and "to walk humbly with God if they would walk wisely with men." He talked to them about the love of God and the wonderful ways of God. He told them to have faith and to remember that *all things are possible to him that believeth.*

All the old precepts? All the old verities? Yes, all the old precepts, all the old verities, because Samuel Trexler believed that the moral principles and spiritual truths which had been handed down from old are the most dependable.

In a ministry marked by pioneering, his student pastorate work stands out as one of the most impressive of his achievements. In the two years devoted to religious work among students he developed techniques, formulated principles, created a pattern which made possible a rewarding and fast-moving program in the years ahead. The impact of his work as Students' Pastor was forceful and enduring. Between young Lutherans in the university world and the Lutheran Church Samuel Trexler built a soaring bridge.

Student pastorate work is today regarded as one of the most significant responsibilities of the Church. The work of the National Lutheran Council of which Paul C. Empie is executive director and the Reverend Donald R. Heiges executive secretary, is nationwide. In the 1953–54 directory of representatives serving some 100,000 students in non-Lutheran colleges and universities, are listed 25 full-time campus pastors, 15 women counselors, 20 assistants and 500 parish pastors, who work in cooperation with leaders of the Lutheran Student Association of America. Facilities for the ministry to students include student centers, parsonages for university pastors and chapels. More than a million dollars have been invested in these projects and another million is slated for their completion.

In 1915 the Lutheran students of Cornell asked the Synod of New York and New England for help in creating a center of worship at the university. Ten years after Samuel's arrival in Ithaca as Students' Pastor, ground was broken (May 13, 1923) for the beautiful Lutheran Chapel which stands at the gateway to the campus. Samuel, then president of the Synod, threw himself wholeheartedly into the campaign for funds. In less than thirty days he had helped to raise $90,000. Built of stone hewn from the university quarries, the chapel was completed at a cost of $145,000.

The spirit with which the money was given was as significant as the money itself. Among those who contributed heavily to the project was Mrs. Oscar Zollikoffer (Lady Emily, we called her). As soon as funds to complete the building were assured Samuel began to think in terms of furnishings and equipment. One morning the telephone rang. "Good morning, Lady Emily," I heard Samuel say. Then, "Well, we need an organ." And then, "Well, it will cost about ten thousand dollars."

"Did I *thank* Lady Emily?" he asked after he hung up. "Thank her for what?" I asked. "For the organ," he said excitedly. "She called to inquire what we needed for the chapel and when I told her an organ, she asked how much it would cost, and when I told her, she said 'I will give ten thousand dollars for the organ.' I was so happy I'm not sure I thanked her."

"In 1912 our Lutheran students scarce had the courage to register themselves as such," Samuel told the joyful young people who assembled in the chapel for the Service of Dedication in June, 1925. The work he began in Ithaca forty years ago is today being carried forward with ability by one of his younger friends, the Reverend John H. Sardeson.

In Cambridge where in 1913 Samuel rejoiced in a meeting at which "seventeen splendid men were present," an impressive chapel and student center—the Harvard University Lutheran Church was dedicated in April 1951. The Reverend Henry E. Horn is today pastor of this church and ministers also to students at Massachusetts Institute of Technology, Radcliffe College, Boston University, Northeastern University, Simmons College and Suffolk University. To the realization of this student dream Samuel also gave time, energy and support across the years. At the Service of Consecration, tribute was paid his memory by the Reverend Dr. Frederick R. Knubel, president of the Lutheran Synod of New York and New England.

"The work inaugurated in 1913 by the late Reverend Dr. Samuel Trexler," said Dr. Knubel, "has from those early formative days borne the stamp of his devotion and vision. During years of discouragement, even despair, he kept the fires of enthusiasm burning—to the end that this longed-for student church has finally been brought into being. In a sense, this church is a memorial to his confident zeal and unfaltering faith."

It is remarkable what faith can achieve. The student churches at Cornell and Harvard universities are unique. It would be difficult to gauge the spiritual influence of these churches on the lives of students who worship at their altars—the children and the children's children of men and women for whom Samuel Trexler lighted sanctuary lamps when no altars had yet been built.

Many of our universities had their origins in the tenets of religion. Yale was organized by ten clergymen in 1701, Harvard was founded in 1636 as an independent divinity school. Syracuse was founded and fostered by the Methodist Church. Columbia, established by British royal charter, is traditionally Episcopalian. In his work as Students' Pastor Samuel reaffirmed the dreams of the founders, replanted the seed of faith in these great institutions of learning.

Grateful for the vision granted his Synod in initiating the student pastorate work and for the far-sighted wisdom of leaders who continued to support the work in times good and bad he observed with joy growing numbers of young Lutherans leaving the universities strong in the faith of their fathers. It was for them that he built a bridge to span the tide of "a chasm deep and wide." In the pocket of the diary in which Samuel recorded his farewell to the universities I found this well-known poem by an author unknown.

An old man traveling a lone highway,
Came at evening cold and gray,
To a chasm deep and wide,
Through which there flowed a sullen tide.
The old man crossed in the twilight dim,
For the sullen stream held no fear for him,
He turned when he reached the other side
And built a bridge to span the tide.

"Old man!" cried a fellow pilgrim near,
"You waste your strength with your building here;
Your journey will end with the ending day,
And you will never again pass this way:
You have crossed the chasm deep and wide,
Why build a bridge at eventide?"

And the builder raised his old gray head,
"Good friend, on the path I have come," he said,
"There followeth after me today
A youth whose feet will pass this way,
This stream which has been naught to me
To that fair-haired boy may a pitfall be:
He, too, must cross in the twilight dim.
Good friend, I am building the bridge for him."

CHAPTER FIVE

A GOOD SOLDIER

With good will doing service,
as to the Lord, and not to men

EPHESIANS 6:7

HAPPY IN his ministry to students as he had been in his Greenpoint pastorate, Samuel Trexler was again without thought of change when the Church of the Redeemer in Buffalo, New York, asked him to become its pastor.

He had preached in this church in February 1914 describing to the congregation his work in the universities and appealing to the young men to consider the ministry of the Gospel—"the high calling of God in Christ Jesus"—as a vocation. When he preached there again in March he made this note in his diary: "Mr. Franklin W. H. Becker, president of the Church Board, consulted me with a view to becoming their pastor. Discouraged him. I made the reply that my loyalty to the student work would prevent any change."

Nevertheless he found that he could not readily dismiss the invitation from the Church of the Redeemer. The desire to again shepherd a flock was too strong. ("I still believe," he said years later, "that the work of the pastor is the most satisfactory in the church.") Again he faced a difficult decision, and again asked the question: Where can I best serve the interests of my Church?

"It is not clear to me what is best to do," Samuel said with a sigh on his return from upstate. He was more and more disquieted too by disturbing letters from home as the months passed. Seventeen years had gone by since his vigil at the deathbed of his brother Martin. They had been years crowded with work, full of blessings. Life had gone happily . . . but now the home he loved so dearly was shadowed by anxiety. His father was failing rapidly. For months his letters had reflected growing weariness and sadness of heart.

> *Bernville*
> November 5, 1913

Dear Son,

These few years I have to live—I have an idea they will not be many more—I desire to see my brothers and sisters as often as possible. On Saturday Mama and I went to Grimsville and after lunch to the cemetery to visit my dear parents' graves. I imagined it was the last time for me . . . Afterwards we went on our way past the old homestead and down the valley we used to travel in the morningtime of life.

Time is passing swiftly by and we are but pilgrims and strangers here. Last evening I sent my check for $1,000 to Muhlenberg College, to found the Martin Luther Trexler Scholarship, endowed by his Parents, the Reverend Daniel D. and Agnes A. Trexler that the God of Luther be honored and Martin Luther Trexler remembered.

> D. D. Trexler

Bernville
November 12, 1913

Dear Son:

Today, fifty-three years ago, I left my parental roof. My destination was above Lewisburg, where I had hired out to work on a farm mornings and evenings for my board while I attended public school. The public schools in Union County were better than in our county. I attended 63 days making good progress and on March 14th, I returned thinking *now my school days are over,* and behold! they had really only commenced.

My father—through my mother's coaxing—permitted me to go to Freeland Seminary at Collegeville to prepare for teaching. In time I obtained my Certificate and also a school at $20 a month. I was thus enabled in due time to enter the Lutheran Seminary at Philadelphia and after three years was ordained in the ministry June 10, 1868.

On this day 20 years ago, my dear mother was buried, and 16 years ago this same day, your brother Martin was buried, which you will remember as long as memory serves you. Before that time I had hoped that I might have three sons in the ministry.

God's blessings be with you in your outgoing and your coming home, and be with you wherever you are.

Your Father

The dreaded summons to "come at once" arrived in March. Together, Samuel and his brother Charles made the journey, traveling all night in a day coach. In his diary Samuel wrote with a heavy heart:

March 21, 1914

Father was awakened and recognized us with a smile. He mentioned my name and then again sank into a stupor from which he never regained himself. The invincible seemed finally compelled to yield. We watched by his bedside all day—his life gradually ebbing out. Through the night we watched from midnight until 4 when Mother took our place.

Mother woke us at 7 and with great calm told us that father had gone home. The end had come peacefully at five-thirty. It is a sore loss but with the glorious hope of the Resurrection it can be borne. Father has left us a splendid heritage in his noble life, and I pray that it may ever be a stimulus to us in our ministry.

Now again Daniel Trexler's house was filled with sorrowing relatives and friends, disarranged by the heavy-laden activities of preparations for the dead. The funeral was largely attended.

March 28, 1914

By ten o'clock the house was filled with family and friends as well as representatives of all of father's congregation—come to pay their tribute to love. Eleven ministers were present. The funeral service at the house was conducted by the Reverend L. R. Miller. At the church, Dr. E. S. Brown Miller preached a strong sermon on Daniel 12:13. *But go thou thy way till the end be: for thou shalt rest, and stand in thy lot at the end of the days.* He had known father intimately and spoke most highly of him.

Then we had our last view of that stalwart form and strong face and took him to his last resting place in the grave. Surely he was the sailor home from the sea, the hunter home from the hill. It warmed my heart to see the many old friends and their devotion to father.

By four o'clock everyone had gone and we were quite alone. Mother had borne herself with great courage through it all.

Never shall I forget that day! Bleak, curtained by rain, and full of mourning. Not knowing how to express condolence in words (how futile in the presence of death!) I had ordered a blanket of American beauty roses to be placed on the casket. When it had been spread I was taken aback. (The roses are too flamboyant, I thought, dismally, standing beside the austere coffin in which the remains of Daniel Trexler, clad in black, reposed on cream silk. White roses, I fretted . . . or even gold, would have been better. But it is too late now.)

For a long time, joined at intervals by Samuel and his brother, I watched the unbroken procession of buggies, carriages, spring-wagons—all manner of vehicles—making their way toward the lighted door. They kept coming and coming very slowly, splashing through the mud and the rain—water streaming from the horses, the wagonwheels . . . From Millersburg, Rehrers-burg, Shartlesville, Lenhartsville, Slatington, Kutztown, Topton, Sinking Spring, Myerstown, Robesonia, Reading, Philadelphia, Brooklyn, New York City—the mourners came. It was a wonderful testimony to the affection in which Daniel Trexler was held by those to whom he had ministered, and I thought with gratitude of the privilege that had been mine in having known Samuel's father.

In September after preaching again in Buffalo, Samuel told representatives of the Council of Redeemer Church that he would give fair consideration to their urgent invitation to serve as their pastor. Two weeks later on his return from Cornell University he found the formal letter of call on his desk. "The call is unanimous," he recorded, "and I feel strongly urged within me to accept it."

"I have come to trust the providential hand of God in men's affairs," he wrote many years after his resignation as Students' Pastor. "Each step of my life has been taken with strong forces impelling me on, rather than of my own choice. The changes in my life were not of my making. They were in the control of a stronger Hand than mine. There seemed, in the end, to be no choice."

His resignation was received by university presidents, professors, and students with genuine regret. The Lutheran Club of Harvard had some weeks earlier forwarded a petition to university officials requesting a Lutheran representative on the Board of Preachers. Harvard's Professor E. C. Moore told Samuel that in his opinion he would be the suitable man. "I made a brave effort to keep my equilibrium," Samuel wrote me. "I said that while I should deeply appreciate the privilege of serving on this distinguished Board, I felt that older men in the Church should have the honor. He however said that the students cared naught for a man's age or position in the church, but wanted a man who understood and was in sympathy with them . . .

"Dean Hurlburt told me he was sorry to hear of my going and then added in his friendly way, 'I congratulate Buffalo, but we need you here.' I thanked him, of course. It is a joy to be needed."

During the summer Samuel spent as much time as possible with his mother, hitching up the team and driving with her through old valleys of memory—calling on relatives and old-time friends, making pilgrimages to ancestral graves, and in the twilight of a soft September day arriving at his father's boyhood home . . .

"Mother and I left at nine in the morning for Grimsville where we visited the church and grandparents Trexler's graves. Then we drove to father's boyhood home and came down the old valley to Uncle Reuben's where father's only aunt, Aunt Kitty, is still living. Everywhere we found kin and friends of the most real type. It was a joy to feel their sincerity. The entire day was memorable by reason of being in the bosom of father's family.

"Mother and I drove to Eagle Point where we stopped overnight. It was a real blessing again to see Aunt Mary and to hear her sweet kindly voice. We talked quite late, as father used to do when he visited there. In Rehrersburg we met many of father's warm and loyal people. Mother bears up bravely, noble soul that she is . . ."

That fall the days were again occupied with the details of departure, filled with farewell receptions and dinners. "To Columbia for tea at the deanery with the Grosvenors . . . Tea with Margaret Woodrow Wilson . . . To Garden City with the G. H. Gerards . . . Dinner with Gertrude Atherton at the Sesrun Club . . . A delightful dinner with the Gertrude Robinson Smiths . . . Breakfast with Kate Douglas Wiggin . . . Tea with Miss Belle Greene at the Morgan Library . . . A delightful farewell party at Betty Hammond's . . . Dinner with the Honorable Charles A. Schieren who gave me his blessing . . ."

In November, Samuel departed for Buffalo. I shall always

remember his smiling face at the window as the train pulled out. God bless him in his great work, I thought, standing on the platform at Grand Central Terminal, torn by conflicting emotions. Parting is a powerful and a painful thing. It was difficult for me to contemplate the future without his companionship. I would miss his words of cheer. It would be lonely . . .

From Buffalo he wrote me the following morning:

Dear Edmund:

I could not tell you all I thought last night. Four hundred miles will not break or even lessen our friendship. I never told you, but I told many others that no man could be a truer friend than you have been. My life would have been so much poorer had Milton Street never brought you to me. You go on bravely at your duty in New York and I in Buffalo—and what jolly times our reunions will be!

Trexler

The while a friend of many years wrote him:

New York City
November 2, 1914

My dear Mr. Trexler:

And now comes to a close a chapter of your life. Oh what a happy and growing time it has been for you and Edmund Devol both! And how much larger life is than it would have been for either of you if you had missed each other! You have twenty of the best years of your life before you—twenty wonderful years of work, faith and struggle, for, of course, struggle there will be. Perhaps you will have to fight to win the people whose pastor you are to be, away from materialism, pride and caste into a true Christian brotherhood with their fellows. If so, I know you will choose to fight rather than to yield to any lesser good, whatever that may be. You are one of the few men who, like Bishop Spalding, so deeply mourned, are ready to risk all in pursuit of the things that are best and worthiest.

Eliza Witham

There is a word that flashes on almost every page in the diaries recording Samuel Trexler's pastorate at the Church of the Redeemer. The word is *splendid*. No word more perfectly describes his ministry in Buffalo. "The first session of our Advisory Committee met with splendid promise . . . The Church Council had a splendid meeting . . . The Thanksgiving Service brought a splendid audience . . . Splendid morning service . . . Splendid Vesper Service."

The congregation of Redeemer Church was eighteen years old when Samuel began his ministry there "under happy promise." The new church and parish house on Elmwood Avenue had been completed only the year before. "When I met for the first time with the Church Board—all outstanding men," he recorded, "I felt the strength, poise and purpose of the congregation."

There was an immediate and vigorous response to his leadership. He looked forward with happy expectation to the services of worship. "I have striven to maintain the highest standard for my services," he wrote me, "and the result tells. We had a beautiful service of worship this morning with a congregation as near perfect as they come."

His letters were full of enthusiasm for the church and the people of Buffalo: "Mr. Koons took me to the Greater Buffalo

Club—met many Buffalonians . . . Mr. Becker took me to a meeting of the Rotary Club—met many Rotarians . . . Mr. Koester took me to a Chamber of Commerce luncheon—met many business men . . . Pastor Kahler (Dr. F. A. Kahler) took me to a meeting of the Buffalo Ministers Association— met many ministers." At the Albright Gallery, the Automobile Show, the Flower Show, the Country Club, Elmwood Music Hall, St. John's Orphan's Home, the Lutheran Church Home, Samuel "met many people." It was not long before he knew nearly everybody in Buffalo.

As usual he made many calls. "Called . . . on Mr. Ed. Hengerer, Mr. Henry May, Mason Chace, Miss Cornelia Sage, Miss Katherine Dreier, Lady Wolcott, Mrs. Dexter Rumsey, the Corning Townsends, the Clarence Littells, the Henry Zellers, the Herbert Wadsworths, the Soren Kiellands, the Park-Lewises . . ." "I last week walked exactly 40 miles by my pedometer," he wrote me Thanksgiving Day. "Made 68 calls all over the city. Our members are distributed among 270 families." People said Samuel took Buffalo by storm. Certainly, Buffalo took Samuel by storm. He made his residence at the University Club, but spent few evenings there. The doors of Buffalo's hospitable homes were always open to him and he seldom dined alone.

"I feel sure the people of Redeemer Church will try their best to make you feel at home and happy," his mother wrote him, when she received word of the cordial welcome they had extended. "It is so wonderful that no matter where you go you make friends."

"Dear Ed, Mother is having the time of her life," Samuel wrote happily on the occasion of her visit a month later. "Of course everyone is falling in love with her and she has more invitations than we can accept. This morning we motored with Mr. Henry May to their beautiful home on Crescent Beach and in the late afternoon to Niagara Falls with the entire family. Waited for the moon to rise . . . Mother is much pleased with everything. She thinks the city beautiful and the church the most wonderful of all. She sends her love."

When he assumed his pastoral responsibilities at the Church of the Redeemer the congregation was confronted by an indebtedness of $38,000. After carefully surveying the field Samuel decided this debt could be cleared and with every expectation of success made long-range plans to this end. Again the record of his busy days is filled with financial anxiety. "Made financial calls . . . made financial calls all over the city." At a luncheon meeting with Messrs. Henry May, Charles H. Stolzenbach and Edward L. Koons he was assured $10,000. His enthusiasm and determination challenged the men of the congregation. Others came forward. It took time but by 1917 the success of his effort was assured. "The conviction prevailed in every heart," his diary states, "that it could be done and must be done." In the spring he wrote me:

Buffalo
April 2, 1917

Dear Devol:

I have been so enthusiastic about our work these days that I can hardly contain myself. I am on the go continually, but everything is working out happily. I have just finished one great task here. We have raised $35,000 for our debt and need but $3,000 more. Mr. May came into my office this evening and told me he would give what was needed on Sunday morning. This is not to be breathed—but you can know it. After church tonight I attended a patriotic meeting. Otherwise this week means hard work—but did you ever complete a fund of $38,000?

Always,

Trexler

The goal was reached on Easter Sunday. "Easter Sunday was a day of great rejoicing for the congregation of Redeemer Church and one of the happiest days of my life," he records. "The services were perfectly glorious. The church is so beautiful and the people so appreciative. The entire congregation was thrilled by the announcement of the consummation of the debt payment."

The day before that Easter Sunday in 1917 President Wilson had signed the Senate Resolution declaring a state of war with Germany. Three years of uncertainty as to what position America would take in the conflict in Europe ended with a call to arms. We had listened for many months to reports of conditions in hospitals and prison camps abroad, to appeals by the Red Cross for money and men and to eloquent speeches on Preparedness.

We will be in this thing, I thought, when the black headlines thundered from the presses of the nation. It cannot be otherwise. We will be needed over there. *Shall your brethren go to the war, and shall ye sit here?* We men who fought in World War I believed that we knew what we were fighting for . . .

"I came to the conviction that I must get into this work wholeheartedly and at once," Samuel recorded in May after a visit to the Officers' Training Camp at Fort Niagara to see what work his church could do in the training camp there. Returning to Buffalo from Fort Niagara, he found a message at the University Club: "Please call Edmund Devol."

"Ed informed me," the diary states, "of an invitation to accompany the Post Graduate Hospital Unit to France as a chaplain, and told me that this unit, organized by the Post Graduate Medical School and Hospital of New York City as Base Hospital Number 8, had accepted his services as physician." When Samuel informed the officers of Redeemer Church of his desire to serve as chaplain they gave immediate consent. "All gave me encouragement in my mission," he records, "and were in agreement that their Pastor should give himself where his services would be most needed—in ministering to the wounded." He was the first clergyman from Buffalo to leave for the front.

After reporting to the Surgeon General and the American Red Cross in Washington, he hastened to Bernville to break the news to his mother. "I left mother reconciled to my going to France," his diary tells us, "although when she first heard the news she said: 'It cannot be . . .'"

"Hurrah!" telegraphed Margaret Wilson, knowing Samuel's eagerness for this news, when confirmation of his commission came through. Mrs. Edward Brown, a cousin of Miss Wilson's, also happy that the commission had been granted, wrote me:

Atlanta, Georgia
July 10, 1917

My dear Boy,

I cannot tell you how happy I was in your announcement that the Pastor is going with you. I could see the steady, gentle purpose that is so strong in him arriving at Decision.

Now that you are to be together, I shall not feel sorry for you any more, dear Doctor, but just glad for the fine companionship you will have, welded together past breaking, as it will be, by mutual hopes and struggles, by weariness and danger, and by meeting whatever may come shoulder to shoulder.

I rejoice in what the youth and courage and skill of both can mean to the thousands of boys who will be brought to you—you skilled to heal the body, the Pastor not less skilled to heal the wounds that souls suffer on the battlefield—all heartened against the future by the combined strength of you and the Pastor, allied in a friendship so perfect that in all my long years of knowledge of people and hearts I have never seen another like it.

Write to me when you can, dear Boy. I envy you a little, the chance for "high surprise" which is a gift from above. Joy and courage go with you, and the loving thoughts and good wishes of

Yours always

"Mee Mee" Brown

Samuel had planned to preach a farewell sermon but was compelled at the last moment to wire his church: "Sailing. Will not have time to return to Buffalo and preach farewell sermon." After what seemed interminable days on Governor's Island, sailing orders (as generally happens) took us unawares. In his War Diary Samuel describes the embarkation:

Sunday
July 29, 1917

The morning was filled with feverish preparation. I went to the Chapel of Cornelius the Centurion at 10.30 for brief worship. At noon we struck camp and marched down to the landing. Detail of preparation has done much to divert us from the main purpose of our going, but when we finally were on board the lighter, and had a moment's time to think of our sober mission, I realized that I was embarking on one of my life's greatest adventures.

At 2.30 we went on board the "Saratoga," an old Ward liner of 7000 tons. In addition to our Hospital Unit, she carried a Baggage Train, the 5th Field Artillery Regiment, and many unattached men. There could be no evening service owing to the constant excitement of new detachments arriving.

After the tension of the day, I suggested a Song Service, but the Commanding Officer (Major Joseph F. Siler) advised against it on the theory that the sound of voices might carry to enemy ears. So instead of hymns, ribald songs of land and sea rang from ship to ship in our convoy . . . far into the night.

The following day the *Saratoga* was rammed amidship by an incoming liner (the *Panama*). The cause of this absurd accident as far as I know was never determined. Lifeboats were lowered. Tugs, torpedo boat destroyers and launches rushed to the rescue. Samuel and I had barely time to climb over the nose of the *Panama*, landing on her deck too excited to be scared, when she withdrew from the *Saratoga* which promptly sank with all our equipment and belongings aboard. Back then to Governor's Island, to wait until new supplies and equipment could be assembled. It was a week before we boarded the *Finland* and again set forth on our voyage in darkness.

There were three other transports, two torpedo boats and a supply ship in our convoy. The crossing took thirteen days. "Met many of our men and immediately felt very much one of them," recorded Samuel. Among the enlisted men was Alexander Woollcott, then dramatic critic of *The New York Times*. After his own fashion, between boat drills and setting-up exercises, Woollcott instructed us in French. Many of the men on board were from Eastern universities and friendships were quickly forged. Woollcott, Harold Ross, founder and late editor of the *New Yorker*, and others who were to win recognition in journalism and the field of literature were already thinking in terms of an army newspaper—*The Stars and Stripes*.

Lights were ordered out on the *Finland* at 7.30 as a precaution against submarines. Samuel spent the evenings observing the skies: "In the evening watched the wonderful skies . . . It was a glorious night with stars and a bright moon . . . Everything in the sea and in the skies is so peaceful that it requires an effort to realize the possibility of lurking danger . . ."

"A perfect Sabbath morning," he recorded August 12th, "glorious sky and sea. At 10.30 we held a service of worship on the forward deck. The congregation of 2,000 soldiers covered every rigging available. I spoke briefly on Prayer. It was necessary to speak through a megaphone . . ." ("I look back with amazement at my presumption in dealing with so devotional a subject as prayer by methods employed on a baseball field," he said later in recalling that wartime service at sea.)

The sea was calm. The transport ploughed on. A week later, at 4.30 A.M. (it was just beginning to grow light) we sighted the coast of France. Before we had time to breathe a sigh of relief, the dreaded six whistles sounded (Submarine Sighted). "I was below decks," Samuel recorded, "and before I could reach the deck I heard a tremendous explosion, and then another and another. The transport dispersed and the torpedo boats went into action. Shot after shot was fired. French aeroplanes flew out from the shore and dropped depth bombs. The firing continued for forty-five minutes; then it ceased and we were credited with having sent one submarine to the bottom of the sea. I thought of those who had gone down with her . . ."

When General Mason Patrick, commander of troops on the *Finland* (later Chief of the Air Service) asked Chaplain Trexler what his reaction had been to the engagement with the submarine, Samuel confessed that it was his first time under fire. To his astonishment the general replied quietly, "Mine also . . ."

We docked at St. Nazaire, Loire-Inférieur and marched inland to our station in the Breton town of Savenay. That march—some twenty kilometers—is still, when I think of it, a remarkable one. How we stood up under it I do not know. We were altogether unprepared for any such strenuous exertion. At least I was. Samuel's comment (diary): "It was my first military march and very enjoyable. We reached our destination in six hours. Our quarters were very crowded so Ed and I decided to go into town though we were somewhat tired."

Among the first 25,000 Americans to land in France ours was one of the pioneer units of the American Expeditionary Forces. In the midst of almost unbelievable confusion Samuel went calmly about organizing the work for which he had come overseas. "My first thought was for the religious services," his diary states. "Instead of allowing these to be the victims of the emergencies of army life I determined that there should be at least one hour dedicated to worship each Sunday."

He wrested this hour from war despite hell and headquarters. But it was a continuing struggle. "In the beginning the hour of worship was hindered by so many obstacles that I finally went to the commanding officer and demanded reasonable right of way for the service," he recorded. The time and place at which services were held was almost never the same. "Some fatality seemed to arise at the hour of worship," the diary continues, "some order, some incoming or outgoing convoy, some exigency that would throw the whole port into confusion."

The first service was held in the mess hall. "A cold rain greeted us," he recorded, "but at least we were all under one roof. I spoke on the Sword of the Spirit." A cold rain greeted us many times; and usually with every building taxed to capacity, services were perforce held outdoors.

A Belgian soldier presented Samuel with a wooden altar cross which he had carved with great skill and constructed so that it could be taken apart and carried in a brief case. Vivid in my memory of Samuel's ministry to soldiers is this cross, glistening in the rain on improvised outdoor altars in Savenay. Notwithstanding the difficulties under which we worshiped (or perhaps because of them) the numbers attending services increased from week to week. Notes like these appear in Samuel's diary more and more frequently as the weeks passed: "The service was crowded to overflowing . . . There was not standing room at the service . . . I explained to the colonel that we must have more benches . . ."

Samuel was not of the opinion that war affirmed faith or contributed to religious aspirations. Indeed after two years with the AEF he was convinced that war mitigated against religion, depreciated spiritual values, and often destroyed the fabric of faith beyond mending. "It is more necessary to speak of soldiers to God," he said on his return from Germany in 1919, "than it is to speak of Him to soldiers."

The anxious and cheerless winter of 1917–18 was one of waiting. Along the road on which our base hospital was located trudged day after day a desolate procession of refugees with crying children, bedraggled pets, and pitiful odds and ends of household belongings in tow. We were dispirited and restless. When the day's work was done Samuel walked in the country roads and lanes. Sometimes I accompanied him. We said little, each occupied with his own thoughts of impending misery.

When distinguished visitors came to Savenay, as many did that winter for one reason or another, we welcomed the opportunity to show them about the Post. Among those who came were General Pershing, Secretary of War Newton D. Baker, Bishop James de Wolf Perry, Julius Rosenwald, Herbert Adams Gibbons, Hamilton Holt, Heywood Broun and, to our even greater pleasure, a number of the fair sex—the daughter of the prime minister of Belgium, Mademoiselle Dalviella, Gertrude Atherton, Ruth Hale, Mary Roberts Rinehart, Margaret Woodrow Wilson . . .

A letter from Margaret arrived at the post only a few days before she herself did. "Dear Doc," she had written on her silver-gray notepaper, "I want to sing for the soldiers. But I do not know whether my father will permit me to go to France. Doc, I want to do this more than anything in the world! Do you think we can gain his consent? I am counting on you to help me do so . . ."

She was wearing a white evening gown the night she sang at Savenay. Her eyes were like stars. She sang till she could sing no more, pouring her generous heart out in her lovely voice.

"Now I can die happy," she said as we left the barracks, ringing with cheers for the President's daughter.

Samuel adjusted himself quickly to army life. Except for the assistance of Father Le Clair, chaplain to the Catholic soldiers, the entire religious work of the post, which eventually sheltered 14,000 wounded men and 8,000 prisoners, rested on his shoulders. Much of his day was necessarily given to hospital calls. In addition (it had not taken his superior officers long to discover that the chaplain was willing to work) he had charge of the post office and with one assistant was also responsible for censoring the mail—no small assignment on a post of 20,000 men. "My job at the post office offers splendid opportunity for coming to know the men," he wrote during Christmas week, "even if it is a staggering one. Being armed with a letter which sometimes has been traveling from post to post for months transforms the chaplain into an angel of mercy."

In the lull before the German offensive in the spring of 1918 we worked with feverish haste to expand our hospital facilities. By fall our bed capacity was 18,000. The wounded, at first transported by ambulance, then by a fleet of ambulances, were in the end brought to our hospital doors in Red Cross trains—sometimes as many as 600 men in a day.

To lead men into battle is a searing responsibility. To receive their broken bodies after the battle is over is a task freighted with such sorrow that it rends the soul. This task war imposes upon physicians and chaplains. Their eyes behold not the glory—only the abomination of war. Before the full tide of horror had yet rolled over us, Samuel wrote my brother:

Somewhere-in-France
February 1918

Dear Robert:

Sometimes we are much depressed. At present we have fewer patients than we have had for months. But if the much heralded spring drive comes we will be overtaxed before you receive this letter. In military hospitals the most terrible consequences of war are to be seen.

Both Edmund and I feel that instead of making a sacrifice to come here it has been a privilege to do even a little to make the heavy burdens of the wounded a little easier to bear . . . As you can easily imagine we see many, many things every day that fill our eyes with tears. But on the other hand, Edmund especially, has the opportunity to do much good. He is in the wards from morning till night . . .

Yours,

Trexler

How weary we were in body and soul! And how grateful for a brief leave of absence from hospital wards. Recalling a much earlier invitation from the Prince of Monaco, we decided to spend our few days of respite on the Riviera. Cordially welcomed by His Highness, we spent enchanted hours on his famous yacht *Hirondelle,* wandered peacefully about the beautiful old palace. As guests of His Highness at the Royal Opera in Monte Carlo, we had as much attention as four star generals. Princess Charlotte de Valentinois, charming, nineteen-year-old granddaughter of the Prince thought Samuel the handsomest soldier in the AEF and as a token of her admiration and affection presented him with a button-hook on the handle of which is engraved the Seal of State.

It seemed to us that we had never seen water quite as blue as the Mediterranean, villas as magnificent as those on the terraced hillsides, mountains as spectacular as the glittering Alps. To our tired eyes, the Riviera that faraway February was a scene of unbelievable beauty. When we left—the scene, fugitive as a dream, quickly faded from mind.

Returning to Savenay, we soon found ourselves face to face with the fearful aftermath of the March offensive. Our hospital staff was at a loss to know how to contend with the influx of wounded men from the front. We lived in the midst of a hideous nightmare to which was added the scourge of pneumonia and influenza.

The French government provided a caisson upon which to bear the dead. At the graves, Samuel read the services and when the last lonely echo of the bugler's notes had drifted down the Loire valley, he returned to the hospital to make the same sad journey again. And again. . . .

In the American Cemetery cross after cross was planted. Where once the seed of timothy had been broadcast, now was sown the flower of youth. In one section (in conformity with military proprieties) were buried the American officers, in another the enlisted men, and in their own isolated corner German prisoners of war. Over all the sun shone equally. All slept under one blanket of green. And in the light of the stars the white crosses were indistinguishable one from the other.

"You are now possessed of an opportunity for service the greatness of which you could never have conceived when you were ordained for the ministry," Dr. Frederick H. Knubel, president of the United Lutheran Church in America, wrote Samuel.

"May our Saviour sustain you through it."

One of Samuel's most painful duties was writing to those whose sons would return no more, and it was with a heavy heart that he opened letters from grief-stricken fathers and mothers:

"It pierced our hearts when news came that our dear boy was taken from us. Only Jesus knows our sorrow. We thank you and all who helped to care for our dear son. May God's blessing rest upon you. By what you have said in your kind letter we know that our boy passed Beyond a faithful soldier of the Cross and that his soul is safe in the hands of God. His loss is a greater sorrow than can be told . . ."

"Our grief is great. Our dear son was a wonderful happiness to us and an only child. We pray God's blessing upon you in the sorrows you see all about you and thank you for your words of comfort . . ."

"Our loss is great and we are heartbroken. Words cannot express how glad we are to learn from you that his last days in France were happy ones. The work that you are doing, Chaplain Trexler, cannot be measured in words . . ."

"We are deeply touched by the sentiments you expressed in regard to the death of our son who left all and gave his life, as he believed, in the cause of justice and freedom. Your letter was the Shadow of a Rock in a weary land. We are thankful to God you were with our beloved son when the end came . . ."

In his concern for the men entrusted to his spiritual care, Samuel heeded neither weariness nor peril. When everything was confused and unanswerable, he made this entry in his diary: ". . . and although conditions are new and extremely difficult I know that the Father's hand still guides and keeps."

Samuel Trexler was not afraid to die, and the men knew this. In some measure his serenity was transmitted to those around him. There was an assurance in his bearing that quenched fear. When the men—mutilated, blind, insane—cried Oh God, what is this You have done to me! he could only offer them the consolations and promises of God as revealed in His word. He could only turn their minds and hearts to Christ The Comforter: "*Lo I am with you all the days, even unto the end of the age.*" He spoke to them gently of the providence, the peace and the presence of God. It was not so much what he said. It was his calm faith that whatever came to pass God's grace would be sufficient, that imparted to the men strength to bear the cross of tragedy.

We were working under heavy pressure when Bishop Brent, chief chaplain at Chaumont, requested Samuel to minister to the German prisoners of war at our post. "Barracks which held a thousand men standing were soon filled," Samuel records. "I placed my cross at one end of the building and someone kindly provided candles. Thus the room was not unchurchly in aspect. I read the Scriptures to the men: *God is our refuge and strength,* and led them in prayer in German. Then I announced that great Lutheran hymn: *A Mighty Fortress Is Our God,* and it seemed as though the tide of full German voices would rip the roof from the barracks." He ministered to the German prisoners with the same solicitude, buried their dead with the same rites as our own soldiers.

On the eve of his departure from Savenay ("I never left a parish with more poignant regret," he said) he held a farewell service of worship in the prison camp. The men swarmed about him all talking at once, begging him to carry messages to wives, mothers, sisters, sweethearts in the Rhineland. He recorded each address, each message carefully: "I shall return to you . . . Do not fear for me . . . I live. I *live!*" and promised to make every effort to deliver them to dear ones.

Samuel Trexler was a good soldier. Bishop James de Wolfe Perry of the Red Cross Chaplain's Bureau, called his work "admirable" and Bishop John J. Brady, base chaplain at St. Nazaire, wrote: "Captain Trexler is an officer who would easily qualify for the hardest type service at the front—he is of the DSC type."

His long-awaited transfer to Third Army Headquarters in Germany finally came through in December 1918. Historic events then being enacted on the shattered stage of Europe are recorded in his diary:

December 8, 1918

When we came to Metz, President Poincaré was entering the city with Clemenceau, Pétain, Joffre, Foch, Haig, Pershing, and French and American Generals beyond counting—an altogether unparalleled aggregation of the military. They marched to the square where Pétain was given the baton.

The whole effect was a study—German spoken only in low tones, and German signs everywhere erased. We waited before the Hotel de Ville for the Grand Procession. It was like a medieval triumphal entry. The entire scene was a page from the Middle Ages . . . The parading continued all afternoon. The day was one of the most impressive in my life.

From Coblenz he wrote to me a few days later.

December 20, 1918

Dear Major Devol,

When I reached here my first request was for mail. Your two letters were my reward, bless your heart—there never was such a friend. My trips over the battlefields were a revelation of the waste and havoc of war—ruined villages, destroyed bridges, gaping shell holes, crosses marking fallen soldiers . . .

Despite more than four years of combat, the Christmas spirit still lives on in this ancient city. The shops look Christmaslike, and the trees remind me of home. Nature has completed the festival by covering the earth with a mantle of snow and the effect on the Rhine valley and the German architecture is fairylike. Coblenz has more color than dear old Savenay—God bless her—I have given her a good part of my life. I am to hold services on Christmas Day in the Royal Chapel. Its white marble altar ornamented in gold and exquisite appointments will provide a beautiful setting for our service celebrating the birthday of the Christ Child.

Yours,

Trexler

Expectations when we had sailed for France in July 1917 that it would soon be over Over There were not realized. In September 1918 Samuel wrote the president of his Church Council: "I dare not leave the work at this present crisis. My own conscience tells me unalterably that for the present my work is here and I cannot rid myself of this conviction . . . When I ask myself as to why our Church should be asked to make this special sacrifice I invariably feel that few churches can so ably stand without a pastor as we. Every department has faithful and trained workers. For these reasons I feel the very distinct call to remain in the work here and ask you to place the matter before the Church Council and secure their blessing."

The congregation assured him that although they felt his absence keenly, they realized the importance of his work in France and granted him the privilege of remaining until such time as he conscientiously felt he could be spared. They inquired what he needed. "Books," he wrote, "books for the sick and the wounded, books to vary the tedium, to conquer loneliness."

At evacuation hospital number 9, new problems presented themselves with the homeward movement of troops and the army of occupation. Months passed and Samuel was still in Germany when I sailed from St. Nazaire for the United States on the tenth of January 1919.

From the American University Union he wrote:

Dear Edmund,

I am dreadfully tired. The day has been full and fatiguing. I am still waiting—the hardest and most frequent demand. What have these years not brought us! Yes, it has been a wonderful experience, and I suppose in the distance will stand out more clearly. We have come through the war—which is no small reason for thanksgiving— are perhaps wiser men and have, I trust, been of some service.

This morning I conducted two services and then made my hospital rounds. The Prince of Wales is in town—an attractive, shy boy of twenty-five. We are to entertain him tonight at our club. I had an interesting day and a half in Weisbaden and Mayence with the French. On Friday I was at Bonn with the British. I even attended a lecture at the University—which is now more crowded with students than ever before. I am hoping each successive letter will be my last from Germany. I am so eager to return to my congregation. Give my friends my love. God bless you.

Trexler

In Paris during the peace conference, his diary relates the eventful days when the Stars and Stripes were "an emblem of new faith and hope to millions in many lands."

February 10, 1919

Representatives of all colors and races have come here to seek support, to plead for help from the American delegation. The most impressive thing about the peace conference is the great influence of America among all the peoples of the earth. America—as the defender of justice and right—is the hope of the civilized world. The world is here anticipating a re-creation. As President Wilson stated in the Palace D'Orsay—America has come to the unique position of being trusted by all the world. The Stars and Stripes are an emblem of faith and hope to millions.

On the third of March after repeated delays and postponements ("Waiting . . . Continued waiting . . . Still waiting . . .") 50 officers and 500 men boarded the Japanese ship *Awa Maru*. "She was small, overcrowded and very dirty," recorded Samuel. "Not one of us however but was willing to risk himself in any craft so we might again be home."

"The bright sun was a fitting accompaniment to our reaching the U. S. A.," he wrote joyously after a two weeks' crossing in rough seas. "We docked at five. After some disappointment saw Ed and shortly after was with him." A month later his brother

· 136 ·

Charles who had served as chaplain with the 320th Field Artillery returned. In the homestead at Bernville with her two sons back from the war Mrs. Trexler was radiantly happy. "And my doctor son, too!" she said, turning to me, her voice trembling with tears. "It is almost too good to believe! Peace! Peace! And my boys home . . . !"

In Greenpoint Samuel was welcomed by a large and happy turnout at the Church of the Messiah. "The founder of the Church of the Messiah is bronzed and muscular," reported the *Greenpoint Star*, "his dark tan accentuated by his hair, which has turned gray . . ."

"In our work at the base hospitals," Samuel told the congregation, "we experienced the full horror of war, witnessed such anguish as no man can realize who has not seen it with his own eyes. The courage of the men was remarkable. They were valiant beyond belief. They were ready and willing, even eager to give their lives that justice and right might triumph. But they will have fought a losing fight unless the principles for which they died are made the cornerstone of a better world, a better way of life for all peoples of the earth. In striving toward this goal the Church must lead the way . . ."

War makes a breach in the minds as well as in the affairs of men. It is difficult (sometimes impossible) to mend this breach. Our homecoming was a bright blur of hysterical reunions, gay parties, gallant parades, returned heroes, committees of welcome, banners and flags. We were emotionally overwrought, and disinclined to settle down to work. It was hard for us to readjust ourselves to the pursuits of peace.

Samuel had been absent from the Church of the Redeemer for nearly two years. There was a happy reunion with the men of his Council at the University Club in Buffalo. "Then I went to my study at the church," his diary states, "and was quite alone with the past. It seemed somewhat vague and shadowy. My feelings were indefinable . . ."

It was months before he could readjust himself to civilian life. "Spent the entire day in a vain effort to get ready for tomorrow," the diary discloses. "It is very hard to readjust oneself. It requires great effort . . ." "I was grateful to the Church of the Redeemer for many things," he later wrote, "but at that time primarily for the fact that it took hold of me immediately and compelled me to conform to the normal routine of life."

As time passed, his letters and diaries again reflected his joy in pastoral work, his pleasure in friendships old and new, and his happiness in the progress of the church. The congregation, delighted to have him at the helm again, were proud of their pastor, of the role he played in civic and community life, and his leadership in affairs of the church at large. He was on the reception committee to welcome King Albert and Queen Elizabeth of Belgium. He helped entertain the French Lutheran Commission. He spoke at mass meetings of the Inter-Church Movement, presided at meetings of the World Service Campaign which had been organized to assist in reconstruction work abroad.

His letter describing the visit of the King and Queen of the Belgians recalled to my mind the visit of President Wilson to Buffalo in November 1916. On that occasion Samuel had also served on the Committee of Escort. "I loved the dash with which the Presidential party moves," he had written me. "The day was ideal and I had several visits with the President and Mrs. Wilson. She has a great deal of charm and the President seems more wonderful the more one sees of him. His tender feeling is a constant pleasure. In the evening I motored Margaret and her cousin, Helen Bones, to the Broadway Auditorium where the President made a memorable address to 15,000 cheering citizens. It was a Red Letter Day for me . . ." He was always so proud to represent his Church at affairs of state.

That summer the congregation had presented him with a Reo car to facilitate his work. The first trip he made in it was from Buffalo to Bernville. ("Showed my gift-car to mother.") On his return, Margaret Wilson and I met him in New York and the three of us drove to Shadow Lawn, the summer White House near Long Branch, New Jersey. The President and his train were due about nine that evening. We had enjoyed the drive immensely and were in high spirits. About eight-thirty (we were still at the dinner table) word came that the President was due to arrive shortly. Secret-service men, servants, the household and its guests began bustling about, setting things to rights, opening and closing doors, turning on lights in the house, porticoes and driveways. In a few minutes the mansion and grounds were ablaze with light.

Margaret, Samuel and I walked out on the lawn and, looking up, noticed that the lights had not yet been switched on in an upper wing. "I'll do it," said Samuel to Margaret, and disappeared within. The next instant the house, the lawn, the driveways, everything was in total darkness. The Secret-service men, not knowing what had happened, fanned out into the trees and shrubbery. Everyone else stood perfectly still. Samuel had blown a master fuse. Before the lights could be restored, the President arrived. When Samuel was finally able to explain what had occurred the President was amused rather than upset.

But when he discovered that Samuel, a novice at the wheel, had driven his daughter to Long Branch that afternoon, he looked at us reproachfully. "How could you have undertaken the responsibility for so precious a passenger!" he said. Neither Samuel nor I could think of an adequate reply.

As always, Samuel found it impossible to say no to the demands on his time and energy and I suppose he felt too that he wanted to make up for time lost at the Church of the Redeemer during the years he was serving in France. "This is to tell you I am still going strong," he wrote me from Buffalo at Christmastime. "Life is very strenuous these days—mostly on account of big drives. I have been speaking all over. I really should have a booking agent. The Church is opening a drive for reconstruction in Europe—$1,800,000. I am the chairman for Buffalo and we shall have the opening mass meeting here in April . . . Then the Muhlenberg men are going after $1,500,000. They want me to assist them in Allentown—also here and in New York. In addition to these problems the regular parish work demands thought and administration. I am feeling fine though at times somewhat weary . . ."

"Another year of goodness and mercy from above," he noted in his diary at the year's end. "May the new year be for me one more consecrated to Thee . . ." A few days later he collapsed. Dr. Fred Rice, fearing pneumonia, ordered him to the hospital. "This is my first Sunday in bed since my ordination twenty-one years ago," he recorded. "But my hospital prison is quite cheerful in the face of the bitter weather outside."

It was thought wise for him to go to Atlantic City for a few days of rest and sunshine. But he was restless, anxious to be back at his desk. "I must be doing something," he wrote me.

"I become so impatient to be up and working that I can scarcely stand it. I am leaving here in the morning . . ." The following day he telegraphed: "Reached Buffalo at ten-thirty. Immediately went to the Church happily to take up the threads of work."

In June 1920 the course of his life again abruptly changed. He was in Binghamton, New York, attending a convention of the Lutheran Synod of New York and New England. His diary reports briefly three days that marked the opening of a new and greater phase of his career.

June 2, 1920

Finished writing my report while the Synod discussed the salaried presidency. At the afternoon session this was adopted, and before I could get my breath, I was elected. I withdrew my name, but was compelled to take the chair. The final decision I deferred . . .

June 3, 1920

Completed the business of Synod and then took the train for home. On the way saw the Buffalo papers which already had the story of my election. Went to the Church. Came home and tried to rest after the strenuous days.

June 4, 1920

Went downtown in the morning to consult some of our men. The Church Council met in the evening and unanimouly took the larger attitude to my new work. None insisted upon my remaining in the parish.

A few days later he wrote me: "I at times hesitate to leave my beautiful church and our loyal people. It requires courage and faith to venture out upon the new field but I suppose the doing so will develop those qualities . . ."

After conferring with the Reverend Doctor Franklin F. Fry in Rochester, New York, he made the following entry in his diary: "After my consultation with Dr. Fry, yielding to forces which could not be gainsaid, I definitely decided to accept the synodical presidency . . ." From Buffalo he wrote "The congregation is taking it in characteristically generous fashion. They do not want to stand in the way of the progress of the Church at large."

In September he held his farewell service in the Church of the Redeemer and said good-by to the many friends gathered to bid him Godspeed. "Thus ended my happy life in Buffalo," he recorded,—with what feelings of regret and inevitability, who can know!

CHAPTER SIX

WIDER HORIZONS

Behold, how good and how pleasant it is
for brethren to dwell together in unity

PSALMS 133:1

FROM THE beginning of his ministry as a young mission pastor at the turn of the century, Samuel Trexler was in accord with forward-looking pastors who realized that if the Lutheran Church was to make the glory of its faith a more vital force in the life of America, the language of the land must be used in her services of worship and in the instruction of her children.

Associated in separate synods,* ministeriums and conferences organized by immigrants from Germany, the Scandinavian countries and other areas of Europe, the church was divided in America as it had been for centuries past in the old world, by linguistic, ethnic, cultural and confessional differences. There was no effective unity of forces and little interest on the part of the average congregation beyond parish boundaries. Young

* An old Christian word defined as "on the way *together,*" *synod* designates a number of Christian congregations united in faith, fellowship and service.

Lutherans reared in churches holding to the language of the country from which their forefathers had come were gradually drifting away to other Protestant churches or to no church at all.

Fifteen congregations in the New York Ministerium were using the English language exclusively in 1902. These petitioned permission from the Ministerium to organize an English Conference on the grounds that their work could best be accomplished if they were so organized. References to early meetings of the English proponents are noted in Samuel's diary in June 1901: "Spent the entire day at the English Conference session in The Church of the Reformation (Rochester) . . . Took considerable part in the business of the day . . . In the evening laid plans for our work to come at the New York Ministerium . . ."

The plans laid for "work to come" were rejected: "Went to Zion's Church where the New York Ministerium convened . . . The Germans manifested their disaffection . . . In the evening had an English caucus at Reverend W. J. Miller's home—most delightful to have all our young brethren stand up so nobly for our common cause . . . Went to a meeting of the New York Ministerium today prepared for anything in this conflict of English versus German. In the P.M. the storm broke in all its fury. No definite settlement and considerable hot blood . . . Yesterday's questions again arose and hinged around our starting an English mission in South Brooklyn. The Germans would not give us a respectable hearing and our matter was lost 90-18. No telling what may arise out of this defeat . . . At 3.30 P.M. the English ministers had a private conference in the Church of the Reformation as to the grave problems confronting us. We decided to use every means to avert the almost inevitable rupture . . ." Meetings continued throughout the year.

In January 1902, the English Conference withdrew from the New York Ministerium for the purpose of organizing an English synod. "The former English Conference met in the Church of the Redeemer, Albany, New York," Samuel records (January 28, 1902) "to further the organization of the new Synod. There was intense interest in the work before us and I was delighted with the thorough devoutness of everyone concerned. The questions as to organization required the entire day and arguments on all sides were excellent. At six in the evening we finally found the true compromise—a most happy outcome—showing clearly the hand of God in our affairs."

It was a happy and enthusiastic group of young pastors who met in September to adopt a constitution for the new body. "We decided to call it the Synod of New York and New England," the diary states. "Our work will cover the area from New York to Boston and from Boston to Buffalo. The constitution is a carefully prepared document and gives more power to the president than ever yet held by any Lutheran president." The new synod which represented a merger of the English Conference, the New York Synod and the New York Ministerium was an important step toward unification. It comprised 30 parishes and some 10,000 members. Said President William Bacher in his sermon to the delegates, "Our faces are set to the future . . ."

As the work of the synod widened in scope and the responsibility of directing its affairs increased, President Bacher and his successors, the Reverends William M. Horn and Franklin F. Fry recommended that the presidency be made a full-time, salaried office. At the annual convention in Binghamton, New York in 1920 this recommendation was adopted. "It came like a thunderclap in a clear sky," said Samuel, "when the synod decided that it would have a full-time president, and that I should be the president."

It was decided to establish headquarters for the new synod in New York City and office space was arranged for at 16 East 48th Street. Samuel had demonstrated his capacity for leadership in many phases of religious work and was thoroughly familiar with problems of the church both in this country and abroad. He had the unqualified support of the men who had chosen him to preside over the destiny of a Lutheran synod. "Enthusiasm reached a high pitch when Dr. Trexler was escorted to the chair," declared *The Lutheran* (June 24, 1920) in reporting his election in Binghamton. "The new president will have the co-operative support of the entire Synod." Samuel was in his early forties, experienced and alert to the needs of the church in a changing world.

With characteristic zest he plunged into administrative and executive duties. From a convention in Washington, D. C., of the United Lutheran Church in America (a merger effected in 1919) he wrote in October 1920, "We have been so busy that I have scarcely a moment's breathing. I have been thus far unable to call up a single soul. The important matter however is that the Church is moving along in a wonderful manner and one is constantly being thrilled by its advance."

Celebration in 1917 of the four hundredth anniversary of the Protestant Reformation, and in 1920 of the four hundredth anniversary of the publication of Luther's Small Catechism focused attention on common loyalties and a heritage of faith far more significant than the language in which it was voiced. Little by little, differences rooted in nationalism and old-world cleavages were overcome. In the tragic aftermath of the First World War,

American Lutherans, after more than three centuries of going their separate ways, closed ranks.

Except by some scholars and a few zealous pastors the religious life of Europe and the Lutheran Church in Europe had been but vaguely comprehended in America. The same was true of the religious life of America on the part of fellow churchmen in Europe. The Lutheran Church neither knew her sister churches nor enjoyed the benefits of cooperative endeavor with them. The war brought this largest group of Protestant believers into a closer fellowship, challenged American Lutherans to a wider vision of their responsibilities to a world-wide Lutheran family.

As president of the Synod of New York and New England, Samuel Trexler was in a strategic position to serve as liaison between the churches of Europe and America at a time when financial help was vital to sustain life in the mother churches across the sea. In raising funds to restore and rebuild Lutheran churches on the continent he was an eloquent and tireless speaker. Visiting the various churches in the territory of his synod and preaching from many pulpits, he portrayed to shocked congregations conditions he himself had seen as chaplain overseas—churches in ruins, pastors at their wits' end, their congregations scattered like chaff from the seed.

He reminded Lutherans of their debt to the past. He pleaded with them to repay this debt at all cost and to rear new churches in Europe on the old indestructible foundations of their heritage and faith. The people responded generously. In the years following the First World War some six million dollars were contributed by Lutheran churches in this country toward rehabilitation work abroad. The Synod of New York and New England alone was responsible for some eighty-five thousand dollars.

When new and far greater sacrifices were called for after the Second World War, American Lutherans were prepared to make them. They had been brought to full realization that their faith meant more than the salvation of their own souls, that it meant meeting need as wide as the world, that they were indeed their brother's keeper and that they were brother to millions.

It was through desire and willingness to aid the war-stricken churches of Europe that the foundations of Lutheran world unity were painfully constructed. What is today referred to as the ecumenical (wide as the world) Lutheran Church was born out of this desire, this will to meet human need, to mitigate human suffering in a time of great crisis.

To organize and carry forward the work of relief and reconstruction the National Lutheran Council was organized in 1918. In raising funds for the vast program in which the Council was engaged, Samuel Trexler worked very closely with Dr. John Alfred Morehead who was spearheading the work in Europe, motivated by the dream of creating a Lutheran Church of the World. As head of the European Commission, Morehead made the recommendation that the National Lutheran Council call a Lutheran World Convention. This was the beginning of ecumenical Lutheran planning which resulted in the First Lutheran World Convention at Eisenach in 1923. Dr. Morehead, a central figure in this international gathering which was attended by delegates from twenty-two nations, said on behalf of the American churches, "We would help one another." In his biography of Dr. Morehead, published in 1936, Samuel gives a firsthand account of the historic convention in Eisenach. "No one listening to those present could fail to note the deep faith, the heroism and yet humble spirit of these men," he wrote. "At Eisenach was made the first attempt to *demonstrate* that there is a Lutheran Church of the World."

The service which Dr. Morehead and many other valiant churchmen here and abroad rendered to the cause of unifying Lutheran forces throughout the world was materially strengthened by the leadership which Samuel Trexler gave to the Lutheran Church in this country during those years. The merging of forces in which he played a pre-eminent role in 1902 (and again in 1929) strengthened the hand of the church in America and thereby intensified her ability to cope with the overwhelming problems two world wars imposed on the churches abroad.

The transition from Lutheran isolationism to Lutheran world federation was achieved by men of faith working under extraordinary difficulties toward an ideal—a united Church. In this stirring religious drama Samuel Trexler was a prominent figure. Years were required before a Lutheran World Federation was organized in Lund, Sweden.in 1947 and the task of bringing 80,000,000 Lutherans into global accord is by no means completed. But it was through the vision of men like Morehead and Trexler that the foundations were laid for the most powerful Protestant federation in the world today.

When European churchmen came to this country Samuel was at pains to entertain them, to make their stay here enjoyable, informative, memorable. I recall an evening when he had as guests in our home in New York City three church statesmen from Germany—Bishops Marahrens, Meiser and Hanns Lilje. After dinner some twenty young clergymen and their wives attended a reception at which Samuel introduced them to his distinguished visitors. In pleasant ways like this he bound American clergymen to their brethren from other lands, forged friendships between Lutherans of diverse nationalities. The strength inherent in Lutheran world unity stems from international friendships and understanding between church leaders. There were many distinguished visitors to this country during those years, among them that fearless church statesman, Bishop Dibelius of Berlin. A letter to Samuel from Bishop Kapi is typical of similar letters from all over the world:

Györ, Hungary
August, 1930

Dear President Trexler,

I was very glad indeed to receive your kind letter from Budapest. I appreciate very much your loving-kindness and I wish to assure you that I cherish the recollections of your goodness and your love. It is always with sincere joy that I think of America, of the privilege of meeting you in New York, and of our excellent fellow workers across the sea.

Bishop Kapi

Samuel not only had the respect and confidence of Lutheran clergymen but of church leaders of all faiths. His personality, broad sympathies and deep understanding of human beings enabled him to cross barriers that proved stumbling blocks to those unaware of the ease with which the fine balance in human relationships can be destroyed. Few clergymen, during their lifetime, received the accolade from Lutheran clergymen and from leaders of other denominations and faiths accorded Samuel Trexler.

The executive and administrative work of synod was even more arduous than he had apprehended in the prospect. These notations in his diary are typical of hours in the office: "Was busy with many administrative matters all day . . . Spent the entire day with perplexing problems . . . The day was occupied with many small details . . . After a heavy day at the office took the seven o'clock train for . . ."

The paper work was staggering—bulletins to pastors and congregations regarding the work of synod and the church at large, reports, letters, public addresses, and, of course, sermons. Almost never a Sunday that he did not preach. Yet his office door was always open and he was never too busy to share with pastors who came for counsel and encouragement, their hopes and aspirations, plans and problems.

"To work with you really helps to make a pleasure of what might well otherwise be a burden," a young pastor wrote to him. "Many a man in the ministry is deeply indebted to you for help and inspiration that have done much to make his ministry effective. How you ever find time to give so much of yourself to so many people, I shall never know."

The only regret Samuel voiced as president of synod was that his official duties left him so little time for reading and study. Visiting the various churches of synod necessitated almost continual traveling. "It is fortunate you like trains, or so you have said," I remarked one night when he was packing a bag he had unpacked that morning, "since you practically *live* in them." Thinking of his destination and what he was going to say to the congregation which awaited him at his destination he was almost always missing some item when he arrived. "You will find my 'bands' in the box behind the collars in the upper drawer," he would write me. And again, "After carefully putting in the razor strop, I found this morning that I had forgotten the razors —you will find them on the second shelf in the cabinet . . . The only necessity I have thus far forgotten is my white dress tie— send me the one washed by Susie last week . . ." So it went. However, he was not by nature careless. Quite the reverse; he was orderly and methodical. He kept his papers in beautiful order, his dresser drawers neat as a pin. Fortunate that with all the comings and goings, everything was in its place and that he knew exactly where everything was. Only once was there a mixup. He wrote me from a convention meeting in Rochester that he had forgotten his sermon manuscript, giving me exact instructions as to its whereabouts. After I had ransacked the file in which he said I would find it, I wired him that wherever the manuscript might be it was *not* where he said it was. He requested me frantically to make a more thorough search. I did. Still I could not find it. "Stop looking," he wired the next day. "I have the manuscript with me."

He was almost never in the same city two days in succession. On a tour of the churches in northern New York in 1924, he wrote me from Syracuse: "These one-night stands have been fatal to making definite plans. My week will be very crowded—my desk, I know, is piled high with matters to be cared for. This means work by day and by evening. I feel that I am equal to it but fear I must forego the pleasure of accompanying you to Washington . . ."

There were churches to be dedicated, pastors to be installed, cornerstones to be laid. "You seem to be forever wandering in a forest of cornerstones," a friend wrote him apropos of newspaper clippings reporting his varied synod activities.

"Lutheran Leader of Note Coming . . . Well-Known Lutheran Clergyman Expected . . . Lutheran Bishop of New York to Speak . . . Synod Head to Lay Cornerstone . . ."

There were church anniversary celebrations that demanded his presence and, also, social and civic affairs in which the church was directly or indirectly interested. There were conferences, luncheons and dinners in behalf of hospitals, orphanages and homes for the aged. There were meetings of various clubs and organizations to which he belonged—Koinonia, Philothean Society, Sigma Chi, the New York Lutheran Ministers Association (which he served as president), the Clergy Club of New York, the Sons of the Revolution, the Pilgrims, the Buffalo Historical Society, the Pennsylvania Society (which he served as chaplain), the University Club. He was a trustee of various educational institutions and philanthropic foundations including Hartwick College, Endicott Junior College and the Josiah Macy Jr., Foundation.

There were those who envied the President of synod. But of course these were under the erroneous impression that the president's role was a delightful round of gay dinner parties marked by adulation and applause—a job calling for graciousness and platform presence, but not dulled by *work*.

Fifty thousand Lutherans of New York and New England rejoiced in the progress that had been made in a quarter century toward deeper fellowship and greater unity when the Synod of New York and New England celebrated its silver jubilee in the Church of the Reformation, Rochester, New York, in 1926.

"The Empire State was declared a lost cause for the Lutheran Church when I was doing missionary work in 1896," said the Reverend Dr. Frederick H. Knubel, president of the United Lutheran Church in America, in greeting the delegates. "In their missionary zeal to save the day several young ministers of our denomination of whom your president, Dr. Samuel Trexler, was one, formed the Synod of New York and New England. Its progress has been remarkable . . ."

When Samuel rose to address the convention, he spoke with visible emotion:

"We humbly thank God for the group of men who organized our Synod, for the struggle and sacrifices which have been made and in the enjoyment of which we work and live. It was not self-glorification that prompted these men, but a serious sense of responsibility—a strong compulsion quite outside themselves that guided and animated them.

"The life of the Synod has developed into a strong current, the refreshing influence of which is now felt all around the world. During this quarter century, we multiplied our figures in churches by two and our membership by three. We started with thirty-seven congregations, and while dismissing eleven in 1910 to form the Synod of Central Canada, yet have a total number of congregations today of seventy-six. The Synod has grown from a membership of 10,000 to 30,000 and property owned by our churches has increased in value from $800,000 to $5,000,000.

"We are in a community of large universities and colleges. These have called to us and our Synod has responded, making a contribution in ideas and services that has enriched not only our Church but the Church throughout the land. The fruit of our work at Cornell and Harvard has been so satisfying that there is no longer any doubt that the Church has no more effective way of ministering to our young people . . ."

Samuel's contribution to the silver anniversary was a book in

· 154 ·

which he recorded the history of the Synod of New York and New England during its twenty-five years of growth. Published by Macmillan, and entitled *Crusaders of the Twentieth Century*, the volume is dedicated "to the memory of my father who so magnified the ministry that his three sons followed him."

The *New York Times* called *Crusaders* a "story of enterprise and achievement that may well make any executive envious." Dr. Trexler as a churchman, the reviewer stated, "had that experience of development through initiative and vision which in the business world would have transformed the young man from Main Street into a New York bank president." Lutheran pastors welcomed the book with gratitude and praise. Wrote the Reverend W. L. Hunton, Secretary of the Parish and School Board of the United Lutheran Church in America:

"Out of your own rich experience, you have presented the uphill fight of English Lutheran pastors to establish English-speaking churches in New York and New England at a time when the church was divided by almost insurmountable barriers of nationalistic loyalties, confusion of tongues, estrangement and dissension.

"When I think of those earlier days when I was a member of the New York Ministerium and prior even to the time of the English Conference, I recall that if we English-speaking pastors with timidity attempted to express opinions we were likely to have someone in the opposite part of the church call out: *Deutsch! Deutsch!* intimating that if we could not speak German we ought not to speak on the floor of the convention and when I realize what a radical change has been made in the Ministerium in this respect, and how meanwhile the Synod of New York and New England has grown up in that territory, then I appreciate the progress that has been made under your leadership in the entire state within the short space of my own memory and experience."

Swept from one anniversary function to another with the day's work running like a swift tide beneath the bright lights and the incessant talk, Samuel looked a tired man when he stepped off the train after the anniversary convention in Rochester.

A few days later, Crown Prince Gustaf Adolf and Crown Princess Louise of Sweden attended services in the Swedish Evangelical Church of Gustavus Adolphus in New York. A crowd of 2,000 persons were gathered outside the church to cheer and applaud the royal couple. Dignitaries of the Lutheran Church and representatives of the 451 parishes in this district were present. At the conclusion of the services, Samuel as president of the New York Lutheran Ministers Association presented the Crown Prince with a specially prepared copy of *The Lutheran Church in America* written by Professor Abdel Ross Wentz of Gettysburg Lutheran Theological Seminary, and bound in the Swedish national colors. The rituals and ceremonies at the church lasted for two hours. Samuel was at his gracious best. But he had been at his gracious best too long. After three weeks in the hospital he was compelled to spend three more weeks under the watchful eyes and tender care of his mother in Bernville. "Mother was surprised to see me looking so well after the operation," he wrote cheerfully.

A great triumph had been scored at the Silver Jubilee Convention of Synod. A plan to merge the Synod of New York and New England with the New York Ministerium and the New York Synod had been approved. This was another major stride toward collective strength and during the years following Samuel gave much time and thought to effective consummation of this merger. It was declared a reality in June 1929 by unanimous vote at a meeting in St. John's Church, Albany, New York. There was great rejoicing on the part of all who had helped bring the new synod into being. The church rang with the hymn of thanks "Now Thank We All Our God." The name chosen was the United Synod of New York.* Let us open Samuel's diary and look in on the proceedings in St. John's Church:

June 5, 1929

Spent much of the morning in a meeting of the incorporators of the new Synod and hectically gathering the final papers. At two o'clock the long-looked-for meeting opened. St. John's Church crowded from pit to dome—the eight incorporators entering in robes and taking places in the chancel—the audience breathless.

The merger was effected and then came the election. I led on each ballot and was declared elected on the third—227—209. The vote was made unanimous. I made a brief statement and then took the gavel . . .

"The merger brings together a wide variety of churches in the busiest thoroughfares of our largest cities as well as at the country crossroads," Samuel told the happy delegates, "all the diverse life of Lutherans from Boston to Buffalo, from Cape Cod to Niagara Falls. There are congregations in the United Synod of New York which celebrated their centennial when Muhlenberg arrived in this country in 1742, and there are new missions still in their swaddling clothes. The United Synod of New York comprises 416 congregations and 220,000 Lutherans! We will face

* Now designated as the United Synod of New York and New England.

many difficult problems, but these can be solved if we earnestly strive, with the help of God, in all humility, to find a meeting of minds . . ."

"It was the work of God," he recorded in his diary when the convention closed. "Unity and hope everywhere. Took my berth early and was asleep before we left Albany."

Smiling faces, excited greetings, telegrams and telephone messages awaited him in New York City. Everybody was happy that this new honor had been conferred upon him. Congratulations cascaded on his desk—a shining waterfall of words like these:

May I offer you my hearty congratulations and best wishes upon the high and important office to which you have been appointed. Your election is a matter of congratulation not only to the Lutheran Church but to all who are laboring for the upbuilding of the Kingdom of God. With high regard,

William T. Manning

Kindly permit a well-wisher from another denomination to express to you his congratulations upon your election as the head of this great section of the United Lutheran Church. We will continue our prayers that you may be given an unusual measure of grace, tact and diplomacy as you carry on the work of consolidating these hitherto separate units into a united working force for your Church.

The Reverend Willard L. Robinson

Allow me to congratulate you with all my heart. You have truly magnified your office and I, as one of your fellow alumni of Muhlenberg College, tender you my meed of praise with profound thanks to God that He has let your life so shine among men. It is a wonderful thing so to live that, because we have lived, the world is better for our having lived.

Edgar D. Shimer

There are many things that I could say in your praise today. But there is one thing that stands out. It is your confidence in God. If anyone were to ask me "What kind of man is Samuel Trexler?" I would answer that he is a rare kind of man—a man who is sure in his God. It sounds simple. It is simple. But it is illuminating. Does it not indeed make everything clear?

Samuel Strauss

Letters from people in every walk and circumstance of life. Letters from all parts of the world. What joy Samuel Trexler had in them. He liked to be appreciated—who does not? He reread them many times, treasured them, filed them carefully in leather bound books.

Among the letters he received was one from his mother. She wrote concerning his election:

Bernville
June 7, 1929

To the President,
Dear Son,

Just received your telegram. My congratulations. It is a great honor and a grave responsibility. You have had glorious weather, such weather as your father would have enjoyed for Synod. When will you be coming home?

Love,
Mother

· 159 ·

She had that day received a letter from the Reverend Franklin F. Fry which must have brought her happiness beyond words:

June 7, 1929

Dear Mrs. Trexler,

You must be one of the happiest mothers on God's planet. Your cup of joy is overflowing. Like Cornelia who spoke of her two sons as her chief jewels, so with you. Your oldest son has been chosen as leader of the United Synod of New York and your youngest son has been called to a great opportunity in the largest city of the United States. Neither of your sons could have come into being without you, and your training and example has been their constant guide and their inspiration. They are the first to acknowledge it . . .

Franklin F. Fry

In October that year the Church of the Messiah celebrated the thirtieth anniversary of its founding. The date also marked the thirtieth anniversary of Samuel's ordination. At a dinner in his honor many expressions of gratitude and affection were voiced. Because the words spoken were from the hearts of the people they were extremely moving. When Samuel stood up to respond there were tears in his eyes. Turning to his mother who was sitting at his right hand, fragile and lovely in black silk, he said gently, "Mother . . . you have heard the wonderfully kind things the people have said . . . no more can be said when I am gone . . . no higher praise given than the tributes it has been my humble joy to receive, with you, this night." She looked up at him with her sweet shy smile, her face suffused with happiness in his happiness.

· 160 ·

In an impressive service in St. John's Church, New York, "before many witnesses" on December 10, 1929 Samuel Trexler was formally inducted into office as president of the newly formed United Synod of New York. The sermon was preached by the Reverend Frederick H. Knubel, president of the United Lutheran Church in America. The Reverend Herman Brezing, president of the former New York Ministerium, officiated. To the question "Will you endeavor to administer your office to the glory of God, to the advancement of His Kingdom, in fidelity to the constitution of this body (the synod) and in charity to your brethren?" Dr. Trexler answered, "Yes, the Lord helping me with the power and grace of His Holy Spirit."

The Synod was then addressed as follows:

"Brethren: You have heard the obligation solemnly assumed by our brother whom we have called to the presidency of our Synod. We are exhorted by the blessed apostle, to know them who labor among us and who are over us in the Lord and admonish us; and to esteem them very highly for their work's sake. Will you therefore receive him and show him the honor and obedience in the Lord due to a shepherd and guide placed over you by the Lord Jesus, the Chief Shepherd and Bishop of our souls?" The congregation responded, "Yes, by the help of God. Amen." The office was then committed to Dr. Trexler in the name of the Father, the Son and the Holy Ghost.

The territory of the United Synod of New York included the state of New York, northern New Jersey, Connecticut, Massachusetts and the adjacent New England communities, with headquarters at 39 East 35 Street, New York. It was imperative at the outset that the divergent views of more than 400 pastors and some 250,000 members be reconciled. The texture of the new merger of congregations was complex and loosely woven. Samuel's first concern as president of Synod was to draw the threads together to firm the fabric. This required patience and time, and skill, too. The year's end found him, as noted in his diary, "pulling a new and heavier load."

When the curtain rose on the thirties, the stage was set for a calamity known as the depression. As the darkness of the years ahead deepened, merely to support the financial structure of the Synod became a serious problem. It was a time of suffering, shock and bewilderment. People were heartsick and weary, confused in mind and spirit. Progress was hindered by anxieties and uncertainties. The Synod's program of benevolence and evangelism lagged. Meanwhile divisions of opinion stemming from old differences in backgrounds and viewpoints rose to the surface of the troubled times. Discontent spread. There was growing apprehension on the part of those who respected Samuel Trexler's leadership that the men disinclined to "show him the honor and obedience in the Lord due to a shepherd and a guide," were not only weakening his position but jeopardizing the future of the new synod as well.

In 1931 Samuel made a synod-wide tour of the churches, conferring with their church councils on vital problems affecting church life, in an effort to restore hope and confidence in hardpressed pastors and discouraged congregations. Although endowed with unusual talent for finding solutions to problems that concerned the church, there was little he or any other church leader could do to alleviate the misery and despondency that trailed in the wake of continuing economic crisis.

The Synod's income steadily declined. The number of workers was reduced from nine to three. Samuel suggested and obtained approval for a reduction in executive salaries, his own included. It was proposed by the Long Island Conference as a depression measure, that salaried officers be eliminated altogether, but this recommendation was rejected by the delegates as a fatal backward step. Conventions of Synod were marked by constraint, mounting dissension, short tempers and growing unrest. Diverse currents of thought that had prevailed before the consolidation flowed back into old stream-beds.

Samuel Trexler was a reasonable man. He felt that human beings were entitled to their own points of view and readily allowed that every man had a right to defend his opinion. But while he brought to the sessions of Synod considered judgment and forbearance he would not sacrifice basic convictions for uneasy alliances. "I have to restrain myself not to inject caustic remarks into the various discussions," he wrote me. "But I succeed quite well by the grace of God. They propound many questions but can give the solutions to few."

In his annual report to Synod in 1933 he charged that funds pledged by member congregations for benevolent and mission work of the Church at large were being misused by some of the churches. "Funds contributed for work of the Church at large dare not be diverted to local purposes," he told the delegates. "That we should not divert funds so received, no matter how urgent the local necessity, permits of no controversy. It is fundamentally wrong to use funds gathered for one purpose for another . . . Such diversion is morally cupable and spiritually degrading . . ."

"Your views of the situation so clearly and courageously set forth have been read by me with great interest," one pastor wrote. "If all the church leaders of America would speak out in this way we might hope for a transformation in a distressing situation." But there were others who did not like the President's rebuke at all. Back and forth, like dark birds in the convention halls, swooped angry words of blame and fault. "I am sorry to find myself so utterly out of agreement with your views . . . Speaking furthermore, and having in divers moods considered your statement, I feel constrained to . . . As to the working out of Christ's plans, let me remind you . . ."

In May 1934 when the flowers in her garden were coming into bloom, Samuel's mother stepped into eternity. Her dress had caught fire when she was trying to light an oil stove in the kitchen that had been her loved domain for sixty years. Critically burned, she lingered awhile, but all the ministrations of skilled physicians could not save her life. Both her sons were at her bedside.

"Then we went to the church," Samuel wrote sadly, "where the service was held and where we for the last time looked on her lovely face . . ." His grief was like a crushing weight that he was too weary to push aside. To live without her sweet presence, to know that she waited his homecoming no more, was a grievous thing for him to face. I thought of his many letters from Bernville: "Mother and I are having a wonderful time talking it all over . . . Mother and I are having a wonderful time entertaining old friends . . . Mother and I are having a wonderful time . . ." The only occasion on which I saw Samuel give way to his emotions was when he returned from the cemetery the day his mother was laid to rest. Reading the letters of condolence from those who sought to comfort him, he buried his hands in his face and wept bitterly.

Two weeks later the United Synod of New York met in convention in St. John's Church, Albany. "Well the worst is over," Samuel wrote me on May 29th. "We had a hard day of it— tangled up in all sorts of snarls. The election comes tomorrow. I have constant expressions of support. Unless something unforeseen happens I am quite certain of being elected. We can only wait . . ."

"The scheduled business proceeded during the day," his diary relates the following day. "At noon there were the elections and I was surprised not to be elected on the first ballot. At the close of the session the third ballot was counted and I had lost the presidency to Dr. Ellis B. Burgess of Pittsburgh. I was dazed and tried to reconcile myself."

When he returned home, Samuel came into the living room and sat down wearily. "Trexler, I . . ." But he silenced me with a gesture. "I'm not so sure, Ed," he said composedly, "that this isn't the best thing that could have happened. There have been times of late when I felt that I could not carry the burden of Synod responsibilities much further . . . Someone who has not been worn down by the struggle of the past five years may do the job better . . ." "Trexler, I . . ." "Things do not always go according to plan," he said.

When the newspapers reported the results of the election a storm of protest broke. Letters poured in from indignant, surprised, bewildered men and women.

"You will always be 'a King in the camp' for us. God continue to bless and empower you," wrote the Reverend S. Parkes Cadman.

"History will make you an heroic figure for no man in our time has done so much for the Lutheran Church as you," declared Carl W. Ackerman.

"I am prepared for any turn of fortune's wheel," stated Dr. Ralph W. Sockman, "but I confess that the transactions in Albany are beyond my power of understanding."

"I do not understand the reasoning in Albany," Dr. Harry Emerson Fosdick wrote, "but your devoted friends love and admire you more than ever. Blessings on you."

And Miss Margaret Wilson wired him: "This just marks the end of work nobly accomplished and the beginning of a new work for God's servant of love."

Day after day an avalanche of letters and telegrams descended on Samuel's desk. It was a long time before the storm cleared. Everybody was indignant—except Samuel. He went to Bar Harbor, Maine to rest, read and meditate. There was no place he enjoyed more. The rocky beauty of the Maine coast appealed to him, and we had a host of friends in and around Bar Harbor. The long summer days were ideal for visiting back and forth with friends whom we had little or no opportunity to call on during work-filled winters. There was Professor William Adams Brown, William Lyon Phelps, Mary and Katherine Dreier, the John D. Rockefellers, the William Jay Schieffelins, the Henry Morgenthaus, Mrs. Morris Loeb, the Edwin Goulds, Mrs. Shepard Fabbri, Bishop Manning, the Harry Emerson Fosdicks and others.

Wherever Samuel went he had great pleasure in visiting the churches. About a hundred miles from Bar Harbor near Waldoboro, Maine, there was an historic and picturesque little German meetinghouse. One of the five oldest churches in the country, it was founded in 1773 by General Samuel Waldo. When Samuel discovered it in the summer of 1932 it had not been used for services for many years. Situated on a hill in the midst of tiger-lilies and crumbling headstones, the forsaken little building pulled at his heartstrings. "Wouldn't it be *wonderful*, Ed," he said, walking toward the weathered doors, "to reopen this old church and hold summer services here!"

The next morning he called on the Waldoboro town officials and with their enthusiastic co-operation and the aid of friends, the meetinghouse was reopened the following summer. Every year thereafter, when he was in Bar Harbor, Samuel conducted a service of worship at the old Waldoboro church, preaching to an overflowing congregation of summer residents and townspeople. Many drove considerable distances to the service.

One Sunday morning as we were walking up the hill to the church we met Harry Emerson Fosdick, also climbing the hill. "Why, Dr. Fosdick," exclaimed Samuel, delighted to see his friend, "what on earth are *you* doing here?" Dr. Fosdick smiled. "I've come to hear *you* preach," he replied. "I've just driven fifty miles with that in mind . . ."

"Imagine Dr. Fosdick driving fifty miles to hear me preach," Samuel observed later, shaking his head. "Does that surprise you so much?" I asked. "Why yes," he answered, "yes, it does."

Of the gifts and graces that were plain to others Samuel Trexler seemed entirely unaware. Genuinely humble, he was without personal conceit. Power and prestige only deepened his humility of spirit. It never occurred to him to inform people whom he met that he was the president of a synod. High honors had come to him from his church when he penned these lines by Kathleen Wheeler in his diary in 1929:

He came to my desk with quivering lips
*   The lesson was done*
"Dear teacher, I want a new leaf," he said
*   "I have spoiled this one."*
I took the old leaf stained and blotted
And gave him a new one all unspotted
*   And into his sad eyes smiled*
*   "Do better now, my child."*

I went to the throne with quivering soul
*   The old year was done*
"Dear Father, hast Thou a new leaf for me
*   I have spoiled this one."*
He took the old leaf, stained and blotted
And gave me a new one all unspotted
*   And into my sad heart smiled*
*   "Do better now, my child."*

When we returned from Bar Harbor in the fall of 1934 Samuel sailed for Europe to make a firsthand study of religious conditions in Germany and in Russia. In 1935 he again went to Europe, this time for the purpose of attending the Third Lutheran World Convention in Paris.

In January 1936 at a public lecture in Syracuse under the auspices of the Lutheran Pastoral Association of that city he made the prediction that war would engulf the world within five years and that the United States would find it impossible to remain neutral. "Dr. Trexler told reporters (*Syracuse Herald,* January 16) he believed another world conflagration to be inevitable as the result of the activities of five or six men who at the moment wield the power that controls the world's destiny.

These men, he said, are Adolf Hitler of Germany, Premier Mussolini of Italy, Joseph Stalin of Soviet Russia and one or two Japanese warlords . . ."

"None of these men is one whom anyone in his calm judgment would select to lead the world," the distinguished churchman observed sadly, "but the fact remains that if no one else leads it, they will do the job. It is all very well for us in America to say that we will remain neutral, but alas, it will, I am afraid, be impossible for us to remain out of it. The world is so small that whatever affects one nation or group of nations affects every other . . . The world is divided between those nations which have and those which have not. It is those which have not, whether it be territory or markets or power, wherein the danger lies . . . The lengthening shadow of totalitarianism gradually falling upon a large part of Europe means so much to the Christian church that the entire church must stand together to resist its dread possibilities. Ecclesiastical isolationism, like that of nations, is doomed."

The following year Samuel journeyed to Oxford for a Conference on Life and Work, and to Edinburgh to attend a Conference on Faith and Order. At home and abroad he continued to be "busied all the day in the work of the church." He was in constant demand as a speaker and his appointment calendar was as crowded, if not more so, than it had been when he was president of Synod. He was always available when called upon to address young people or to attend meetings of Camp Trexler— a boy's camp he had founded in 1930 on Lake Stahahe in the Ramapo Mountains near Southfields, New York. This youth church project which is carried forward under the auspices of the Boys' Work Foundation of the Lutheran Church was one to which Samuel gave happy personal attention and direction from the summer day when he dedicated the camp to the development of Christian leadership among boys. His interest in the camp continued to the end of his life.

He served also on the Board of Foreign Missions of the United Lutheran Church in America. When he was elected as a member of the Board in 1935 the following newsnote appeared in *The Foreign Mission*: ". . . No doubt the complexity of the numerous items of our foreign mission business will appeal to Dr. Samuel Trexler, who for so many years has dealt with numerous and varied problems of administration."

Yet, with all the demands upon his time during these years he succeeded in writing two books—both of them regarded as important contributions to the history and literature of the Lutheran Church. *Out of Thirty-Five Years:* "Leaves from the life book of a Lutheran pastor who looks out on the world and sees both good and evil," was published in 1936 (Putnam) and dedicated to his mother's memory: "To my gentle mother whose love and strength encompass me as they did throughout these thirty-five years." In 1938 the same publishers presented his biography of John A. Morehead, of which August Marahrens, then Bishop of Hanover and president of the Lutheran World Convention, said: "It is my desire that this book may find its way into the congregations of our Lutheran churches throughout the world."

In 1939 the United Synod of New York again met to elect a president. "The sessions of synod continued on an even keel," the diary relates. "In the P.M. the second ballot was announced with 170 votes for me. The third ballot was taken at five o'clock and my success was almost certain. I knew that the young men behind me . . ."

The final ballot returning Samuel to the presidency, was announced the following morning (June 8, 1939). "It was a great victory," he wrote, "and a great challenge. Letters and telegrams in endless numbers poured in and friends came to rejoice with me." Rachel McDowell, Religious Editor of the *New York Times* who had followed his career from struggling mission pastor to synod president telegraphed excitedly: "Congratulate Lutheran Synod electing you President. God bless all."

"The sun shone gloriously on the day of my Induction," Samuel recorded October 10, 1939. "Ed and I went to St. John's Church * where the clergy were gathering. At eleven, in a majestic procession of pastors and the Wagner College Choir we entered the crowded church. The Reverend Dr. Paul E. Scherer preached a powerful sermon. Dr. Burgess inducted me into office in the presence of 800 people . . ."

As of old, when honors had come to him, as soon as he could do so he left for Bernville. "The country was glorious in autumn foliage," his diary relates. "Reached Bernville at four and placed my Induction flowers on mother's grave."

"The Synod is eagerly awaiting your direction and encouragement," the Reverend Ernest J. Mollenauer, pastor of St. John's Church, New York City, wrote him. "Your congregation of pastors has many members who love and admire you, and look to you to instill the confidence we all need so badly now. Some of us come home nights, heartsick and weary and we all need a pastor to whom we can go for guidance and encourage-

* Christopher Street, New York City.

ment. Our flocks are so far away from God in their daily living that the problem of merely maintaining our organizations are far heavier than they should be. It is much harder to reach into the soul life of men today than it was five years ago. The men of Synod are looking to you as never before and you will feel a surging support that will gladden your heart. You have the gift to succeed in everything you touch, and former occasions have given proof of your firm and beneficent course in dealing with situations, conditions, and men. I am so hopeful for the future that I can hardly wait for September first when you resume your post . . ."

Again "letters and telegrams in endless numbers . . ." Typical is the following from the Reverend S. De Lancey Townsend:

New York City
June 9, 1939

My dear Brother Trexler,

A notice in the morning *Times* sounds "good news" to me and I am sure brings a thrill to you. Your Christlike reception of what seemed bad news to your multitude of loving friends here and everywhere five years ago showed such a Christlike spirit to all concerned that a repercussion was inevitable, if God still reigns and if the Cross is truly the key to the realm of Heaven.

Five years ago your innumerable friends were keenly disappointed. Today we can give three cheers for that very disappointment and wind up with the Doxology: *In your endurance ye shall achieve your souls!* To us the darkness—but to you the heaven above was alight and alive with stars!

Thus have you preached a sermon to us your brethren in the pulpit and at the altar; a sermon we shall never forget. Before, I admired you; today I am tremendously grateful to God for you! How true it is that a good man is always better than any sermon proclaimed from the pulpit.

Yours,

S. De Lancey Townsend

As unwilling, or unable, to "slow down" in his sixties as he had been unmindful of his mother's pleas in former years, Samuel's strength and endurance during the years ahead were taxed to the breaking point. Illness repeatedly struck. He was in and out of Roosevelt Hospital thirteen times in 1944. He would not give in to pain. He dreaded illness, not because he feared pain but because pain was a deterrent to the day's work. "I was fearful lest I could not do the day's work." Notations like this appeared more and more frequently in his diaries. For years he vanquished the implacable foe. "I think I'm going to be all right now," he said to me confidently each time he left the hospital. "I think they've got it now . . ."

In the midst of his busy preparations for the meeting of synod in June 1944 he was again overtaken by illness. We had been invited by the Metropolitan Museum of Art and the Netherlands-America Foundation to a special preview in honor of Her Royal Highness Princess Juliana of the Netherlands. The occasion (May 24) marked the reopening of the Paintings Galleries at the Museum, and we had looked forward with pleasure to meeting old friends.

When I came home that evening, I found Samuel lying on the bed. "Better hurry and get dressed," I said, "or we will be late getting to the Museum . . ." "If you don't mind, Ed," he answered quietly, "I don't believe I'll go . . . I'm not feeling very well . . ."

I looked at him more closely, and immediately telephoned Doctors Howard F. Shattuck and Henry W. Cave. After they had examined him Dr. Cave said casually, "I'm going over to the hospital, Dr. Trexler, and you're going with me." "All right, Doctor," Samuel replied agreeably. None of us knew the extreme pain he was in. He was rushed to Doctors Hospital in an ambulance. At midnight when Dr. Cave operated he found that the appendix had ruptured. While the operation was under way, the anesthetist said, "Doctor, Dr. Trexler's pulse is imperceptible." His condition was reported as "serious." Pneumonia followed and further operations.

I had taken a room at the hospital in order to be on call. Samuel was recovering, but very weak, when Rachel McDowell telephoned me from Albany where the United Synod of New York was in convention, "The 'Bishop' has been re-elected!" Naturally I rushed to relay the news to Samuel. "I'm so happy that my men stood so loyally behind me," he said, his voice trembling. "How long will it be before I can leave the hospital? There is so much to be done."

The next morning I was again called to the telephone. Again, Albany calling. Miss McDowell had been over-confident. The vote had been close and when the third ballot was counted the Reverend Dr. Frederick R. Knubel had been elected. How to break this news to a sick man! But I had no alternative. Bracing myself and summoning what courage I could muster, I went at once to Samuel's room. Propped up on pillows, he was chatting amiably with his nurses.

"Samuel," I said with a supreme effort to sound offhand, "I

have just learned that Fred Knubel has been elected president of Synod." Samuel did not say anything for a few moments. I walked over to the window and stared out at the rooftops. After a few moments he calmly asked us to bow our heads in prayer. When I joined the nurses at his bedside, he raised his thin hand, and lifting his voice, tranquilly, trustfully to the throne of grace, asked God to give Dr. Knubel the wisdom and the strength needed to carry on the work of Synod.

The Church was his life. He loved and served her with his whole heart, seeking always her greater influence and wider usefulness. In the Church he lived and moved and had his being. To her altars he brought the flowers of fifty springtimes.

The melody of church bells called to him joyously. From near and far, from slender spires and majestic towers the music of bells fell like bright rain on his heart. Best of all music, Samuel loved the sweet melting music of church bells on Sunday mornings. He was ever glad when they summoned him into the House of the Lord.

CHAPTER SEVEN

AT HOME ABROAD

The heavens are thine,
the earth also is thine:
as for the world and the
fulness thereof, Thou hast
founded them

PSALMS 89:11

SAMUEL TREXLER loved the face of the earth. He never wearied
of gazing at its restless, mobile features, its enigmatic ever-
changing countenance weathered by wind and water, scarred
by violence, mellowed with age. The green horizons of plains
and prairies, peaceful valleys, massive mountains thrusting upward toward the clouds, stirred him deeply. Very often he told
me of the intense happiness he had in observing nature.

From land beyond land and from city to city he traveled
across the bewildering, beautiful earth, observing with wonder
and delight soaring peaks and pinnacles, deep canyons cut
through layered rock, high eternal snowfields, mighty rivers
and secretive forests. The majesty and grandeur of the earth,
the mystery of creation, filled him with longing to journey to

all countries and continents, to visit all cities and to know all the peoples of the world.

His eagerness made him a restless traveler. But it was hard for him to tear himself away from one place to travel on to another, for he had happiness both in cities full of memories and the associations of friendship, and in cities whose gates he entered for the first time.

Every country captivated him by the beauty and strangeness of its landscape, by the historical and religious associations that were ever present for him, and by the opportunity afforded to meet his fellow human beings, so different and so alike all over the world. His longing to know more about human beings was insatiable.

No journey was ever perfunctory to Samuel. Each moment was filled with eager expectation, crowded with new experiences that enriched his life and gave fuller, wider and deeper meaning to his ministry. How he delighted in observing the people of other lands, talking with them, coming to know them, reading their faces, learning their thoughts. "How wonderfully kind people are everywhere!" he said again and again. "What a privilege to know the people of England, France, Germany, Scandinavia, Russia, the Balkans, South America, Asia."

His home was the world, and from its wide windows he looked out on varied scenes, some lovely, some forbidding. Through some windows he beheld radiant vistas; through others what he saw was dark and terrifying. But although he saw chaos, he also saw order and beauty and the harmony of creation. There was so much he wanted to know, so much he wanted to see. Always he wanted to see and to know for *himself.* "The days are too short," was his lament. "How I wish I could remain longer in this land where I am, to learn more fully the genius of this people . . ."

"Not many ministers have crossed the ocean as often as you . . ." his father wrote somewhat dubiously when he learned that Samuel was planning a fourth voyage to the old world in the first decade of his ministry. Travel afforded Samuel needed change, rest and recreation, renewal of his physical and spiritual resources. Travel provided opportunity for him to read and study, observe and reflect, enjoy world-wide friendships, acquire knowledge and understanding. But the most important reason for travel from Samuel's point of view was this—that it contributed to his usefulness as an ambassador for Christ.

Although he had not enjoyed the perspective and inspiration that travel affords, Samuel's father made these advantages available to his sons when they were young men. He knew what the cultural and educational benefits thus derived could mean to a pastor and pointed this out to them. He believed too that journeying should begin early in life and so "color and leaven all that a man does afterwards." He therefore projected trips for his sons which he hoped and expected would serve them in good stead in years to come.

The first "distant" journey that Samuel made was in 1893—destination Chicago. Probably no boy of fifteen ever set out with keener appreciation for a welcome opportunity. The city of Chicago in the year 1893 was thronged with visitors to the widely heralded Columbian Exposition. Eager and excited in the midst of flying flags, fanfare of trumpets and converging notables, Samuel covered every inch of the Fair Grounds, industriously writing down in a small paper-bound notebook (Compliments of the Oliver Chilled Plow Works) everything he saw with his grave, brown eyes.

This little notebook, entitled "Daily Diary of the Visit of Samuel Geiss Trexler, Bernville, Pennsylvania to the World's Columbian Exposition, held at Chicago, 1893" is a prologue to diaries in which he recorded journeys that crossed seas and embraced continents. He was to make many journeys, each one thrilling, each one brimming with excitement, but none more memorable than this journey to the "Midwest Metropolis" in the summer of 1893.

Weaving in and out of the colorful crowds on the boulevards ("people from all parts of the world—many strangely attired"), he spent endless hours in the Palaces of Art and in the monumental State Buildings examining carefully and at length the assembled treasures displayed.

"Visited the Galleries of Holland, Denmark, Italy, Germany and Austria," the diary tells us. "Spent a long time in the Pennsylvania, New York, Costa Rica, Guatemala, Haiti, Canada, Sweden, Norway and France buildings . . . Examined interesting Fish and Fisheries exhibits, Leather and Forestry exhibits (saw a Redwood pine 270 x 30 feet), the Hall of Mine exhibits (saw the Tiffany Diamond) . . . the Electrical Display, Buffalo Bill's Wild West . . . Watched arrival of the Vikings and arrival of the Spanish caravel (boarded the *Santa Maria*).

"Visited the Manufacturers and Liberal Arts Building . . . the Anthropology and Agricultural buildings . . . the Transportation and Machinery buildings . . . Inspected the Government Building which covers an area of 350 x 420 feet and cost $400,000 . . . Visited the Administration Building, 'the Gem and Crown' of the Exposition palaces.

"Went through the buildings of Florida, New Mexico, Arizona, Oklahoma, Iowa, New Hampshire, Connecticut, Rhode Island, Massachusetts, New Jersey, Delaware . . . Passed through the Midway Plaisance and took a ride on the Ferris Wheel . . . Finished Art Galleries and State Buildings . . . Shook hands with Governor Pattison."

A trip around the world could not have been more thrilling to Samuel at fifteen than the nine kaleidoscopic days he spent exploring the World's Columbian Exposition, wandering happily among the bright blooms in the Horticultural Gardens, watching fireworks shower stars and flowers into the dark waters of Lake Michigan. He must have covered every building and scrutinized every exhibit on the 666 acres devoted to "commemoration of the 400th anniversary of the discovery of America." He also made side trips to "points of interest" in the city— the zoo, the parks, the shops, bookstores, libraries and, of course, churches. His travelogue concludes with this recapitulation: "Was absent sixteen days—four on the road, three in Chicago and nine at the Fair. Travelled 800 miles, passed through five states and spent $55."

Other youthful journeys followed—to New York City on the eve of his graduation from Muhlenberg College in 1896; to Washington, D. C. with his brother Martin in 1897; to Northfield, Massachusetts to attend a conference presided over by the famous evangelist, Dwight L. Moody; to Buffalo to view the Pan-American Exposition in 1901.

As long as he lived, Samuel Trexler's enthusiasm for travel never waned. "My Western trip was in every way glorious," he wrote me from Yellowstone Park in 1914. "I have gained new strength from the awe-inspiring Rockies . . . new energy to work." And from the Island of Mackinac in 1916: "The island is quaint, beautiful and rich in history—conducive to peace, reflection and tranquility of soul. The sail through the thousand islands was an experience of rare beauty. I was particularly happy sitting alone in delightful recollection and anticipation— the glorious moonlight giving a nice color to my thoughts . . ."

Many letters from many cities and not one city which he did not find pleasing for one reason or another—"a delightful old city . . . a sparkling, beautiful city . . . a city of energy and progress . . . a splendid city . . . a city of enterprise and beauty . . ." It was the good and the beautiful that he sought— and found. He was aware of the un-beautiful both in surroundings and in people—but he did not look for the ugly and the mean, and seldom did he record disappointment or disapproval.

I do not recall ever receiving a letter from him in all the years of our friendship that contained a discouraging word. Samuel had the gift of happiness. He instinctively looked on the bright side and his letters never failed to enliven the day for me. I knew before I opened them that they would bring good news. The same could not be said of my letters to him. Whereas he was never anxious, I was inclined to be impatient and apprehensive, and to register my dissatisfactions and disquiet—all too apparent in Samuel's comments: "I was happy to receive your letter for various reasons but chiefly because you seemed in better spirits. You are indeed an afflicted person—a Job transplanted into the twentieth century . . ." "Your letter came this morning—I am sorry for your discouragement but I know from past experience that you have the faculty of quickly mounting up to the clouds . . ." "I am free to confess that your letter of Friday morning upset me. What a time you must be having between a trying cold and a hurt of the feelings. Cheer up. Everybody loves you. The 'good old times' had their thorns too."

When we were young men our incomes did not leave much margin for travel. Money or no money, we found ways and means to go abroad. "Sailing for foreign parts" often necessitated dipping into our savings accounts. No matter. Samuel was earning about $900 a year as pastor of the Church of the Messiah in Greenpoint when we made our first crossing on the *Kroonland* in 1905. "As we sailed, the magnitude and the opportunity of the undertaking gradually dawned upon me," Samuel noted in his diary.

The voyage was a pleasant one. The sights and sounds of the sea were new and strange to us, the fresh salt wind exhilarating. The friendships Samuel forged on ocean voyages were many. Over the years he corresponded with hundreds of people in all parts of the world, and not merely at Christmastime either.

"It is remarkable how quickly one becomes acclimated to life on shipboard," he wrote his mother in 1905. "In a very few hours one has a speaking acquaintance with a large percentage of passengers and has perhaps found common acquaintances. Life is free and care-less—no callers, no letters, no morning newspaper. The days are pleasantly occupied in reading, studying Baedecker, walking the deck, playing tether ball or shuffleboard, and conversing with fellow passengers. The charm of a ship voyage lies largely in freedom from care and responsibility and in the new friends one makes. The ship goes on irrespective of what the passenger does or does not do. But the *glory* of the voyage lies in the opportunity it affords to watch the starlit sky and to allow the ocean to speak to you in its grandeur and mystery . . . The days are not long enough and the end of the voyage is too near. We reach Antwerp tomorrow morning . . ."

"Arose at six, long before the ship was astir," his diary relates. "As we came on deck Antwerp presented itself. Put foot for the first time on the Old World." We secured a pension at *La Fleur D'Or*. The Gold Flower was the humblest of hostelries—sanded floors, crude furnishings, minimum comforts. Samuel's diary, however, describes the inn as one "constantly affording new and delightful surprises." "In Antwerp," he writes, "we went first to the Cathedral. In the Royal Museum we saw many marvelous Rubens. In the evening at the Zoological Garden we had an interesting view of the Belgian people—free, gallant, cordial."

Thence to Brussels, Waterloo, Rotterdam, The Hague, Amsterdam, Leyden, Haarlem. "Holland is a fairyland of windmills, canals, wooden shoes, cream-colored houses, flower beds and window boxes," the diary tells us. "Left this charming, tranquil land regretfully . . ."

In Germany there was the magnificent Cologne Cathedral, the historic cities of Düsseldorf, Mayence, Weisbaden, Coblenz, Weimar, Trier and Stuttgart. "Stuttgart has a special interest for me," he noted, "because of the repute that this is the cradle of the Trexlers, of whom there are still numbers of families resident." With what intense interest he explored Eisleben, where Martin Luther was born, Worms, where Luther took his stand, Wittenberg, where Luther affixed his "Ninety-five Propositions concerning the Power of Indulgences" to the door of the parish church, Eisenach . . . "Eisenach has a charm entirely its own," he wrote. "In the twilight we drove up the mountain to the Wartburg Castle. The impression is beyond words. In the soft evening light, with the fabled hills and valleys about us, our pilgrimage to this historic spot was an event never to be forgotten."

Time was always "entirely too short" for Samuel in art galleries hung with great paintings, in palaces, museums, universities and cathedrals, and in the houses and haunts of the poets. "Inexhaustible riches present themselves here," he wrote in Dresden. Likewise in Leipzig, Berlin, Munich, Paris, Rouen, Versailles . . .

"How *beautiful* is the country of England!" he recorded when we reached London. "How wonderful her glens and forests, cliffs and shores, her historic abbeys and churches!" Drake, Raleigh, Shakespeare, Cromwell, Coleridge, Thackeray, Dickens, London and Stratford, the Thames and the Avon—every step full of associations with a living past." How eagerly he viewed the rooms which bore traces of poets, soldiers and statesmen of bygone centuries. "This is the land of Lorna Doone!" he exclaimed full of excitement, "the land of the Druids! The land where John Wesley once held in a great meadow the world's largest prayer meeting!"

How different the face of Europe in those days! And the crossings too, marked by a sense of high adventure. It was a joy to travel with Samuel. His enthusiasm vested everything with sudden beauty, brilliant colors, intense interest. Sometimes on arrival in Europe we would travel together. At other times we would part company—Samuel following the roads that led to churches, and I those that led to the medical centers and clinics of London, Berlin, Vienna. In 1908 he journeyed to Italy while I remained in Berlin. I still have his letters describing an audience with the Pope ("a lonely, old man") and setting forth his impressions of Rome which he assured me was "magnificent . . . wonderful . . . and the more wonderful because of a friendly, hospitable people who set a splendid example of thrift, industry, cheerfulness . . ."

In June 1911 we were in England as guests of special ambassador John Hays Hammond to witness a high moment and an historic spectacle—the coronation of a King. The day, June 23, dawned gray and cold to the thunder of the saluting guns, the mutter of drums, the shrilling of fifes. Then the church bells began to ring joyously. About ten-thirty, at the moment of the King and Queen's departure from Buckingham Palace, the sun shone through the clouds, and the courtyard echoed with God Save the King!

The great array of princes and potentates who had assembled from "Dominions beyond the Seas" opened the progress to Westminster Abbey. They were followed by the five royal children—the Prince of Wales, the three younger princes and Princess Mary. Five landaus with escorts of guards bore them into the Mall and a charming picture they made, bowing gracefully to the cheering, applauding multitude, their serious-smiling faces full of interest, surprise and curiosity. Fair little Princess Mary was in white with a white ribbon in her hair, the Prince of Wales, looking dignified beyond his years, wearing the Order of the Garter, Prince George in the uniform of a naval cadet, Prince Henry and Prince Albert in Highland dress with feathered bonnet. Then came the King and Queen in the ornate golden state coach, drawn by cream horses.

The interior of the Abbey was draped in deep-hued blue velvet with brilliant masses of color glowing between the gray-brown Gothic arches and columns. The flashing jewels and diamond tiaras of regally robed peers and peeresses, the colorful dress of princes from every part of the world, glittering gold epaulettes, flowing trains of crimson velvet, white veils and capes of snowy miniver, presented a scene of breathtaking splendor. When the organ thundered out its announcement that the king was close at hand a thrill ran through the hearts of the spectators. Here in the presence of the nobility of his realm and heads of the royal houses of Europe, the Crown of Dominion was placed on the king's head.

We viewed the returning procession from the Burdette Coutts house, one of the great houses of London. "The coronation procession left the Abbey at two-thirty," Samuel recorded, "their Majesties George V and Mary, bearing their sceptres and insignia of State and wearing their gem-studded crowns, followed by an impressive array of the high-born from many lands—a stately and moving spectacle—unique for its medieval pomp, picturesqueness and symbolism. At the palace, over which flew the Royal Standard, the King and Queen presented themselves on a little center balcony draped with crimson and cloth of gold to the cheering crowd . . . At nightfall the jubilant city, gala in decorations and brilliantly illuminated, blazed with bonfires in honor of the coronation."

Samuel and I were speechless as we gazed at the ordered ranks of scarlet-uniformed dragoons and glittering bayonets that stretched in a double line from the palace to the gates, the guards mounted on black horses, and resplendent in gleaming breastplates and nodding plumes, the cadets from Australia and Canada, the Irish guards, the Indian detachments, the British South African police, the Abyssinian princes in their state dress of lions' skins and plumes, the retinues of princes, soldiers and seamen, and Lord Kitchener, his Majesty's Master of Horse, a commanding figure on a matchless charger. Our eyes were swimming with color and the symbols of sovereignty. We had never before witnessed such an array of majesty and might, such dazzling splendor and grandeur.

The days that followed were a whirl of coronation festivities— dinners and receptions at the Hammonds', the Milhollands', the Ambassador Reids', a garden party at Buckingham Palace, the Horseshow, a Thanksgiving Service for the Coronation in St. Paul's Cathedral.

That summer I remained in London while Samuel journeyed to Norway and Sweden from where he wrote a great many letters recounting happy days with the "most friendly people in the world," and his pleasure in the "wonderfully picturesque scenery—snow-capped mountains . . . mysterious rocks and fastnesses . . . ice-blue fiords."

"A wild and romantic country, dotted with beautiful old Lutheran churches," he informed me. "This morning I worshipped in the oldest church in Scandinavia," he wrote. "The days are full of startling and unexpected turns. I have explored Trondheim, Christiana, Stockholm, Upsala and little towns far in the interior. Journeying in the interior is rugged and yet, had I not gone on foot and by post through the hinterland, I should not have come to really know this land of the Midnight Sun and its splendid people."

Of the many voyages Samuel made he regarded his journey to the Holy Land as the most rewarding. He had long looked forward to visiting this country sacred to the memory of Jesus, this land where Jesus had lived and taught and preached and died. In the summer of 1923, full of happy anticipation, he sailed for Palestine on the *Tuscania* accompanied by his brother Charles. The journey was a memorable one. They went first to Portugal and Spain, then to Genoa, Naples, Pompeii, Venice, Constantinople and Beirut, Samuel recording his impressions of "the vari-colored life in ancient and pregnant civilizations on the Dardanelles . . . the Black Sea . . . the Aegean . . ."

Damascus, where Scripture is interwoven with every scene, brought to mind many incidents in the life of St. Paul. The brothers gazed at a window in a wall recalling Paul's words: "In Damascus the Governor, under Aretas the King, kept the city of the Damascenes with a garrison desirous to apprehend me: and through a window, in a basket, was I let down by the wall, and escaped his hands." They walked the street called Straight where Judas lived. They saw the house of Judas, the house of Naaman the Syrian, and the site of the House of Rimmon. They followed the road into Damascus on which Paul, called Saul of Tarsus, was blinded by a vision of Jesus. They visited the house of the disciple Ananias through whom Paul's sight was restored.

In Samuel's diary he recorded every impression as the journey proceeded, and though his expectations were high he was not disappointed.

*

August 6, 1923

Started out from Damascus at seven going southwest past the place of Paul's conversion and onward to the plain where snowcapped Hermon came in view. Rough roads on which we met only caravans and Bedouins led at last into the Valley of the Jordan. Standing on the shore of Galilee, looking across the beautiful peaceful water, green and still, I felt the nearness of Jesus . . .

In Capernaum, where one drinks in the spirit of Our Lord most deeply . . . In Tiberius . . . In these hills so sacred in His Life there is a sweet serenity . . .

They mount to the Plain of Gennesaret, visit the Chapel of the Annunciation, the workshop of Joseph in Nazareth, travel on to the Plain of Esdraelon and cities and places rich in Biblical history and steeped in oriental heritage—Nain, Endor, Shunem, Mt. Carmel, Ebal, Gerizim and Samaria. One evening at dusk they came to Jerusalem, Samuel recording his joy in the scenery, places and monuments identified with Scripture history—the Temple, the Pool of Bethesda, the Via Dolorosa, the House of Caiaphas, the Tomb of Rachel. He enjoyed intensely seeing these monuments of Old Testament history and walking in the hills and valleys where Jesus had walked. They spent quiet days in Bethlehem, saw the hills where David watched his flocks, the plains of Boaz, Jericho, Bethany, the Jordan, the Dead Sea. They journeyed to the gate where Stephen was stoned; the Mount of Olives; the Garden of Gethsemane; Calvary.

"Regretfully did we face toward Egypt," Samuel wrote, "where we had planned to spend a brief interlude before proceeding to Germany to attend the first Lutheran World Convention at Eisenach." To this momentous gathering of Christian leaders Samuel brought the inspiration gained in the hills and plains hallowed by the presence of Jesus. Every detail of these hills and plains, every scene in the drama that had been witnessed there twenty centuries before, was before him as he took his place in the Thuringian town of Eisenach that August.

The delegates, representing 22 nations, met in the hall of the Fürstenhof, a hotel in the city of Eisenach. In his diary the day's proceedings are thus recorded.

August 21, 1923

At ten o'clock the delegates convened—a most impressive gathering —one of the first international gatherings since the war—a meeting of Christians on a parity, whether from vanquished or victorious peoples. Bishop Ludwig Ihmels of Saxony welcomed the group. President G. A. Brandelle of the Augustana Synod spoke for America. Archbishop Soderblom of Sweden expressed the purpose of the gathering in these words: "We have come together to edify one another and to strengthen one another in our common faith." Dr. John A. Morehead gave the main address, stressing the importance of unity and a common organization among the Lutherans of the world. The unity of the Lutheran Church, here expressed, is not based on the will to create a big Evangelical group. It has its origin in a common faith, a common need and common desire.

The excitement of departure and farewells never lost their charm for Samuel Trexler. Nor did the years diminish the happiness with which he returned to America, the joy of seeing the Statue of Liberty come in view. "Ed," he said, as we gazed at the lofty torch from the deck of the *Europa* on our return in 1930, "you know of course that the Statue of Liberty was a gift from the French government in commemoration of the 100th anniversary of American independence—but do you know that the Statue is the work of . . ." "A *Lutheran?*" I interposed, "*Exactly,*" he replied. "A French Lutheran—Frederic August Bartholdi." "Isn't it wonderful to be home again!" he added happily. "How beautiful the skyline is in the sunset! In fact the whole United States of America is beautiful. There is no country in the world as beautiful as America . . ."

When Samuel Trexler lost the presidency of Synod in 1934 to Dr. Ellis B. Burgess there was much speculation as to how he would take the defeat and many conjectures as to what he would do next. I myself wondered.

One of the first questions I asked him when he returned from the ecclesiastical-political upset in St. John's Church, Albany was: What will you do now? "You mean *immediately?*" he parried. "I shall go abroad. I am more and more concerned about the growing conflict between Church and State in Europe. Two powerful men are at cross purposes in Germany—Adolf Hitler, shouting from the Wilhelmstrasse and Martin Niemoeller preaching from the pulpit of the Church of Jesus Christ in Dahlem. The cleavage between these two men is deep, far deeper than meets the eye.

"I wish to see my friend Niemoeller as soon as possible and discuss religious trends in Germany with him. Niemoeller is well aware that everything Martin Luther fought for is being challenged by the Nazi government and has taken his stand in defense of religious freedom. As a matter of fact, more than religious freedom is at stake. The freedom of mankind is in jeopardy and the struggle to preserve it may well plunge the whole world into another war . . .

"From Germany I shall go to Russia where the church is in a sorry state. Perhaps you would like to go to Russia with me, Ed? It is a land I have long wanted to visit. Do you know that there were five million Lutherans in Russia before the war? Five million! What has happened to Christians in Russia since October 1917 is appalling . . . In 1923 Bishop Meyer estimated only a million had survived the hardships and suffering that followed the overthrow of the Czar. In the past ten years this number has been greatly reduced. We used to have 400 churches in Russia. Last year we had 40. Now we have, perhaps, ten. It is very sad. The Orthodox Church of Russia has been similarly decimated. Just think, Ed, the Lutheran Church was planted in the plains of Russia four centuries ago. Our first congregation, named after Saint Peter and Saint Paul, was organized in 1576 in Moscow . . ." He paused a moment, and then continued his musings.

"Moscow! Burnt and sacked by the Golden Horde, destroyed by the armies of Napoleon, blasted by German machine guns, racked and ruined by revolutions. A city of perpetual strife and bloodshed, violence and unrest. Time and again leveled to the ground and time and again risen from ashes. A city mentioned for the first time by chroniclers in 1147 and said to have had *forty times forty* churches. What did you say, Ed?" "I didn't say anything," I replied. "I was just thinking." "Thinking about what?" Samuel asked impatiently. "Moscow," I answered. "Churches."

"Of course all that is changed now," he continued, sighing. "Old Moscow has been superseded by a new Moscow—in which a subway is being built. The projected stations coincide with the sites of churches, and of course, the churches must go. So I am told and further, that this is a jest among the people. I only wish I had gone to Russia fifty years ago . . .

"Fifty years ago, looking north over the Kremlin I would have beheld a skyline of breathtaking oriental splendor. Great bulbous domes, sheeted in burning gold and gorgeous eastern colors . . . lofty towers ornamented with Saracenic arabesques and bands of glittering stone . . . shining minarets bearing aloft

balustraded balconies . . . a thousand crosses lifted imperiously
to the vast green-blue Russian sky . . .

"Gone," he said, and sighed again. "Gone . . . No longer do
churches throng the horizon beyond the Kremlin. One by one
the crosses fell from the sky . . ." "Yes," I said inadequately.
"As for the remaining Lutheran pastors in Moscow and in
other Russian cities," he went on, shaking his head sadly,
"whether it is in my power to help them in any way I do not
know, but I can at least go to see them . . ."

I remarked then that the Synod convention must have been
an exhausting business, that he had been working too hard too
long and that time out from responsibilities was in order. He
acknowledged that he was tired. "Yes, I am tired," he said. "Trying to hold the men together during these depression years has
been like trying to keep dry leaves from scattering in a wind-
storm. You have no idea . . . But a few days of sun and sea
at Bar Harbor will rest me . . ."

Then, as if even the thought of sunshine and salt spray had
dispersed tiredness, his face lighted up. "By the way," he said,
"I have another book in mind . . . Thirty-five years in the
ministry have taught me a few things I would like to pass on to
younger men headed for the road I have been over. You know
how full my days have been and that I have had little time for
study and reflection, let alone writing. But now . . .

"The point is this: The ministry is not an easy road at best,
and it seems to me that it might be worth while to indicate some
of the hazards of the road—the blind crossings, the dangerous
curves—to put up a few warning signs. Remember the old automobile Blue Books—our trusted guides in the days of dusters,
goggles and no windshields? All roads began and also ended

at Columbus Circle. Remember? Well, a sort of Blue Book for men headed for the ministry is what I have in mind. I thought I would . . ."

Knowing that his defeat in Albany had been a blow, I was prepared to find Samuel depressed. On the contrary, he had returned in a calm if not exactly happy frame of mind. No resentment. No bitterness. No indecision. I had listened with admiration and some amazement to his plans for the months ahead. "Samuel," I interrupted, "you are a courageous man . . ." "What has courage to do with it?" he demanded evenly. "Rest assured that I do not have to be president of Synod to be useful to my Church. There are other ways, many ways in which I can serve—and perhaps to better advantage."

He rose from the brown velvet sofa on which he was sitting. Above the sofa hung a painting of him by Albert Herter. Herter had captured that same serenity of spirit that was in his eyes at this moment. He smiled. "I'm going for a walk in Central Park," he said, picking up his stick and gloves. "I must *think* . . ."

We sailed on the *Europa* the third week in October. Berlin was in a flag-waving, heel-clicking mood. Hotels and cafés crowded with visitors. "Where on earth do all these people come from!" I exclaimed when we were checking in at the Kaiserhof. "From the six continents, I should say," Samuel replied, glancing at the faces of the men and women in the lobby. "Looks as if Berlin has become an international crossroad."

We were astonished by the number of men in uniform and startled by the hard insolence in their eyes. The city was a stage: Bands playing, loud speakers blaring. Traffic flashing by in the crowded streets. Planes glinting overhead. Horns honking. Sirens screeching. Everywhere clamor and confusion. Everywhere The Party and Der Führer. A new regime . . .

After we had unpacked, or as Samuel used to say, "settled" ourselves, we decided to have a cup of coffee. In the dining room of the Kaiserhof (as the elevator operator had importantly whispered) was Adolph Hitler, also having coffee. From a near-by table we studied his avid face, and the faces of the two men with him. (Later we were to meet these men, and others, —Propaganda Minister Goebbels, Foreign Minister von Neurath, Alfred Rosenberg, Ernst Hanfstaengl.) Strangers in the room, which was not large, we in turn were scrutinized with interest by the dictator and his companions.

"There is no doubt," said Samuel in a low tone, after his third cup of coffee, "that the man is possessed." "Possessed?" I asked. "By what?" "The devil," he muttered, continuing to watch Der Führer out of the corner of his eye. "Hitler is the devil's advocate . . ." "For the love of heaven, Samuel," I exclaimed, glancing uneasily about. "That is my opinion," he said, "*understated.*" He looked at his watch. "Let's go, Ed, or we will be late for the appointment with Ambassador Dodd . . . I believe the English ambassador, Sir Eric Phipps and Kermit Roosevelt are to be at the Embassy too . . . Also I promised Mrs. Adlon to motor with her this afternoon to Potsdam where we are to call on Crown Prince Wilhelm . . ."

We were in Berlin three days. Samuel's visits to pastors confirmed his anxieties regarding the difficulties the church faced. "I do not expect to be in Russia for any length of time," he told Martin Niemoeller on leaving. "When I return we will talk further. Fortunate for our people that they have leaders such as you in this crisis when the very life of the Church is threatened by an apostle of brute force."

A Russian consul to whom we had been introduced on the *Europa* had urged us to visit Moscow if possible on November seventh. "Stalin will review the troops that day," he explained, "in celebration of the seventeenth anniversary of the Revolution." Although passports to the Soviet Union were not readily obtained even in 1934, we were agreeably surprised to find our papers in order at the Russian consulate in Berlin. A telephone call from the Consul to Moscow, and we were on our way.

We flew from Tempelhof Field November sixth. Every seat in the plane was occupied by (it seemed to us) very important people. Koenigsberg was the last flight stop. Hugging their brief cases, our fellow travelers funneled through an exit and disappeared. Samuel and I were transferred to a Russian plane on which we found ourselves the only passengers. With the suddenness with which things happen in the skies, we rushed headlong into a heavy fog and in a slashing rain roared down to a forced landing at Welikiye Luki.

Welikiye Luki proved to be a barren Russian outpost at which an airport was under construction, but where as yet there was no provision for passengers. We were cold, hungry and wet. Night had fallen. The rain drummed on the metal roof, and outside the hangar the winter winds howled like wolves. Two German engineers who had come to the airport to repair a damaged plane were good enough to share the food they had in their knapsacks. Following their suggestion we stumbled through mud and darkness to a small cottage about a quarter mile distant where we were given shelter for the night. At daybreak we stumbled back through gray wetness to the airfield. The outlook was far from favorable for flying. Our two pilots, one Russian, the other German, held a "visibility" consultation. "We will attempt it," they announced finally, "seeing it is the day of the Festival in Moscow." Whereat we climbed into the plane and roared back up into the storm.

Skies bolted with lightning were an interesting spectacle to Samuel. Not to me. My nerves frayed by the stress and excitement of the previous day plus a sleepless night, I was in no mood for the storm-ridden skies, in which we were bouncing about like a ping-pong ball. Leaning unsteadily across the aisle I put my hand on Samuel's shoulder. "Samuel, if ever we reach Moscow alive," I said (and meant it), "I will devote the remainder of my life to righteous living and good deeds." His thoughts were clearly far away. He regarded me briefly, gave me a faraway smile and said nothing. When the storm passed we could see beneath us the spectacular forests and rivers of Russia. Absorbed in their immensity, my fears vanished.

"Moscow," Samuel announced cheerfully a few minutes later. We fastened our belts. Instead of descending, however, the plane began to circle the city, round and round, banking, tilting her wings like a monster bird in the brilliant sky. Peering down we could see great numbers of soldiers converging on Red Square. We were puzzled. Why did we not land? Perhaps our pilots wanted to show us the host of marching men in the spacious Square? The dense crowds assembled for the Festival Day events? We were wrong, the reverse was true. Our pilots had received word (we later learned) to seize this opportunity to display the huge new plane to the multitude below.

No sooner had we landed than my pious pledge, like so many resolves made under stress, was forgotten. "Delay, delay, delay," I thought. "Red tape and more red tape," I fretted. "When moments count if we are to witness Stalin review the troops," I fumed. With mounting irritation I watched the inspector (a woman) mauling the contents of our bags. Suddenly my patience, never long, snapped like an overdrawn bowstring. I hurled an outburst of ill-tempered words at the inspector. Whether she understood what I was saying, I do not know. Be that as it may, she continued her mauling and her paperwork unhurriedly. At long last the bags were closed. "I'm sorry," I said to Samuel in a contrite tone, at the same time giving the woman a venomous look. He threw me a long glance, gave the inspector a kindly nod and walked away.

Pushing our way through the milling crowds we struggled toward Red Square. Stalin was standing near the tomb of Lenin, his dark face impassive, watching the Russian Army and Navy pass in review. It was a stupendous spectacle that we witnessed in the Red Square that November day. It was more than a mass demonstration. It was a delirious dedication of the spirit of a people to a new heaven and a new earth. We watched disturbed, and a little frightened. What heaven? And what earth?

Afterward we walked across the great Square to the red marble tomb wherein the body of Nikolai Lenin, founder of the Soviet State, lies exposed to the gaze of worshipful throngs—a venerated symbol for world communism. We stood a moment beside the glass coffin. His face drawn, Samuel turned to me. "Shall two hundred million Russians be subject to an entirely Godless life?" he lamented. "Will the embalmed body of Lenin suffice to give this great nation the inspiration and hope which every soul needs? It cannot be . . ."

The following day, again with considerable difficulty, we pushed through the crowds gathered to watch the parade of the civic organizations, and made our way slowly and indirectly to the historic Lutheran Church of Saints Peter and Paul. It was one of the few churches remaining after repeated liquidations. "The building was so dilapidated," Samuel's diary records, "that it spoke volumes for the dying condition of religion in the Soviet Union. The pastor (Pastor Strek) was so fearful of the future that he would rather not have spoken and charged me not to quote him either in Russia or America."

Accompanying us as interpreter was a young Russian Communist said to have belonged to the old aristocracy. So close did she keep to us that constructive conversation with Pastor Strek was virtually impossible. It was with difficulty that he managed to whisper to Samuel in German as we were leaving: "Kommen Sie morgen in die Kirch, ohne den Dolmetscher." (Come to the church tomorrow *without the interpreter*.) "The pastor told me of experiences of the church in Russia only to be described by the language of the Book of the Apocalypse," he noted in his diary after their visit in the church. (The following year the pastor was "liquidated" and the tenuous life of the congregation was snuffed out.)

In Leningrad which had been a strong center of the Lutheran Church since the seventeenth century, the outlook was slightly, but only slightly, more hopeful. The pastor (Pastor Reichert) of the Church of St. Peter on the Nevski Prospect (organized in 1710) invited six of the younger clergy—all graduates of the Lutheran Seminary in Leningrad—to meet Samuel. "A finer group of young pastors one would not see in any church in any land," he told me. "They informed me sorrowfully that only a skeletal work is being carried forward by the stricken churches and that pastors are constantly being arrested and deported, sometimes executed. Nevertheless, they spoke with great courage and even hope . . ." St. Peter's Church, once a powerful influence as a congregation and rich in schools and institutions of mercy, still retained its beauty of interior. Samuel gazed long at its famous Holbein altarpiece. "But the glory of the congregation has departed," he said sadly.

"The situation is worse than I feared," he moaned after a visit to some of the rural congregations. "The pastors are helpless and many are desperate. Some with whom I spoke seemed dazed. Some have suffered such anguish of mind and spirit that they would welcome death. Countless numbers of men and women have given their lives for the sake of Christ in Russia. To what length will the rulers of this land not go in their mad determination to extirpate the church! Her suffering is beyond endurance. Yet she lives . . ."

While we were in Moscow Samuel visited the grave of Bishop Meyer (Theophilus Meyer, elected Primate in 1924). Worn out with the struggle in behalf of his fellow believers he had died a few months before we arrived in Russia. "How well I remember Bishop Meyer's moving appeal to the Lutheran World Convention in Eisenach ten years ago," Samuel said on the way back from the cemetery. "How with tears in his eyes, he expressed the gratitude of Russian pastors for the 'brotherly love shown' . . . Oh how inadequate our help has been . . ."

He sighed. "There were times when the Lutheran Church in Russia was second in leadership and numbers only to the official Greek Orthodox Church. It was outstanding in numbers, in leadership and in institutions of education and mercy. "Under the Czarist regime, many Lutherans came to Russia from Finland, Sweden, Poland, Germany and the Baltic provinces. At the invitation of Catherine the Great, herself a German, three hundred thousand German Lutherans settled in the valley of the Volga. For more than two hundred years they lived and worked there. Do you know, Ed, that Lenin's grandmother was one of these Volga Lutherans? He proudly acknowledged it. Now the Lutheran Church is at the point of death in Russia . . . It is hard to believe."

Accustomed as I was to a buoyant and cheerful outlook on Samuel's part, and deeply disturbed myself by the harrowing stories we had listened to, I began to wish we had never come to Russia. What good is it, I thought? How can we possibly help? They are beyond help. But then I remembered how Samuel had said, "I can at least go to see them . . ." So I kept silent.

Twice Samuel visited Bishop Malmgren. At seventy-four this courageous disciple of Christ was still struggling to maintain a flicker of life in the Theological School in Leningrad, the school for which Dr. Morehead had enlisted so many American friends. (The flicker was stamped out and the seminary closed in 1934.) "Bishop Malmgren told me," Samuel noted in his diary, "that he has seen and suffered unspeakable things, and sadly acknowledged his fear that the organized Lutheran Church in Russia is nearing its end."

Nor were conversations with statesmen and newspapermen in Russia reassuring. In Russia at the time were Acting Ambassador John Cooper Wiley, Walter Duranty and Harold Denny of the *New York Times*, the Knickerbockers and other friends. One afternoon at the Metropole, Walter Duranty re-

marked that the Soviet regime was the most remarkable economic experiment of the ages. "Much of what is being done for
the people is commendable," Samuel responded unhappily. "At
the same time the Soviet State is a brutal organization. In its
program, the church of the gentle Nazarene has no place."

"I have seen and heard enough," he told me a few days later.
"There is no purpose to be served by staying longer in Russia.
The future of the Church in the Soviet Union will depend on
what is done at *home*—and by statesmen as well as churchmen."

In Riga he called on Bishop Poelschau. At Danzig he talked
with Bishop Beerman. In Dresden he visited Baron von Kirch-
bach (who had been deposed as Court Preacher). In Leipzig
he consulted "very fully on church matters" with the theological
faculty at the university. All, everywhere, despaired regarding
the future of the church in Russia.

When we returned to Germany Samuel conferred again with
Bishops Meiser and Marahrens and Dr. Hans Lilje, Dr. Julius
Richter and other Lutheran leaders. He called on many of
the pastors and spent several days with Pastor Bodelschwing at
Bielefeld. Ambassador Orme Wilson, Frank Gannett, Stanley
High, the Ed Wights, Sigrid Schulz of the *Chicago Tribune*—
all friends of many years—were in Germany that fall. Talk,
talk, talk. Exchanging views on things seen and heard and
feared. Like the good reporter he was, Samuel was eager to hear
all sides of the story.

In Dahlem he listened to his friend Martin Niemoeller,
former U-Boat captain and champion of the Confessional
Church. "I followed the crowds to Pastor Niemoeller's church,"

he recorded in his diary. "They came by subway, by bus, by taxi, and on foot. Long before the service started the church was crowded to overflowing. Young people came willingly and in great numbers. On Buss Tag (Day of Public Repentance) I heard Niemoeller preach to a congregation of ten thousand in the Tennis Hall at Wilhelmsdorf on the text: *Unless ye repent ye shall likewise perish.* He was magnificent."

"The most vivid picture of my stay in Germany," Samuel told Lutheran clergymen on his return to the States, "is of a noble army of martyrs and heroes of the faith rising up in every part of the Reich, conscious of the trials the Church must go through and waiting patiently the leading of God in Whose word alone they trust. One cannot feel that the German nation will dispense with the Gospel which one of her greatest sons, Martin Luther, restored to the world."

In 1935, Samuel again crossed the ocean. Dr. John A. Morehead, then president of the Lutheran World Convention, had requested that he present a paper on "The Church and Youth" at the Third Lutheran World Convention to be held in Paris. "After a day or so (his diary records) I wrote to Dr. Morehead that if this was the way I could serve the Church and be of help, I should be glad to comply with his request."

From the sixty-nine-year-old widely loved church leader he received the following reply:

Sept. 11, 1935

My dear Dr. Trexler:

With assurances of very particular appreciation I am acknowledging your letter advising me that you have decided to attend the Third Lutheran World Convention to be held in Paris, France, October 13–

20th, 1935. The fact that you are to be with us for this ecumenical gathering of Lutherans is a source of great joy to me because of my personal attachment to you and because your presence should add to the value and fruitfulness of this world Lutheran event.

We have felt that the opening address on youth—a subject vital to the future of the Lutheran Church in the world—should be made by a man experienced in work among the youth of the church and equipped by training and gifts to present the subject. Knowing your experience as a successful pioneer in the field of spiritual and churchly care of Lutheran students in universities, and also your experience as a church executive accustomed to think and plan for the advancement of the Church, we are persuaded that you are especially equipped to make this address.

Fraternally yours,

John A. Morehead
President, Executive
Committee
Lutheran World
Convention

Dr. Morehead was determined, despite the pleas of his physicians, to preside over the Lutheran World Convention in Paris. The crossing was rough and he was seen on deck only once. Samuel, who sailed with him, did what he could to relieve him of the mass of detail preparatory to the tasks ahead. "His cabin took on the appearance of the headquarters of a commanding officer," the diary records. "Radio messages were dispatched to all parts of Europe, and many conferences were held with the delegates on board in preparation for the convention in Paris, where representatives of 80,000,000 Lutherans throughout the world waited his welcome."

The American delegates numbered many churchmen, including the Reverend Dr. Frederick H. Knubel, president of the United Lutheran Church in America; the Reverend Drs. George Linn Kieffer and Ralph H. Long of the National Lutheran Council; the Reverend Doctors G. A. Brandelle, president of the Augustana Synod; C. C. Hein, first president of the American Lutheran Church; Astrup Larsen, president of the Iowa District of the Norwegian Lutheran Church and N. C. Carlsen, president of the Danish Synod of North America.

The sessions of the convention were held in the church house of the Church of St. Jean situated on the Rue de Grenelle, from where Samuel wrote:

Paris
October 5, 1935

Dear Edmund:

The apostolic injunction "Be given to hospitality" has its most generous expression in the welcome of the French Church. There are many friends here, including Bishop Bursche of Warsaw, one of many whose battles Dr. Morehead has fought in the struggle against famine, disease, and death. Bishop Popp and Bishop Starke are here from Jugoslavia; Dr. Erich Wehrenfenig from Czechoslovakia, and Bishop Glendys from Roumania. Hungary is represented by Professor Dr. Prohle of the University of Sopron. Holland sent Professor Dr. Pont; Austria, Church President Dr. Victor Capesius. It is a brilliant assemblage—Archbishops, Bishops, Presidents, Superintendents, University Professors, Pastors, Senators—all under one ecumenical roof.

No fewer than sixteen men are here from the land of Luther, including Bishop Marahrens, a leader whose strength is well known, Bishop Meiser and Dr. Hans Lilje. From Sweden there is Archbishop

Eidem (you will recall he succeeded the late Nathan Soderblom); also Bishop Samuel Stadener and Provost Pehrsson of Gothenburg. From Norway, Provost Johs Hygen and Pastor Normann. From Denmark, the Primate, Bishop Fuglsang-Damgaard of Copenhagen. Iceland, Finland and Esthonia are represented. Spain too by Pastor Juan Fliedner. The foreign mission field also has representatives—India, Japan, China. Altogether an occasion for gratitude and rejoicing.

Dr. Morehead welcomed the delegates with the humility so characteristic of his warm-hearted soul. Throughout the week, there will be discussions on inner missions and practical problems of the Christian Church today and in the days before us. It is intended that this be an Arbeitstag—a working convention. The general discussion is Lutheranism and the Religious Crisis of the Present Day. Listening to the stories of heroism, privation, and sacrifices provides a picture of the Church at once inspiring and distressing.

A number of social events are planned. President Albert Lebrun will receive Dr. Morehead and the Executive Committee at the palace on the Champs-Elysees. We are looking forward also with pleasure to a visit from the Protestant faculty of the University of Paris. Honorary degrees are to be conferred upon Dr. Morehead and Dr. Jorgensen in recognition of the part they played in rebuilding French churches destroyed during the war. A number of delegates present attended the convention in Eisenach in 1923 and in Copenhagen in 1929. May God bless the Third World Convention of the Lutheran Church!

Always,

Trexler

No subject could have held greater appeal for Samuel Trexler than "The Church and Youth," on which he had been asked to speak at the Paris convention.

"The church of Jesus Christ is the church of Youth," he told the delegates. "Our Lord was only thirty-three when He was crucified. His followers too were young men. The men who turned the world upside down in the Apostolic Age were young men and the men speaking out against the evils, the hatreds and the injustice in the world today are young men . . .

"The Young Communist International at its Sixth World Congress in Moscow has just called on the youth of the world to unite against war. What can be more Christian than a call to end this traffic in death even though the call be uttered by those who style themselves atheists? Christianity, and Communism in the proper definition of the word—a system of social organization in which goods are held in common—both inspire sacrifice; both seek to change the world; both are international in concept and in ideology. This youthful organization has voiced an appeal which every Christian knows he should not merely echo, but proclaim with clarion call . . .

"We ask: Where are the leaders of the church of tomorrow? Possibly leaders of the church in A.D. 325 asked the same question at the moment when young Athanasius, at the age of thirty-two, was defending the faith at the Council of Niceae. St. Francis of Assisi is honored as one of the church's greatest evangelists. How many guessed this when he founded his Order at the age of thirty-four? Did the church realize when Martin Luther nailed his thesis to the church door at Wittenberg that this young man would shake the world?

"The church is too much in the care of older men. We need the balance and wisdom which older men give, but we need also the energy and the vision of young men. Young men should be represented more strongly on her councils. The church must demonstrate by wider vision and more loving endurance that the Master's 'Go ye into all the world' transcends Karl Marx's 'Workers of the world, unite!' She must believe and demonstrate that the power of Jesus in the world is greater than that of a Lenin or a Stalin or any other power of darkness. She must prove that Christians of all nations and races can work together to build a better world. This is work for the *Church and Youth*. Elder statesmen dream dreams, but youth has faith to change the world.

"Young people always have, and will always respond to challenging and rewarding opportunity. The church in her worship, her teaching, and above all in her *life* must express completely the glory of Him who is her founder. Too many bearing the name of Christian are not exponents of Christianity. Young people know this. It is true that the church lives in a limited world of social, economic and political conflict. But she also lives in an illimitable and uncharted universe of mystery and miracle, and she is led by One who was Himself a young man when he traveled the road that led from the Mount of Transfiguration to the cross on Calvary. Youth will follow His leadership, be it known to them who He is."

How was his address received? From the Hotel Lutétia, Samuel wrote:

Paris
October 18, 1935

Dear Edmund:

Today I read my paper on The Church and Youth. I was not quite satisfied with its delivery because we were kept strictly to time and I had to abbreviate certain matters. Nevertheless, I had many words of appreciation (and some of dissent). I afterwards supplemented my statements by taking part in the debate in German. All do not have the invincible faith in young people that I have.

Paris has never been so beautiful as it is these perfect October days. If Margaret comes to New York, tell her I spent a half day at Chartres as a compliment to her—and how glorious is that cathedral, its windows unparalleled!

The French people do everything possible for our comfort and happiness. It has been a worthwhile trip. The bond of Christian unity between members of our great Lutheran family has been strengthened . . . I am ready to leave tomorrow night—on my birthday— for Germany. In two weeks more, I shall be home, enriched with wonderful experiences. Dr. Morehead has kept up remarkably well, but tires easily. It is sad to see his strength ebbing.

Keep well and happy.

Always,

Trexler

Leaving Paris he returned to Berlin. "It is with a sense of foreboding that I say farewell to Germany," he wrote. "The struggle between Church and State is bitter and fateful. The pastors are distraught but they are not afraid."

Two years passed and after attending conferences in Oxford and Edinburgh, he journeyed again to Germany. There were many more soldiers on the flag-decked streets of Berlin. Many more planes soared overhead. Martin Niemoeller was a prisoner of Adolf Hitler. Bishop Meiser had been arrested; so had Julius Richter. The skies were darkening. Now and again the rumble of distant thunder could be heard in the Third Reich. *Thunder?*

New ways in the wilderness appealed to Samuel Trexler. The challenge of unknown circumstances, unexplored regions commanded his imagination. The wonders of new worlds compelled him to tasks not premeditated, summoned him to distant scenes in countries he had not known before. Everywhere he called on pastors, talked with church leaders, attended services of worship in Lutheran churches great and small, and in tabernacles, temples and cathedrals of many faiths.

Summer after summer he retraced the steps of former years, or mapped some new area that beckoned in a burst of sunlight, in dusk that was enchanted, or in the glittering light of reaching stars. Scarcely was he home from one journey than he was planning another. Voyages cadenced with church bells, ornamented by crosses dusted with gold, in skies that were strange to him.

In the winter of 1940, he attended a meeting of the Federal Council of Churches of Christ in America. John R. Mott, the great missionary, then seventy-five years old, made an impassioned appeal in behalf of South America. "Latin America, as no other part of the world at this time, summons us to larger evangelisms," said the venerable Mott. "The call in Argentina, Brazil and other Latin lands, little understood by us, is as clear and sharp as the call in the United States two generations ago."

Samuel listened with mounting excitement. John Mott had turned his thought to a new continent. The opportunities for the church, the summons to "larger evangelisms" gripped his imagination. He had heard a command, a word that demanded obedience. I was reminded of something he had once read to me—an inscription on the flyleaf of one of Eucken's books? *Das heist wohl uberhaupt leben, ein Kommande, ein wort hören, das unsern gehorsam fordert.* (This after all, is Life, to hear a command, a word that demands obedience.) With eagerness and anticipation he began at once to make plans for a missionary journey to South America. It was benefits in expectation that enabled him in the latter years as in his youth, to look toward the future, to explore a world beyond his previous experience.

The journey to South America in the summer of 1941 was well timed. The old world was locked in mortal strife, fires raging, roads barred. In Asia doors were closing, especially in the Japanese missions. "If doors close in one country, they should be opened in another," declared Samuel. "At this moment the impact of the church can probably best be made in South America. For many decades our Lutheran missionaries have been working there. The time has come to survey what has been accomplished, to estimate what more can be done . . ."

He was eager to make the journey, in the interests of his work as president of the Board of Foreign Missions of the United Lutheran Church in America and as president of the United Synod of New York. "How much stronger appeals are," he said reasonably enough, "when made by one who has seen for himself what is being done and what can be done. Every meeting of the Board of Foreign Missions will have greater meaning for me and for those whose aid I seek after I have visited this great continent."

His companion in many adventures, I made the journey to South America with him. The weeks preceding our sailing were filled with preparations and excitement. Samuel applied himself to intensive lessons in Spanish and Portuguese, read old and new books on South America, and called on all the people he could think of who had any knowledge of the climate, customs and people of South America, including his friend and admirer, Mrs. Sara Delano Roosevelt, who was deeply interested in the work of the church in South America.

The United States was then engaged in a "Good Neighbor Policy" on the theory that many South Americans did not like us because they did not know us very well and that visiting back and forth in neighborly fashion would be productive of good will. Mr. Nelson Rockefeller, coordinator of cultural relations between the Americas, telegraphed from the State Department in Washington, graciously making an appointment for Samuel to confer with him in New York. Unfortunately, Samuel was called out of the city that day, and at his request I kept the appointment for him. "What did Mr. Rockefeller say about South America?" he inquired on his return.

"All I could extract from Edmund concerning the South Americas," he declared later, "was that they were mostly Catholic—one of the few things I already knew. Beyond this, he intimated that Mr. Rockefeller thought that I, as a Protestant minister, would have to be a bit tactful. Subsequently I was to find that this warning was quite unnecessary."

On the fourth of July, in a heavy downpour, we taxied to the foot of Canal Street. As we walked up the gangplank of the *Santa Lucia* on the first lap of a fifteen thousand mile journey— six thousand by ship and nine thousand by plane—we were aware in the hubbub of conversations on deck, that our Spanish dictionary was going to be the most useful book we had packed. Simply to be able to say *Gracias Muchas* was not going to do at all.

From New York southward to Valparaiso (Valley of Paradise),

a voyage of eighteen days, we engaged in the usual occupations on shipboard, especially (as Samuel noted in his diary) "the luxury of reading and talking in the cabin." As always, he quickly made friends among the passengers. Among them was Lieutenant-Commander Lincoln Ellsworth, explorer of both poles, en route to Mount Misti, near Arequipa, in quest of the lost tombs of the Inca emperors. Not until we were bidding farewell to the Commander and the beautiful Mrs. Ellsworth in Lima did Samuel discover (with the pleasure that seems always to attend unexpected encounters with hometown folk on foreign soil) that Mrs. Ellsworth had been born in Pottsville, Pennsylvania, only a few miles from Bernville.

"My first impression of South America and one that lingered with me all through the visit was one of extreme poverty," Samuel recorded in his Journal of Travel, "great areas of people ignorant, superstitious and oppressed by Church and State . . . The City of Guayaquil, founded four centuries ago by the Spanish conquistador Don Francisco Orellana, presented an imposing façade. Alas, beggars crowded the docks when our ship arrived. I had not recovered sufficiently from the indisposition I suffered two days below the Equator to leave the ship. However, Edmund went across on the tender to see the city. His report was depressing."

At Callao, port of Lima, General Cesar de la Fuentes, Minister of War from Peru and Madame Fuentes, were waiting to greet us. Good neighbors in deed as well as in words, they had been waiting on the pier and in the rain for two and a half hours. Furthermore, we discovered later that the Minister of War had little time for gracious gestures, his troops being on active duty at the time in a fray between Peru and Ecuador. But he had taken time to be gracious just the same. The South Americans consider such time well taken.

"In Lima, ancient home of the Incas," wrote Samuel, "the people appeared more hopeful, more purposeful than those we had encountered in the dreary settlements at which we touched on the way to Valparaiso—Talara, Salaverry, Mollendo, Antofagasta. Long, long ago, Lima had lain in the heart of the mighty Inca empire. In the sixteenth century had come the Spaniards, greedy for gold and glory, searching for cinnamon, dreaming of empire. To the adventurer Captain General don Francisco Pizarro is ascribed the enslavement and doom of the Inca empire and the founding of the city in 1535.

"After the murderous conquest of Peru, Pizarro laid the cornerstone for a cathedral in the Ciudad de los Reyes (City of the Kings)," his journal continues. "In this cathedral rest his remains—shrunken bones in a glass casket."

"Francisco Pizarro," said Samuel, gazing at the bones in the light of a taper held by the verger. "Francisco Pizarro who was with Balboa in the discovery of the Pacific, with Cortez in the conquest of Mexico. A handful of bones under glass . . . *Sic transit gloria mundi.*" He was reading Prescott's *Conquest of Peru* at the time.

Leaving the great cathedral and its enshrined dust of power and glory, we went to the home of Rose of Lima, the first person of the new world to be canonized. "Wandering in her lovely garden, reflecting upon her self-inflicted tortures, her garment of spikes and the cell of stones she had devised to shut herself from the world—all to the glory of her Lord," Samuel observed that evening. "I could not but think her heroic devotion misguided. But Rose of Lima thought otherwise. Ed, I tell you, it is easier to bridge two worlds than to span the distance between minds of opposite convictions."

Eager though Samuel was to press on to destinations in the Argentine and British Guiana, it was a matter of deep regret to him that he could not spend more time in the museums and universities of South America. "How I would have liked to spend a long time there," he said regretfully as we were leaving the Inca Museum, "savoring every relic of that fabulous dominion." And, "How I wish I could linger, that I had the freedom of mind to do so," he said in farewell to the Dean of the School of Liberal Arts at San Marcos University.

With reluctant steps he turned from the historic university founded in 1551 and reputed to be the oldest in all the Americas. "I can understand," he said, "why South Americans resent North American patronage in which there is any hint that we are the bearers of culture to benighted younger brothers." He looked longingly back at the centuries-old Moorish buildings. But time was short and we desired before leaving Lima to call on the American ambassador, the Honorable R. Henry Norweb.

Within the embassy the scene was dramatically changed. The rooms were thronged with visitors and officials—alert, confident, capable men and women, intent on affairs of the moment. We had been absorbed for the most part in a veiled cloak and dagger Spanish past. Now the stage was set with the clean-cut, streamlined props of modern America. The sudden change of pace was a little confusing. The same energetic scene presented itself in Santiago, where we called on Ambassador Claude G. Bowers. It was the same all over the world, in all the American embassies everywhere—the atmosphere invariably charged with energy, efficiency, enterprise.

From our rooms at the Carrera Hotel in Santiago, we could see in the distance the snow-covered Andes. For three days while the August winter storms beat about us we waited word regarding our flight across the snowy peaks. Every kind of weather is possible on an Andean flight—fog, clouds, hail, rain, snow, not to mention thin and cold air and treacherous wind currents. On the fourth day our telephone bell rang and we were instructed to be ready to leave in thirty minutes for Los Cerillos airport.

Flying across the Andes was an unforgettable experience. We lifted speedily, because the ascent on the Chilean side is abrupt. Beneath us billowed a shining sea of clouds; above us towered giant peaks shrouded in snow. We followed mountain passes of cataclysmic beauty. Reaching an altitude of 18,000 feet, Mount Aconcagua ascended another 5000 feet to the empty white sky. The wings of our plane almost flicked the granite walls of this highest peak in the Americas as we sped by.

Ice frosted the windows of the plane. Through openings achieved by vigorous scrubbing with alcohol, Samuel gazed intently into the primal universe whirling by—spectacular cliffs curtained with ice, snow-drifted ridges sprinkled with dancing diamonds, jagged crystal-crowned summits, silent, frigid voids.

"Incredible!" he would exclaim. "Incredible!" "Yes, yes," I replied. "It *is* incredible." "I mean," he said, "it is incredible that without scientific data or equipment, without maps, Pizarro's men, centuries ago, encompassed these bitter mountains on horseback and by foot . . . traversed this uncharted solitude, clad in coats of mail and the trappings of knighthood, carrying swords, daggers and crossbows and herding pigs, dogs, llamas and Indians . . . An unbelievable achievement!"

While our plane was flying high in the sky through the mountain passes, Samuel had been knee-deep in heavy snow, stumbling along with Pizarro's men. Travel always made history companion to his thoughts. "By God's mercy," he murmured, still in the snows of yesterday, when the thrilling flight was accomplished.

We alighted at Mendoza, a city of many parks and famous for its vineyards. Sparkling with sunshine, Mendoza brought to mind southern France. A lovely city, where it would have been pleasant to rest for a while—but time as well as our plane had wings. On we flew to Buenos Aires, where, on a Sunday afternoon, Samuel was welcomed with outstretched arms by Missionary Pastors Herman D. Hammer, President of the Argentine Conference, and by John M. Armbruster and Jonas Villaverde of Buenos Aires.

At the Church of the Redeemer in the Villa del Parque, the congregation patiently waited the arrival of their distinguished visitor. Sunday services were held in English, Spanish and Slovak. In the evening Samuel spoke to the Lutheran Colony of Buenos Aires, after which a reception was held for him in the near-by girl's school. "At this reception," he notes in his diary, "I came to realize more fully the cosmopolitan character of our work in Buenos Aires. In the United States the diversified tongues of our Church are spoken in different church buildings, but in South America, dwellers from every part of the earth are united in one congregation. The congregation at Villa del Parque includes not only native Argentinians, but immigrants from every European nation and Orientals as well. It is not a German Lutheran church or a Scandinavian Lutheran church that has been planted in South America. It is truly an ecumenical church, ministering equally to the needs of all people who gather to hear the wonderful works of God."

Samuel summed up his days in Buenos Aires as "exhausting, but happy." He addressed convocations of pastors and "concentrations" of young people ("wearing white smocks and smiles"), concentrations of women ("deeply spiritual and devoted to Christian work"), and concentrations of men ("who offered prayers in Italian, Spanish, German and Slovak for the safe guidance of their guest"). He preached sometimes three times a day in the various churches of Argentina. His voice almost gave out but he could not find it in his heart to decline the warm-hearted invitations from the pastors. Especially was he impressed by the impact of the work being done by Pastor Andrew Mazak who was caring for some 5000 Slovak Lutherans in the Argentine.

He preached in the Church of the Good Samaritan at Villa Progreso, "a new plant of the church with a well-disciplined school of black-eyed, black-haired youngsters." (The mission stations in South America all maintain schools.) He preached at Villa Ballester and at Caseros. In the Temple San Pablo (St. Paul's Church) at San Miguel, assisted by eight other pastors, he ordained to the Lutheran ministry Senor Luis Garcia Izquierdo—a convert from the Roman Catholic Church.

Everywhere greeted by words of welcome and overflowing congregations, he responded cordially, making every effort to converse with the people in a semblance of their own tongues. As was his way, he visited non-Lutheran churches as well as Lutheran missions and attended mass in the Roman Catholic cathedrals. It did not take him long, talking with pastors, newspapermen and officials of Church and State in "full days complete with work and happiness" to inform himself regarding church work and religious life in South America. That Samuel Trexler was looked to as an interpreter as well as an observer of the scene is evident in a letter (July 1, 1941) from Dr. Franklin Clark Fry, later to become president of the United Lutheran Church in America, the office he holds today. Wishing him bon voyage, Dr. Fry wrote:

"There is no more intelligent or discerning pair of eyes in the Lutheran Church in America. Do keep them keenly alert for all of us! For the past eighteen months, it's been almost an obsession with me that we Lutherans should be doing a thousandfold more in South America—not only as zealous missionaries but as patriots . . . You believed it long before I did. And better still, you are *doing* something about it. A Mizpah blessing to you!"

Flying to Rio, Samuel asked me if I knew the derivation of the name Rio de Janeiro. I replied that I did not. "It is very interesting how cities come by their names," he said. "The complete name of the city to which we are flying is São Sebastião do Rio de Janeiro . . . ("Very interesting," I remarked, trying to see over the wing of the plane.) And the word *Rio* comes into it because when André Gonçalves, a Portuguese, discovered the bay on January 1, 1502, he thought it was a river . . . hence, Rio de Janeiro—River of January—popularly called just Rio . . . Ed, are you listening?" "Yes, of course," I answered. (We must be nearing the harbor, I thought.) "Well, then," he said, "there was a city which preceded Buenos Aires for a short existence named Ciudad de la Sanctissima Trinidad . . ."

"Samuel, look! Look!" I cried. "We are entering the harbor

of São Sebastião do . . . ! Look! There is the statue of Christ the Redeemer!" What a magnificent stretch of water lay ahead of us! We were stunned by the glory of the harbor. It has a beauty which can hardly be described. "At this moment," observed Samuel, "I would prefer being on a ship, granted hours instead of minutes coming in."

The heat in Brazil was oppressive. Conferences with churchmen, the press and Brazilian and American officials were attended by a flushed and perspiring president of the Board of Foreign Missions. Returning from a humid, flower-drenched garden party at the Corcovado home of Ambassador Jefferson Caffrey, Samuel mopped his brow. "The party was enjoyable," he sighed, "but enervating. For one with the energy of youth, the climate of Buenos Aires is, to my way of thinking, more stimulating. What fun to run into Chauncey Hamlin at the party!" An old friend from Buffalo, Mr. Hamlin was heading a mission to study the museums of South America.

A week in Rio, and we headed for Belém, a jungle city, spawned at the wide marshy mouth of the Amazon. Enroute, Samuel again inclined toward history. "Do you know who discovered the Amazon, Ed?" he began. I hesitated. "At the moment," I replied, "I do not exactly remember." "Well, listen then," he said eagerly. "The Amazon was discovered in the year 1541 by the explorer Don Francisco Orellana, a one-eyed Spaniard portrayed by some scholars as a scoundrel and by others, in an entirely different light . . .

"Opinions may differ regarding the man's character, but the fact remains that four hundred years ago—savages, reptiles and chiggers notwithstanding—Orellana, together with fifty scoundrels and otherwise, navigated the Amazon River.

An intrepid explorer, this Orellana," Samuel continued, "and strongly suspected of Lutheran leanings, even of *being* a Lutheran. At the time, this of course branded him a heretic. However, he died on the shore of the Amazon before the Inquisition could get their hands on him . . ."

"Orellana? A Lutheran?" I protested. "I thought the Spanish explorers were . . ." "Roman Catholics," said Samuel, taking the words out of my mouth. "So they were. But Orellana had heard of the great Reformer and was in accord with many of his convictions of faith, particularly the doctrine of *justification by faith alone* as distinguished from merit earned by good works." He paused to gaze at the clouds above and below us. Then he went on with fervor, "Not only did Orellana master the mightiest river in the world. He also hacked his way through the jungles over which our plane is now soaring free as a bird. Your mind may picture poisonous swamps, treacherous quicksands, tearing thorns and strangling vines . . . but think of the *mosquitoes!*" "I *am* thinking of the mosquitoes," I replied.

High, high we flew, over the French, Dutch and British Guianas, into Georgetown. Here Missionary Howard R. Kunkle, Acting Superintendent of the Lutheran Church Mission, British Guiana, met us with a hearty welcome and a request that Samuel preach that evening in Epiphany Church, Georgetown.

"Here was a new type of mission work and here were entirely new conditions," the diary records. "Every one of our people here are Negro or East Indian." Every seat was taken and many men were standing at the simple service of worship that evening. Unhappily, in the stagnant waters of the canal near which the church stands, a formidable army of mosquitoes adds to the misery of people already victimized by poverty, ignorance,

· 221 ·

apathy, and disease. Malaria and yellow fever are taken for granted. "I could speak eloquently and at length regarding the enterprise of tropical mosquitoes," Samuel told reporters on his return to the States. "I shall long remember my experiences with the super-stingers at Paradise in British Guiana."

Following the service, the organist, a stalwart black, presented to Samuel a highly embellished address of welcome, afterward making an urgent plea for a new organ. Samuel assured the congregation a new organ would be forthcoming. "Having heard the present one," he told me as we were leaving the church, "I could not do otherwise than promise a new one." "Of course not," I agreed, "but how will you manage it?" "I will manage it," he replied. "It is the least I can do in tribute to the wonderful work Pastor Bowen is doing here." The organ was duly sent through the good offices of St. Marks Church, Van Wert, Ohio, and joyously dedicated the following spring by Epiphany's congregation.

By slow train we proceeded from Georgetown to New Amsterdam—sixty-three miles dotted by impoverished settlements. Gazing at the flimsy shacks on stilts beneath which the inhabitants took refuge from the blazing sun, Samuel shook his head and frowned. "It is clear that more, much more must be done to help our missionaries in their heroic labors here. I am told that our missionaries and catechists frequently hold Sunday School and week-day schools beneath these—these riddled boards. Their courage is remarkable—missionaries never lose hope—but we should do more than preach the gospel to these people. We must provide means for improving their physical existence . . ."

The streets of New Amsterdam were lined with stately palms

and overrun with dogs. Gaunt, hungry, disease-ridden, they wandered at will in and out of the houses as well as the churches. Their attendance at services of worship was taken as a matter of course and occasioned no comment. After sultry excursions in the heat of the day into the dispirited communal settlements, the hospitality of Pastor Kunkle at the parsonage of Ebenezer Church was a welcome oasis.

Succeeding congregations of Ebenezer Church, founded in 1743 at Fort Nassau when Berbice was governed by the Dutch, had seen the struggle for power in Europe reflected in events there. They had seen the Dutch leave, never to return, the French come and go in Napoleon's time, and finally the arrival of the British—a colorful history under successive crowns. One of the oldest churches in South America, Ebenezer Church was full of plans in 1941 for the celebration in 1943 of the bicentenary of the Lutheran Church in British Guiana.

"And now may I ask you to continue to grow in grace and in the knowledge of the Lord," Samuel said in farewell to the congregation. "There remains much work to be done in the centuries to come. The Board of Foreign Missions will continue to help you. Your growth in faith will flower as you walk in the Master's steps and work with Him. Luther put our faith in simple words when he said, 'With one hand holding in trust to God, and with the other serving our neighbor in love.'"

"There is great need in British Guiana for better medical and sanitation facilities and more trade schools," Samuel agreed in bidding good-by to Pastor Kunkle, "and *screens!* Screens to defend these people from the scourge of mosquitoes and black flies . . . As you say," he added with a rueful smile, "how can they give attention to things of the spirit beset as they are by bloodthirsty insects! Yes—screens should have number one priority; our Mission Board should screen all open buildings. Our church buildings should be examples of cleanliness and neatness; afford protection and peace of mind."

The work of sixteen missions in British Guiana was scattered over a distance of nearly two hundred miles and Samuel wanted to visit as many outposts of the work as time permitted. Unfortunately travel was slow, especially when we were compelled to travel by boat.

One morning at seven o'clock we set out for the land of the Arawak Indians—about a hundred miles up the Berbice River. Three miles wide at New Amsterdam, the river gradually narrowed as our steam-propelled, double-deck boat cleaved a dilatory furrow through the yellowish-brown water. Lush verdure encroached on the banks. We stopped a number of times, always in the middle of the river. The natives paddled out to our boat in canoes. Long, narrow and sharp at both ends, the canoes darted about us like dragonflies, clinging to the side of our steamer until letters and freight had been received or delivered. Traveling with us were several Lutheran catechists returning from New Amsterdam to their river stations. The stories they told of their lives and the lives of those in their care did much to enliven the tedious journey.

The sun went down and the stars came out and still we were going up the Berbice River. About ten-thirty we reached Paradise, ultimate destination of our steamer. Here, Missionary Patrick A. Magalee was waiting for us in a little launch in which we continued our journey up the river for another hour. At last we came to Ituni, central village of the Arawak Indians. Here, in the light of the midnight stars we beheld an exquisite little church. Built of wood, hewn and sculptured by the Indians, it resembled a miniature Greek temple.

I shall never forget the service of worship held that morning in the Arawak compound. At four A.M. the church bell rang. Some of the Indians (whose origin in South America goes back beyond recorded history) had paddled a night and a day to greet the visitor from a distant land. They had heard of this white man and had traveled great distances to welcome him.

I watched their canoes glide silently into places along the river bank. I had the feeling that I had observed this scene somewhere before. Where? When? As I continued to watch the grave-faced men securing their boats to the moorings, memory disclosed the time and the place for which my mind was groping. I was a young lad, standing on a grass-grown gravel path. The path led to the open door of a country church. Grave-faced men were securing their horses to hitching posts in a white shed. How beautiful in the sunlight was this country church ringed by green-gold fields! I thought. I could hear the sweet, clear tones of the church bell calling, ringing and then mingling with the solemn overtones of another bell. The picture faded. I turned from the river and listened to the solemn tone of the Mt. Carmel Church bell calling the Indians to worship.

I looked again at the church which the Arawaks and the missionaries had built in Ituni and I thought: The children of the Arawaks will also remember. Far from home, as I am this day, they will see this church in their mind's eye and they will think: How beautiful in the light of dawn was this temple wherein dwelt the spirit of the Christ!

Samuel's voice trembled a little as he offered the prayer and read from the Scriptures. The drone and buzz of insects provided drumlike background music. Sixty sun-browned men and women attended the service. They listened attentively to the sermon. How much English they understood I do not know; not very much, I am afraid. After the service, a chieftain of the Arawaks presented Samuel with a fishing spear as a memento of his visit among them, saying nothing as he handed the spear with simple dignity to the honored guest. Samuel smiled and thanked him in Spanish.

Daylight had come when the reception, held on the coarse lawn of native grass, concluded. Bidding farewell to the church and the Arawaks we proceeded down the river to Maria Henrietta, second oldest Lutheran congregation in British Guiana. Here were gathered a large congregation of Negroes and East Indians. Addressing Samuel on behalf of the vestrymen and the congregation, Catechist W. A. Blair welcomed him:

Notwithstanding this is the first time since the establishment of this Church over forty years ago that we have the great pleasure of welcoming in our midst one who occupies the presidential chair of the Board and Synod responsible for our spiritual welfare, we have never been left in doubt of your great interest in us and we regard your visit at this time, when traveling is fraught with much danger and risk, as overwhelming evidence of a Christlike love and interest in us for which we crave your acceptance of our humble and sincere thanks.

Indeed, sir, for faithful and devoted missionaries and for the kind assistance given by the Board of Foreign Missions to the upkeep of our buildings and work, we are conscious of a great debt of gratitude which we feel can be paid only by our living faith in Jesus our Master, our loyalty and devotion to His cause and our spiritual growth in the Kingdom of His grace—the one reward we believe you seek, and to this end may God help us.

It is regrettable that your stay with us is so brief. We wish you a safe voyage on your return home, and may the Lord use your missionary journey beneath the Southern Cross to His glory . . .

Samuel was deeply impressed by the opportunities the journey had afforded, and looked back upon it with happiness and gratitude. "How grateful I am that I have been privileged to win the friendship of the South American people," he said warmly, "and to gain a clearer understanding of their problems. The Church in the United States must put forth greater effort to help these people." The written record of his journey *A Pastor Wings Over South America* was published in 1941 by the Muhlenberg Press and has enjoyed four printings.

When he arrived home he felt that he had something to convey to the Board of Foreign Missions concerning methods to be pursued in the work south of the equator. "The people of South America," he told members of the Board, "are very, very poor, or very, very rich. There is no middle road. It is this middle road that our missionaries are striving to build, day by day, mile by mile. The faith and the courage of these men surpass the dreams and the valor of the legendary Spaniards who defied jungles in search of El Dorado, the man of gold. I think of consecrated men like the Reverend Mr. Armbuster, our senior missionary, and of the men in all the missions I visited in South America. Brave and humble, and with vision to see the boundless possibilities of their limited endeavors, these men are building roads in South America between wealth and want . . .

"They have given momentum to a work that needs only the intelligent support of Lutherans on both continents to produce remarkable results. While the initiative in South America has been taken by the Catholic Church, Lutherans number some 350,000 and there is no reason why they should not increase in numbers.

"The large inflows of population from every part of the world invite Protestant churches not less than Roman Catholic churches to do missionary work in South America. It is not a matter of transforming Catholics into Lutherans but of helping the average man and woman to walk the Christian way of life, of bringing Christ to the unchurched, the indifferent. That is the all-important matter.

"Our work in Argentina, Brazil and the British Guianas represents more than a mission field in the limited sense of the term—it is the Church functioning in South America. I am convinced that there is a great future for our Church in this great land. I thought Lutherans working in a non-Lutheran land might be handicapped, but the only real handicap is the lack of missionaries. We must increase the number of educators and missionaries. This will mean money, but it is an investment in Christian living."

It was Samuel's wish to return some day to South America. "God willing," he said, "I shall go again to South America, make another missionary journey beneath the Southern cross."

Homeward bound we made a stopover in Trinidad. The curtains of our plane were drawn as we approached the harbor, and unusual care taken with regard to everyone entering. Columbus discovered the island in 1496, Samuel informed me, and named it "in honor of the Holy Trinity." Encamped on the island were British and American soldiers, sailors and airmen, adding to the confusion and congestion in the picturesque streets already overcrowded with Trinidad's English, French, Spanish, Portuguese, Chinese, Hindu and mixed populace. The pastors of Port-au-Spain invited Samuel to a meeting to discuss the problems which the soldiers had brought to the island, notably the social problem. "After much discussion the meeting adjourned," Samuel sighed, "as it would have in any other part of the world in these tragic times without having accomplished very much."

We continued our journey. "Do you know why I am so eager to visit Puerto Rico?" Samuel asked as our stratoliner neared the island. "What land are you not eager to visit?" I answered. "But I have a special happiness in going to Puerto Rico," he said. "I will tell you why this is so . . .

"One morning in February 1899, a howling blizzard kept the students of Mt. Airy Seminary indoors. To while away the time a group of us fell to discussing world events, principally the current Spanish American War and the new lands that had just come into possession of Uncle Sam. One of the students had read an article pertaining to Puerto Rico, and graphically described to us 'the spiritual poverty in this remote outpost.' We became very much wrought up about so sad a state of affairs. Two students with the impulsiveness of youth, vowed then and there to go to Puerto Rico, and in 'this remote outpost' plant the seed of the Word. To us who had traveled scarcely the length of two counties, Puerto Rico was an unimaginable distance away —somewhere on the opposite side of the globe. The magnitude and daring of our classmates' proposal brought our discussion to an abrupt end. In silence, we stared out at the swirling snow, reflecting on their venturesome boldness.

"The two students who committed their lives to the spiritual enlightenment of Puerto Rico were Benjamin Franklin Hanky and Herbert Franklin Richards. Despite many obstacles they did finally reach Puerto Rico. They persisted bravely, and it is to see the realization of their dream that I am so eager to visit this island. The work they started today counts thirteen congregations, eleven pastors and more than 1,000 members."

Immediately our plane touched the ground Samuel was surrounded by Lutheran pastors, shepherded by the Reverend William G. Arbaugh, field representative of the Board of American Missions. The pastor escorted him to the Union Theological Seminary where he spoke to the faculty and students. In this school, supported by the joint Protestant churches of Puerto Rico, the students represented not only Puerto Rico but also South America. The following day he spoke to the pastors, their wives and the women workers in the church at Bayamon. In the Women's Missionary House, he spent a happy hour discussing conditions in the Lutheran world.

"The day was strenuous, but it was a day of wonderful fellowship with the pastors and workers of Puerto Rico," his diary concludes. "Pastor Arbaugh and Pastor Eduardo Roig took me to see every Lutheran church in Puerto Rico, as well as prospects of new work and new missions near the university now being built at Rio Piedras. The harvest of your planting has been blessed, classmates of long ago! The lamp of faith burns brightly in Puerto Rico. The fulfillment of a dream which seemed fantastic in 1899 has exceeded the dream itself. Spiritual poverty is no match for a dream such as yours . . ."

In the summer of 1947 a delegation of seven Protestant clergymen, of whom Samuel Trexler was one, boarded a plane at La Guardia field bound for Yugoslavia. The purpose of their journey was to investigate the status of organized religion in the new Yugoslav People's Republic. I had been invited, as a layman, to accompany the group. The Yugoslav Consul General, M. Markovic was present to see us off. It was probably one of the most strenuous as well as significant journeys that Samuel ever made, and certainly one of the most controversial, ecclesiastically speaking. The genesis of the expedition was as follows:

We had attended a dinner in October 1946 given by the American Committee for Yugoslav Relief at the Hotel Pennsylvania, New York, in honor of the Yugoslav ambassador, Mr. Sava Kosanovich. It was quite a brilliant affair, studded with dignitaries and marked by friendly feeling and fervid speeches, one of the most fervid being that of Fiorello La Guardia, then mayor of New York City. Following an address by Samuel on why men cherish the things of the spirit, Ambassador Kosanovich referred at some length to the Yugoslav "religious issue."

At the crowded press table, Monroe Stern, Information Officer, Embassy of the Federal Peoples' Republic of Yugoslavia, told the Reverend Dr. Guy Emery Shipler, editor of *The Churchman*, that he thought Mr. Kosanovich would welcome an opportunity to discuss more fully with church leaders of America the status of religion in his country. This idea met with Dr. Shipler's enthusiastic approval. In November a luncheon was arranged at the Hotel Pierre in New York at which some thirty Protestant clergymen met with Ambassador Kosanovich, Foreign Minister Simich and members of the Yugoslav United Nations' delegation to listen and to ask questions.

As a result of what was said at this luncheon, especially in connection with the trial (September 30, 1946) of Archbishop Aloysius Stepinac, Roman Catholic prelate who was imprisoned and deprived of civil rights, it was agreed that it would be desirable in the interests of better understanding between the United States and Yugoslavia (then at a low point) if a group of representative clergymen could go to that country and ascertain for themselves the true state of religious affairs.

One thing led to another and in June 1947 Mr. Kosanovich asked Dr. Shipler whether, in his opinion, there were ten outstanding churchmen who would be willing to visit Yugoslavia as guests of the government. Such an invitation was not without precedent. Similar informal groups of religious leaders had visited England during World Wars I and II as guests of the British Ministry of Information. At any rate, Dr. Shipler said that he believed clergymen would not only be willing to make the trip, but would welcome the opportunity to study the religious situation firsthand. Mr. Kosanovich then asked Dr. Shipler to prepare a list of names. No suggestions and no comments were made by the Yugoslav government as to the clergymen invited. Further, they were assured "full opportunity for consultation with religious leaders of all faiths."

Seven clergymen, four of whom were editors of national religious journals, accepted the ambassador's invitation. They included: Dr. Shipler, (*The Churchman*), an Episcopalian; Dr. Emory Stevens Bucke, editor of *Zion's Herald,* of Boston, a Methodist; Dr. George Walker Buckner, Jr., editor of *World Call* of Indianapolis, Disciple of Christ; Dr. Phillips Packer Elliott of the First Presbyterian Church of Brooklyn; the Reverend

William Howard Melish of the Church of the Holy Trinity, Brooklyn, an Episcopalian; the Reverend Claude Williams, director of the Institute of Applied Religion in Birmingham, Alabama; and Samuel Trexler, on behalf of Lutherans.

With us on our travels in Yugoslavia also was Dr. Jean Nussbaum, a Swiss citizen working out of Paris as General Secretary of the International Association for the Defense of Religious Liberty (European Section) with headquarters in Washington, D. C., and co-operating with the United Nations Commission on Human Rights. Dr. Nussbaum had spent thirty years visiting the trouble spots of Europe, testing the degree of religious liberty as it affected Protestant minorities. Further, he was personally acquainted with Archbishop Stepinac, having visited the Balkans several times prior to the war.

All these men were respected for their integrity and sincerity, and well known in religious circles. They were men of years and experience, quite aware of the responsibility they assumed as reporters of religious affairs in the country to which they were flying, and well aware too that it was not an easy assignment they were undertaking. The issues were sharply if not clearly drawn and the whole subject was explosive.

Samuel and I were in Bar Harbor when we received word that the flight to Yugoslavia had been scheduled. (There had been some doubt expressed by the State Department as to whether passports would be issued. Like other members of the group Samuel had received a letter turning down his application. In a forthright reply he made it plain that he did not intend to be pushed around by the State Department.) We returned at once to New York. On July 27th we landed in the Balkans.

During our two weeks in Yugoslavia we visited four of the

country's six republics—Serbia, Croatia, Slovenia and Bosnia. Traveling night and day with every facility at our disposal—motor, train, boat and plane—we had ample opportunity to confer with Roman Catholics, Orthodox, Moslem, Jewish and Protestant leaders. Also, we talked freely with just plain friendly people on the streets and in the shops and hotels. Foreign correspondents in Belgrade told us that we had seen more in fourteen days than they had in several months. We also visited a number of religious institutions and studied many documents, notably the official indictment of Archbishop (now Cardinal) Stepinac who had been found guilty of treason against the government of Yugoslavia.

Making use of every hour, we sometimes traveled as a group, at other times going separate ways. We found no evidence of inhospitality or lack of cordiality and among our most friendly receptions were those given us by leaders of the Roman Catholic Church. We were impressed by the number of monks and nuns on the crowded streets. Ninety per cent of the nurses in Zagreb University Hospital (a state-operated institution) were Roman Catholic nuns. Somehow we had not expected to find them there, especially wearing their religious habits. As a matter of fact, men and women in religious garb were a significant part of the Yugoslav scene in 1947.

A Princeton graduate, Steven Dedijer, who had lived sixteen years in the United States and worked for a year on *Newsweek* acted as our interpreter on official visits and interviews. However, we were free to come and go as we pleased and more often than not were without benefit of either interpreter or guide. Where we went and what we wished to see was proposed by us and arranged by our hosts from day to day. Wherever we went we found the churches open and functioning and were received by leaders of all churches with genuine courtesy and friendliness. Samuel, of course, recorded in his diary the places we went, the churchmen with whom we talked:

In the ancient city of Belgrade we were received by Ambassador Cannon, Counsellor Cabot, Braque Zereckty, Minister of Reconstruction, and other party leaders who asked us what we wanted to see.

We had supper with the theological faculty (Serbian Orthodox) of the University of Belgrade and talked long with the Vice-Rector, Dr. Dushan Glunac and Dr. A. Anastasievich, Professor of Theology . . .

In Zagreb we went to the cathedral where Stepinac was formerly Archbishop and visited the theological faculty (Roman Catholic) of the University of Zagreb, where we were hospitably received by the Rector, Dr. Janko Oberski and our questions answered freely . . .

After a visit to St. Marks the Evangelist—its marvelous altar sculpture the work of Mestrovich—we had an enlightening visit with Monseigneur Dr. Svetozar Ritig, retired Rector of St. Marks, and Minister without portfolio in the Croatian government—a wise old counsellor. At dinner in his beautiful home Monseigneur Ritig said: "Things are not as they are printed in a section of the Roman Catholic press abroad. While the separation of Church and State has caused much feeling, the State nevertheless is giving the Church large amounts for reconstruction and is also helping the theological seminaries . . ."

One hot morning (Yugoslav summers can be torrid) Samuel and I went out for a stroll in the city of Zagreb. About a block from Stepinac's cathedral we came to a Franciscan monastery. The inner court looked cool and inviting, so we entered and asked to speak with the abbot or the superior. Father Guerlion was summoned. He received us courteously but in obvious bewilderment regarding the purpose of our unannounced visit. We soon discovered that we were in company not sympathetic to the regime.

Later we learned that this was the monastery under the chancel of which had been buried gold and jewels wrested by the Ustashi (a Catholic terrorist organization) from those who had resisted the enemy-sponsored conspiracy to set up a quisling government to be called "The Independent State of Croatia." During World War II the Ustashi, headed by Dr. Ante Pavelic, and Zlatko Kvaternik and served by Stepinac as Military Vicar, had engaged in bloody conflict with the partisans led by Marshal Tito. To the accusation of mass murder is alleged the death of more than 800,000 Serbs, Croat anti-Fascists and Jews. It was significant (at least to us) that the religious life of this monastery, despite these ghastly episodes, remained undisturbed.

All clergymen to whom we spoke attested to "equality" of religious groups. The Protestants in particular commended their current status as a distinct improvement. In Zagreb we found Lutheran Pastor Edgar Popp, sitting in his study beneath a bust of Martin Luther. After visiting Christ Lutheran Church of which he was pastor, Samuel noted in his diary: "Pastor Popp told us of his heavy responsibilities in caring for sixteen Protestant communities some of them two hundred miles distant. I was privileged in his beautiful church to ask God's blessing upon these congregations. He spoke of the need for books and vestments and of his gratitude to the government for financial assistance in connection with heavy travel expenses involved in ministering to such widely scattered parishes. He said he was happy in his work and that he enjoyed full enjoyment of religious liberty."

At Ljublijana the mayor and his committee met us at the train and in the midst of dust and din we listened to their speeches of welcome. We then proceeded to Bled, summer capital of Yugoslavia in the foothills of the Julian Alps. After dinner at the Hotel Poplice where the vice-president of Slovenia was our host, we visited the St. Nicholas Roman Catholic Church in the village. Like others, it was crowded.

On the third of August we were the guests of Premier Marshal Josip Broz-Tito, who entertained us around the dining table in his villa on Lake Bled. Conversation was informal, pleasant and lively. The feeling, I would say, was predominantly one of good will. I concluded that our host not only meant to be affable and friendly, but *was*.

During the course of conversation (it was not very tactful under the circumstances) I remarked that "there were those in America who regarded Archbishop Stepinac as a martyr-saint, even having named an American high school after him." Before the interpreter had concluded his translation of this provocative comment, Marshal Tito looked up and, still smiling, replied in a dry tone, "Rather poor material out of which to make a saint . . ."

The visit we made to Lepoglava Prison is recorded by Samuel as follows:

August 5, 1947

After various proprieties we were taken into the warden's office. He received us graciously but somewhat uncertain as to how to proceed

never having had a like visit before. He went to summon the archbishop and returned saying that Stepinac refused to join us having
indicated that he had nothing to impart to a group of Protestant
clergymen. "Does he have the right to refuse?" Ed asked the warden.
To which the man replied, "Yes, he has . . ." However, observing
our disappointment the warden said he would inquire a second time.
In a few moments he advised us that the archbishop would receive
us in his cell.

We found Stepinac in a large clean room, lighted by two windows.
He was wearing a cassock and standing beside a small table on which
was a typewriter. Against the wall were bookshelves containing perhaps fifty or more volumes. I spoke with him in German; Dr. Nussbaum spoke with him in French. Stepinac said he was engaged in
translating the New Testament from the Latin into the Croatian. To
our inquiries as to his health and treatment, he replied, "all quite
satisfactory," saying "the food is very good" and "I have been blessed
with good health all the time I have been here." We were then shown
the chapel (next to his room) where he celebrates Mass daily. He
seemed a weak, unattractive man . . .

On the road from Zagreb to Lepoglava Prison we had passed
a religious procession, the men carrying banners and a standard
surmounted by a crucifix, and singing lustily as they marched
along the hot, dusty country road. On the way back (by a different route) we met hundreds of peasants on foot and in
wagons going (we learned) to the Roman Catholic shrine,
Sveta Marija Bistritza, where an annual festival of cures was
being celebrated. In the village square where the church is
located were booths selling religious art objects, devotional
materials, toys and refreshments. "Makes me think of the county
fair in Reading," observed Samuel, watching the rosy-faced

children waving from a merry-go-round.

At the Hotel Esplanade in Zagreb we had opportunity to talk with leaders of the Serbian Orthodox Church. Seventy or more priests from all parts of the Republic of Croatia were in convention there, all in a jovial mood, planning ahead with obvious confidence and enthusiasm.

An incredibly crowded and very dirty steamer took us to Dubrovnik. "We passively bore the extreme discomfort while we drank in the beauty of the Dalmatian coast and the Adriatic Sea," wrote Samuel. "In Dubrovnik we visited some of the Roman Catholic churches and then took a leisurely walk through the town, talking with residents, pro and con. I had heard much of the beauty of the Dalmatian coast and was not disappointed. I found Dubrovnik a heavenly spot with the blue Adriatic coming up to its very doors . . .

"In Sarajevo which is largely Moslem, a citizens' committee escorted us to the Hotel Europe where we were received by the president of Bosnia, who welcomed us kindly answering our questions frankly," the diary continues. "On the evening of our arrival we attended a dinner of five faiths. There were many speeches by government officials and by churchmen—among them the Franciscan monk, Father Bono Ostojich, representative of the Religious Affairs Committee of Bosnia-Herzegovina; the Moslem leader, Mohammed Ridranovich; the Orthodox priest, Dr. Jankovich; and Dr. Kamliv, president of the Sarajevo Jewish Community. I made the final address. The atmosphere of religious tolerance and understanding was evident to a remarkable degree . . ."

The following morning found us in the heart of Bosnia inspecting the famous Youth Railway project. The work was at its height—thousands of young people of many nations (not including the United States) laying ties, constructing bridges, boring tunnels. The underlying conception of the project was not only to get the railway built (which was urgent) but to challenge young people to take part in voluntary labor that was clearly of service to the nation.

Six hours of work on the railroad was followed by a wide variety of educational pursuits, sports, dancing and games. During the summer some sixty thousand young people were thus employed. They seemed to be having a wonderful time. "We are building a new world!" they shouted, and as we watched them, so happy and confident, so full of zeal and enthusiasm, we could only wish that we were young and building a new world with them.

"During the days and nights of hard traveling in Yugoslavia Samuel Trexler was a constant delight to all of us," wrote Dr. Shipler in *The Churchman*. "Even when we were forced to make a train at 3 o'clock in the morning, after three hours of sleep, he was gay and full of humor. His fluent German proved to be an asset in many interviews, particularly when we visited Archbishop Stepinac in prison."

At the farewell dinner in our honor in Belgrade all the churches in Yugoslavia were represented. Bishop Agoston Sandor of Feketich-Bachta, a leader of the Hungarian Reformed Church, traveled sixty miles by jeep from his parish near the Hungarian border to be present. Dr. Benzion Levi, deputy chairman of the Jewish Religious Community, at the suggestion of Dr. Shipler wrote a message to his friends in the United States expressing the wish for "closer relationship between all men of good will, and for eternal peace between nations." Among our most informative conversations were those with Dr. Levi and with Dr. Henri Urbach, chief rabbi of Zagreb. These representatives of the Jews, whose treatment during the war was lamentable, also spoke with confidence of their current status.

In Belgrade as in Sarajevo we were impressed at inter-faith gatherings by the attitude of church leaders regarding religious opinions, modes of worship and inherited traditions. It was clear that they desired to arrive at a sympathetic understanding of common problems and were willing and able to work together in unity and brotherhood toward this goal.

We had taken full advantage of Ambassador Kosanovich's assurance that we would have "full opportunity to confer with religious leaders of all faiths in Yugoslavia." Talking with many people—young and old, clerical and lay—we had not encountered evidence of tension, fear or restraint. The majority of churchmen, with the exception of the older irreconcilables to whom the People's front did not appeal, had been optimistic regarding the future.

The Protestant pastors had described their status as "a distinct improvement," saying that they "felt a security they had not previously enjoyed as minorities in a Roman Catholic Croatia and an Orthodox Serbia." We had attended (by dividing our forces) some fifty services in churches of various faiths, all of which were crowded.

Everywhere we went we had taken our cameras with us— even into Lepoglava Prison. The only thing we had been asked not to photograph was the outer approach to the prison, nor were we asked to have our negatives developed (we had taken about a thousand photographs) before leaving the country.

As to why Stepinac was arrested and convicted of treason, the American public at the time had little understanding, due to inadequate information on the one hand and misrepresentation of facts on the other. Sources of information relating to his trial were chiefly Roman Catholic. Yet, the most incriminating documents we saw were the files of the Roman Catholic diocesan newspapers, and while we found divisions of opinion among Catholics regarding the archbishop's conviction and imprisonment, many Catholic leaders admitted the truth of this background data.

At the Press Office in Zagreb we had listened carefully to an exposition of his case and examined the documents relating to his trial. Among these were many official Roman Catholic newspapers and periodicals currently reporting the story of the archbishop's collaboration with the enemy during World War II. Sentenced before the regular courts, he had been held accountable as a promoter of terrorism against the Tito government, and for moral and real responsibility in connection with the blood crimes committed against the Yugoslav population, especially of Orthodox and Jewish faiths, by the quisling government.

There was no doubt in the mind of any one of the American clergymen regarding the archbishop's guilt. We left Lepoglava Prison convinced that assertions (for example in *The Catholic Universe Bulletin*, July 18, 1947) that Stepinac was serving a sixteen-year sentence at "forced labor . . . and . . . slowly starving on an inadequate diet" were unfounded.

In their report the clergymen pointed out that the archbishop's trial and conviction represented prosecution of an individual charged with serious collaboration with the enemy of his country; not persecution of his church or religion. The report also stated that the delegates had found in Yugoslavia essential equality of all religious groups, fundamental freedom of worship, and respect for religious beliefs and institutions.

Members of the deputation were men who had given their lives to the Christian ministry and to the extension of the Christian church. Protestants, with a heritage of religious freedom which they cherished, they might reasonably have been expected to be on guard against any denial of that freedom. But the fact remains (as Samuel's father so often said) that people do not like to be told "disagreeable facts." And no facts are more disagreeable than those contrary to what people *want to believe*.

Certain individuals and certain sections of the press, secular and religious, in this country and abroad, did not believe or did not want to believe the facts presented in our report. They saw red, and sought by every means at their disposal to discredit both the delegation and its findings.

The storm of protest, gathering momentum while we were still in Europe, broke with fury on our arrival in the United States, and while the tumult was not altogether unexpected, its violence amazed us. If it had been possible, those in disagreement with the findings would have prevented publication of the report.

However, some three thousand Protestant clergymen endorsed distribution of the report, on the grounds that "both the standing of the authors and the importance of their findings entitle them to an uncensored hearing." The names of these clergymen were made public by the Reverend Dr. Paul E. Scherer of Union Theological Seminary, and the Reverend Dr.

Mark A. Dawber, executive secretary of the Home Missions Council of North America.

"We feel confident," said Doctors Scherer and Dawber, "that our fellow clergy and the public will welcome, as we do, an opportunity of judging on its merits a report covering a matter so closely affecting world peace and international good will."

A series of mass meetings was held so that the embattled delegates could present their conclusions personally to the clergy of America and answer questions on any phases of the report. The first of these meetings was held in the Broadway Congregational Tabernacle, New York City. "We are not here to express agreement with any political technique," declared Chairman Joseph R. Sizoo, president of the Theological Seminary at New Brunswick, "or to fan the flames of intolerance, or to decide whether or not they (members of the delegation) should have undertaken the mission, but to assert their right to state their findings."

We had not gone to Yugoslavia to appraise the Tito government or to pass judgment on the political policies or economic techniques of that government. We sought answers to two questions only: What is the status of religious freedom? What is the truth regarding rumors and accusations in connection with the case of Archbishop Stepinac? In none of our investigations was the government a source of information. Nevertheless, the veracity of our report was questioned and the motives of the delegation impugned.

We were accused of having "whitewashed the Tito government," even of having gone to Yugoslavia with that purpose; of having been deceived by the Tito government and of having deceived the American people. We were charged with being "apologists for a Communist dictatorship," of seeing "only what a Communist dictatorship wished us to see on a conducted tour." At no time had we discussed communism in Yugoslavia much less made any effort to defend it. Yet, we were accused of having been "willing pawns of the Communists." It was said that we had been "under the constant surveillance and well-regimented direction of a police state." Representatives Fred E. Busbey and Martin Gorski of Illinois called for a Congressional investigation, terming the visit "reprehensible."

The Evangelist (August 15, 1947) published by the Albany Catholic Press Association exhorted its readers to "be quick to repudiate these falsifiers . . . ravening wolves . . . in the clothing of sheep."

"I feel bound," declared Archbishop Richard J. Cushing of Boston, "publicly to denounce the systematic and sinister anti-Catholicism of organized groups like the committee of ministers which last week returned to this country from Yugoslavia . . . The damage is being done by men who—may God forgive them—are introduced as 'Reverend' . . ."

The Rt. Reverend William T. Manning (then retired Bishop of the Protestant Episcopal Diocese of New York) indignantly pointed to the presence in New York of two bishops of the Serbian Orthodox Church whom he labeled "refugees from Yugoslav terror." (Samuel particularly regretted Bishop Manning's position in the matter because the two men had long been friends.) One of the two Serbian bishops to whom Bishop Manning pointed was the Rt. Reverend Iriney Georgevich of Dalmatia, who protested that it was beyond his understanding how "as servants of God, the committee could so gladly accept an invitation from one of the most ruthless tyrannies the world has ever known . . ." Nor did it help matters at all when I said truthfully that we had found Tito a gracious host as well as a man of discernment and considerable charm.

Barbed words flew thick and fast jamming typewriters and jumping into print. We were branded "liars," "fellow-travelers," and accused of accepting "blood-money." We were bombarded by letters, mostly scurrilous. "I question the honesty of these seven American preachers who have been blindfolded on their inspection tours," wrote Peter Paul Reiner in a letter to the *Chicago Tribune* (August 21, 1947). "Certainly no man or woman with a speck of decency would close his eyes to the most wicked, tyrannical and inhuman regime . . . Just a few questions to these seven disciples of Tito who are trying to pin wings on this cut-throat . . . Can these seven men face their God with a clear conscience . . . ?"

"Personally I feel sorry a Lutheran pastor of our United Lutheran Church deemed it necessary with the other six divines to issue such a statement in the face of all the open facts to the contrary," wrote Otto Bergfelder, "giving the Catholic hierarchy occasion to reflect in a caustic manner on the veracity of the whole Protestant Church . . ."

Some statements in defense of our report and reputations as good Americans also appeared. But these were voices crying in a wilderness of denunciations. "I have recently returned from a four months' stay in Yugoslavia where I attended the All-Slav Congress in December 1946 as a guest," Anita Price wrote the *New York Times* July 12, 1947. "I also toured the country as an interpreter for the well-known American correspondent, writer and commentator, Robert St. John. I was particularly interested in the attitude of the present government toward religion. I attended a different church every Sunday and found most of them full of worshippers. Never once did I hear from those present that there exists today any restriction on religious freedom . . . One of the first buildings to be reconstructed in many a village has been the church . . . Yugoslavs enjoy today greater religious freedom than ever before . . ."

"One cannot but feel that if more persons of your perception and ability should make friendly visitations to the troubled nations, the friendliness which you demonstrate in your consecrated life might 'give for wild confusion peace,' the blessed peace of God," Sarah Chapman Francis wrote Samuel. "That you regard all forms of totalitarianism an enemy of Christianity, that you reject the Communistic philosophy of materialism and atheism as inimical to the Christian religion is too well known to be questioned." I repeat, these were voices crying in a wilderness.

As for our assertions that we had found Archbishop Stepinac in good health, enjoying religious privileges, and so far as we could discover well treated, the opposition, instead of branding these statements false, used different tactics. They declared that we had doubtless been deceived by "an imposter posing as Archbishop Aloysius Stepinac in Lepoglava Prison."

In the *Catholic Universe Bulletin* there appeared (February 6, 1948) a photograph captioned: Archbishop Stepinac— *actually he*, and a story headlined "Seven Protestant Churchmen Fooled by Fake Archbishop?" The story was alleged to be based on information from an escaped prisoner who was quoted as saying that the archbishop had refused to see the delegation of clergymen.

To me the most irritating thing about the whole affair was the attitude of our friends, which was a mixture of anxiety, pity and embarrassment. Whenever the Yugoslavia journey was a subject of conversation, they would look away, fall silent, change the subject. What they thought (and some confessed to thinking) was: "Too bad. Innocents abroad." The most amusing letter was from a friend whom Samuel and I had known twenty-five years earlier.

> New York City
> October 20, 1947

Dear Dr. Devol:

You will remember me as the old man with the little multigraphing shop in the basement at 12 East 48th Street when you were living with Dr. Trexler at 16 East 48th Street.

I write to ask how on earth did two such fine gentlemen ever fall into the net of the Commies? I can only conclude that being what I know you and Dr. Trexler to be—fine, clean, upright gentlemen— your lack of worldly guile made you easy victims of a group that needs all the clean names it can fool into its web.

> Maurice A. Platt

We were maneuvered into a defensive position where no defense was called for. We were questioned endlessly and became weary of repeating and reaffirming that religious freedom existed in Yugoslavia, even if political freedom did not. It was strange reasoning (as Dr. Shipler observed) to assert that our factual report in connection with freedom of worship in Yugoslavia represented "an open defense of the character and motives of the Tito regime." But that was how the opposition reasoned, if reason could be said to have played a role in charges made.

Samuel had welcomed the opportunity to see for himself how religion and Lutherans were faring in Yugoslavia. This was his sole reason for flying to the Balkans, and he made no apologies for the findings as stated in the report. In the heat of recriminations he was the only one who remained calm. You too! reporters who interviewed him implied with an air of disbelief. "There was not one ripple on the surface that would show there was restriction on freedom of worship in Yugoslavia," he told them with equanimity.

The rest of us (myself especially) were goaded into indignant expletives. I do not say that Samuel was not angered. He was, but more than angry he was shocked by the widespread lack of knowledge regarding the facts and grieved by the unchristian behavior on the part of those—particularly churchmen—who found themselves in disagreement with the findings. Their suspicions, distrust and venom troubled him deeply. But he was not disquieted by the accusations. He had nothing to fear.

At a meeting of the Administrative Committee of the American Section of the Lutheran World Convention in June 1947 it was agreed that if Samuel could secure a visa to enter Russia, he should proceed there from Yugoslavia. "The purpose of your mission is to discover the Lutherans in Russia and the state of their religious life," Ralph H. Long, secretary-treasurer, wrote him. "We should like to know whether there are any Lutheran congregations in operation and especially to discover what the situation is with reference to the Lutherans in the Baltic countries, Esthonia, Latvia and Lithuania. May God accompany you on this mission and speed your way so that it will be possible to bring some comfort and encouragement to the scattered Lutherans in Russia . . ." But a visa to enter Russia could not be secured.

The visit to Yugoslavia was the last journey Samuel Trexler and I made together. A year passed and five months, and then early one morning he departed into the shadows and the peace. I called to him, but he did not turn back.

CHAPTER EIGHT

THE WORD OF GOD

*How beautiful upon the
mountains are the feet of
him that bringeth good
tidings*

ISAIAH 52:7

IT WAS said by Phillips Brooks, renowned Bishop of the Diocese
of Massachusetts, that preaching at its best is an expression of
truth through personality. These words have come often to mind
as I have reflected upon the reasons why men and women in all
walks and conditions of life thronged the churches in which
Samuel Trexler proclaimed the Gospel.

During fifty years of friendship I heard him preach many
times—in small rural churches, in prominent city churches, on
shipboard, in prison camps and army posts, in cathedrals of
this country and Europe, and in mission outposts of Christianity.
Everywhere I saw that he had the confidence and affection of
the people.

As a preacher he was listened to with eager attentiveness. Yet he was no spellbinder. He poured forth no glittering torrent of words in an effort to overwhelm his audience by the impact of eloquent pulpit oratory. I would describe his preaching as felicitous, marked by sincerity of conviction and serenity of spirit rather than by eloquence. True, he had a magnetic voice —warm, vibrant and compelling. Many spoke of the memorable quality of Samuel Trexler's voice. "I can still hear his beautiful voice!" This was said to me time and again after he was gone. True, also, he was a handsome man and when he preached, his face, grave with the import of pleading his Master's cause, seemed to be lighted by inward radiance.

But there was something deeper, something beyond voice and presence that drew people to him. He *believed* in the God he revealed. I think the people knew this and, for this reason, listened so attentively to his expositions of the Word of God. His faith, unshadowed by doubt or fear, banished the doubts and fears of many who heard him.

His tranquil trust in an all-wise, all-loving Father restored and refreshed the spirit. He made the Fatherhood of God seem real. His confidence in the grace and mercy of God gave confidence to others, and his faith in humanity vested the brotherhood of man with sacred privilege. The people came to the church hungry for the bread of Life and went away stronger, better, happier men and women, renewed in strength and courage and in faith and hope. Life appeared more worth living, nobler, finer. This was the inestimable service Samuel Trexler rendered to tens of thousands.

To his sermons he brought his exacting scholarship, his culture and consecration, the riches of his Lutheran heritage, his whole environment, all the varied experiences of his life and being. Everything he observed and contemplated with pleasure or pain he wove into the fabric of his sermons. A rainbow seen through falling drops of rain, the sun on a blackbird's wing, a flower in his mother's garden, a lighted window in a darkened street, the face of a child. I remember vividly the beauty as well as the strength of sermons which touched the heart.

He expended endless patience in the preparation of his sermons, ever fearful that they would miss the mark, that he would fail adequately to interpret some vital truth. He had a poignant sense of man's loneliness and isolation. "I tremble when I think what a responsibility it is to preach the Word of God," he said to me one Sunday morning. "Somewhere in the congregation there may be someone lost, someone in bitter need of the Word, someone *alone*. Somewhere listening to me this morning there may be one who will never again hear the Word of God . . .

"Who knows better than you," he added, "a physician these many years, the heartaches and fears, the despairs of men and women. To enter into the mind and hearts of people, to reveal to them Him who is the Way, the Truth and the Life, to bring *hope* to those who come into the house of God—this is my humble prayer. The message of God is adequate to the need men have for divine love and grace. But the bearer who delivers the message must be able to make its meaning clear. To proclaim the Gospel, to bring to men the glad tidings of mercy, the good tidings of salvation by grace, can serve no useful purpose unless the words are comprehended. Souls can be saved or lost by the success or failure with which the Christian minister interprets the Gospel message. It is no easy task, Edmund. I have listened to some vain and useless expositions of the Word of God. I have also listened to inspiring sermons, sermons that lent wings to the spirit. But these, I can tell you, are not readily achieved. They are wrung from the mind and heart . . ."

Samuel Trexler did not regard himself as a great preacher, thereby escaping the pitfalls of those who do. He used no elegiac phrases, no artificial stratagem to make his point. He addressed himself to the people with simplicity and sincerity, thus achieving a validity that gave unique power to his preaching. Unaffected and unself-conscious in the pulpit, he spoke so effortlessly that no one would have believed the heartsearching, the hours of laborious work that preceded his appearance before a congregation.

Sermon-writing was for him an arduous task, and since it was an unremitting one, he was never free from the anxieties it imposed. "Work *hard* on your sermons," his father enjoined him, "and remember an honest man is much readier to bring judgment to his own efforts than to the efforts of others." Like his father, Samuel did not use a manuscript in the pulpit, but he always wrote his sermons out in full. "You must be working very hard," a classmate wrote him during his early ministry in Greenpoint, "three or more sermons a week is not the work of a few hours a day! Do you still write them out *in full?*"

His diaries, especially during his earlier years in the ministry, testify to long harassed hours spent in sermon-writing. There are many, many notations like the following, giving plaintive voice to his labors.

"Spent the entire day working on my sermon—worked industriously at it and by midnight had the satisfaction of seeing it finished, but not exactly to my liking—some parts good, others not so good."

"At seven in the morning set to work writing a sermon and worked at it assiduously until three in the afternoon—was not well satisfied. In the evening thought over my sermon again— had only one point lacking but the profoundest thought could not supply it."

Rarely a Sunday Samuel Trexler did not preach two or three times and he seldom repreached a sermon. He had an open mind and a hospitable attitude toward other faiths and when not himself preaching, attended services in churches of many denominations. In all parts of the world he studied the work of the churches and the religious life of the people.

"In Leipzig I had a splendid illustration of the European Sunday," he wrote in 1913. "In the morning everything was closed and a Sabbath stillness reigned. When services of worship were over, the shops opened, bands played in the parks and picnic groups assembled . . . On the way to Dresden I saw farms alive with men harvesting grain—they too had heard the Word of God that morning. There is so much we can learn and profit by in this beautiful world." Everywhere he sought the good, the beautiful and the true in services of worship, patiently panning the gold from the gravel of all he heard and observed.

During his fifty years in the ministry changes in the social, political and economic scene were probably greater than in any previous fifty years in history. The circumstances and surroundings of men's lives were vastly different in 1949 than they had been when Samuel Trexler was ordained in 1899.

Through reading and travel and conversation with leaders in

Church and State, he was able to follow and to study the changing trends of thought and thus meet intelligently the spiritual needs of the day. During the first decade of the century the pattern of life was comparatively simple. Men had faith in the future, a will to independent security and a measure of peace. Family life, and to a large extent social life, was integrated in the home and the church.

Samuel and I enjoyed conversing with friends, the theatre, music and art, meetings of the Greenpoint Dickens' Circle, lectures by explorers of the North Pole or the African jungles, walking in the country, and entertaining at home—Samuel presiding over the chafing-dish. He had quite a flair for ruffling the oysters and snuffing the flame. And being young bachelors we were not lacking in invitations to the homes of friends.

Many thought, as had Samuel's father, that his life would have been more complete had he married. He was about fifty years of age when a newspaperman asked him, off the record, why he had not married, whether he felt that marriage and family cares interposed distractions to service in the Church. "No," Samuel replied, "I do not feel that way about it at all. On the contrary, the wife of a minister, as my mother, is often as much of a help in the conduct of his parish as the minister himself. The fact is when I was young I was too poor and too busy to seriously consider marriage and later I was just too busy I guess, too preoccupied with the care of the churches, and then too, my responsibilities necessitated almost constant traveling . . ."

The peaceful, hard-working, confident years ended in 1917. It was a different world to which Samuel and I returned after serving in the army. The rhythm of life had changed. It was a world to which restless activity was the key and mass production the mainspring. A world in which we had difficulty finding ourselves.

During the decade of the twenties when people threw sound judgment, caution and common sense to the winds, Samuel, then president of the Synod of New York and New England, spoke from many pulpits against the "growing indifference to religion and the Church," the "increasing moral and social irresponsibility," and the "corrosive materialism of the times." The texts he preached upon were not at all popular with his listeners: *Enter ye in by the narrow gate for wide is the gate and broad the way that leadeth to destruction . . . Stand ye in the ways and see, and ask for the old paths, where is the good way and walk therein . . .*

"We live in an age intoxicated with material achievements," he said in the pulpit of Holy Trinity Lutheran Church in 1928, "building our tower of Babel, exulting in its increasing height, indifferent to the sounds of destruction which thoughtful men hear above the deafening hammerblows, the roaring blast furnaces . . . We have lost our perspective, our sense of values. We are judging men by what they *have*, not by what they *are*. A day of reckoning will come . . ." But few in those days of easy money heeded a preacher's warning.

In the thirties when the money world went to pieces Samuel traveled from church to church and parish to parish in his Synod, trying to hearten the pastors, to hold the congregations together, to lift people above bitterness, cynicism and despair. A text he used oftentimes during those years of disillusionment and hopelessness was *Strengthen the things that remain.*

"These were the Master's words to the church at Sardis where little did in truth remain of spiritual power and grace," he told the congregations. "His message was one of inspiration and courage, an appeal to rebuild on old foundations of faith. We have been worshipping a god of gold, paying homage to *wealth* . . . The time is coming when homage will be paid not to men of wealth but to those who serve—*Whosoever would become great among you shall be your minister; and whosoever would be chief among you shall be your servant; even as the Son of Man came not to be ministered unto, but to minister.* The 'aristocracy' of wealth will not be the yardstick of a man's worth in the years ahead. The measure of a man commanding the respect of his fellowmen will be his ability to make a contribution to a better world. This is well and good for it is only through unselfish service to humanity that a man's life is either happy or justified."

He understood the weakness as well as the strength of the church, her failings as well as her virtues. When he was still a student in the seminary this note appears in his diary: "The Reverend E. A. Miller made a stirring address on some of the failings of the Lutheran Church. It was powerful—I was so much moved by it that I could not concentrate my thoughts on my work the entire evening." Nothing caused him more distress than spiritual complacency. "The self-centered, self-satisfied, self-righteous church is as hateful to God as it is distasteful to men," he told the pastors of Synod in 1933. "The church must make a heart-searching examination of her purpose for existence. She exists to meet spiritual need and into meeting this need she must throw all her resources. Men are asking: Where is my life going? What am I doing with my life? Is this *all?* They are seeking something which will give meaning and purpose to their lives. The church must answer these questions. And as pastors let us ask ourselves.

"Does the church of our time amaze men by her achievements, by the beauty and power and glory of her life? Are we following in the steps of the Galilean whose abiding work rested in the influence He had on the lives of those about Him? Are we faithful servants of the Master? Let us answer these questions honestly, remembering that it has been truly said that of all vain things the vainest is to labor incessantly for God without the spirit which alone is acceptable to God and effective for God . . ."

Samuel Trexler did not temporize with the truth as he saw the truth. His essential honesty of convictions was well known to his associates. "We owe our fellowmen the truth," he said to a pastor who expressed concern regarding the forthrightness with which he spoke against "the barbarity of war" on the eve of the United States' entrance into the second world war. "Every word ought to be a testimony, a yea that is yea indeed, and a no that is no indeed—an honest revelation of the thoughts and feelings, so that it can be said *as the man, so his word.* Let all who hate war have the courage to say so."

He was convinced that the peace of the world could never be achieved until men had been brought to understanding and acceptance of the Word of God. "We must bring people to the certain knowledge of their responsibilities as children of God," he declared, "and their individual accountability to Him. They must be made to understand that regardless of the teachings of ancient or modern philosophers or the wonders of science, the eternal truth stands that *whatsoever a man soweth, that shall he reap.*"

"Many are the hearts that tremble at the outcome of problems which a confused and troubled world faces," he said in 1947. "Many solutions are offered by statesmen. I am not an apostle of doom but I do not think that statesmen will find the answer to the ills of the world in atom bombs. Only as they enter into the settlement of international problems in the spirit of Christ will the solution be forthcoming. It is the responsibility of the church to see that this is done, to impress upon Christians the sacredness of the individual and the individual Christian's responsibility in the struggle to preserve justice, righteousness and human freedom. We are drifting into a so-called 'welfare state' where individual responsibility is no longer deemed necessary or even desirable. This is contrary to the basic tenets of our faith . . .

"The minister is called upon to do the work of God in a world where the destructive forces have become so powerful that they threaten the very existence of civilization," he told his colleagues. "Who if not Christian ministers will convince statesmen that the ultimate solution to our problems is to be found through brotherhood in Christ? And let us never forget that it is in vain that any man attempt to lead another to Christ unless Christ first be in that man's life."

Samuel Trexler never ceased to be grateful that he had been called to the ministry. He spoke many times of the world-mission of the Church, of her leadership in the establishment of "a realm of good will comprising all men." "It is a project of majestic proportions," he declared, "commanding the fealty of all mankind."

He asked not only an emotional but a full intellectual acceptance of the Christian faith as set forth in the Word of God and the Nicene creeds. "In these," he told his congregations, "you will find comfort, strength and courage in the hour of need . . . *Heaven and earth shall pass away: but my words shall not pass away.* Religion alone can give meaning and purpose to life. It is by faith that man sees all things working together in the light of God."

The sermons Samuel Trexler preached reveal his inner character and beliefs as in a mirror. There is in them the joy of life and the faith and courage of a true-born soldier of the Cross. There was no uncertainty, and no conflicting ideals or purposes in his life. "There was no inconsistency in Dr. Trexler's character or in his career," wrote Dr. Luther D. Reed, president emeritus of the Lutheran Theological Seminary at Philadelphia. "He was always the perfect gentleman, the earnest Christian, the able minister of Jesus Christ, the zealous Churchman . . ."

Samuel Trexler regarded preaching as the heart of pastoral responsibility and preached not to glorify himself but to glorify his ministry. To reflect credit upon his church brought him great happiness. In 1913 when he was serving as pastor to university students he wrote me from Ithaca, New York: "My morning's mail brought me an invitation from Cornell University to be Sage Chapel Preacher on November second. This made me very happy for my Church. The invitation is considered a great honor . . ." When he wrote in November that the sermon had been "well received by a distinguished audience," he added "The service was widely reported by the press—this pleased me greatly because of the attention directed toward the Lutheran Church."

His comment was much the same when he preached in the Cathedral of St. John the Divine, New York City in 1931. The occasion was a Thanksgiving Service for the Patriotic Societies of New York, and it was the first time an American Lutheran clergyman had preached in the Cathedral. "The service was colorful and impressive," he noted in his diary. "I was very happy to have had the honor of preaching the sermon, and especially happy, from the standpoint of the Lutheran Church, that it was considered newsworthy."

Reporters liked Samuel because he was friendly, straightforward and honest with them, and because he had something to *say*. One day a pastor of another denomination asked Rachel McDowell of the *New York Times* how it happened that "Bishop" Trexler appeared so often in the news columns of the *Times*. Miss McDowell gave him a long look and a short reply. "Because he is *news*," she answered.

While Samuel did not seek personal publicity, he welcomed every opportunity to give the church as wide an audience as possible through the press, the religious journals and radio. If television had been invented he would have used that medium, too. His radio broadcasts were a source of much pleasure to his mother. In the Trexler parlor in Bernville, surrounded by many interested neighbors, she listened to his sermons on the "Church of the Air" and wrote him of her "happiness in the good you are doing spreading the Gospel throughout the land."

Samuel even thought of planes in terms of their usefulness to the church. On our journey to South America we saw a milepost at San Pedro Macrois in the Dominican Republic on which was lettered: 2,227 miles to New York—6,391 miles to Buenos Aires. He stood there looking at it for a moment and then turned to me and said, "Quite different from the mileposts of horse and buggy days when I drove with my father from church to church in the Pennsylvania Blue Mountains. The Church can now begin to think in terms of continents instead of countries or counties.

The airplane may some day make possible Christian planning on a planetary basis."

In an old ledger, frayed by time and use, are tabulated the texts upon which Samuel Trexler preached—and the time and the place—a record meticulously kept so that nothing was left to chance or memory. The first entry is dated July 5, 1896; the text Matthew 6:24 *No man can serve two masters:* the place Rehrersburg, Pennsylvania. Fifty-two years later he made the final entry, preaching his last sermon February 26, 1948 at Holy Trinity Protestant Episcopal Church in Brooklyn, New York on the text John 15:17 *These things I command you, that ye love one another.*

Young pastors to whom I have shown this Text Register in which are entered some 3000 sermons, turn the pages thoughtfully, trying to envision the hours, the days, the years, the patience, the diligence and fidelity recorded therein, wondering whether they will be granted the grace so to be faithful to death. Some have asked me whether there was a text Samuel Trexler favored above others. I am not certain, but in studying his Text Register, there is one he chose often. It is from Philippians: *Rejoice in the Lord alway: and again I say, Rejoice.*

So many sermons preached with the prayer that some vital truth from the source of truth would be comprehended, some individual soul challenged, comforted, lifted up. So many words, spoken with the hope that they would impart a measure of faith and hope and love, light the way for one whose lamp had gone out. *The love of God is broader than the measures of man's mind and the heart of the Eternal is most wonderfully kind.* So many, many words . . . But there are no words, no matter how illustrious, no sermons that can match the eloquence of a life lived to the glory of God. The greatest sermon Samuel Trexler preached was the life he lived. His life was a happy one. His ministry was fruitful. His message was one of hope:

They that wait upon the Lord shall renew their strength; they shall mount up with wings as eagles; they shall run, and not be weary; they shall walk, and not faint.

CHAPTER NINE

GOLDEN FAREWELL

I shall not die, but live
and declare the works of
the Lord

PSALMS 118:17

WHEN HIS responsibilities as president of the United Lutheran Synod of New York ended in 1944, Samuel Trexler was not troubled in mind. He felt instead a sense of relief. Satisfied that administration of the office to which he had given so many years was in the capable hands of a man he trusted and loved, he turned his thoughts toward the future.

"Now, at last, Ed, I can devote my entire time to the world work of the Church," he said, "the difficult problems confronting our foreign mission enterprises in Europe, in Asia and the Orient." I shook my head, observing with misgiving how worn he was by illness and by responsibilities that had already put too heavy a demand on his nervous energy and physical strength. But I knew it was useless to argue with him.

"Surely this tragic war must end soon," he went on, his face full of concern. "How I wish I could see my friends in Germany!

It has been nearly seven years since I have heard their voices or clasped their hands, and little or nothing is known of the fate of our people in Russia. I wonder if it will be possible to go to Russia when the war is over, whether the Soviet Union will be disposed to admit a clergyman. And the Balkans, where the war is being waged with such dreadful cruelty, what of our people in Yugoslavia? And what of our missionaries in Japan and in India?"

Anxiety clouded his eyes. He walked restlessly up and down the warm friendly room filled with books, photographs of friends, and small treasures that he cherished—precious possessions from faraway places and from men and women grateful to him for kindnesses beyond words—an exquisite replica of Thorwalsden's "Christ" . . . a communion goblet of flawless crystal . . . a rare Ming lamp . . . paperweights in which were imprisoned fantastic flowers and glistening teardrops . . . an amber chalice, a Malvina Hoffman dancing girl . . . a pair of very old altar candlesticks . . . a golden trinket box gemmed with multi-colored enamel, the gift of a prince . . . the wooden cross he had carried as a chaplain in France, the gift of a Belgian soldier.

For twenty years, as president of Synod, Samuel Trexler had seized every opportunity to depict for American Lutherans the plight of churches and mission stations in war-torn areas. Year after year he had brought to bear in behalf of the church abroad, all the influence of his official position, and all his powers of persuasion. The people had responded. Money had been generously given. But he knew that the ultimate misery was yet to be and that the tasks confronting the church in the years to come would be greater than any she had yet faced. Would she be equal to the challenge and the burden?

The First World War had done great harm to mission under-takings. The destruction that would be wrought by the second holocaust was beyond reckoning. What had taken generations of heroic labor to build up had been reduced to rubble over-night. Hundreds of millions of dollars would be needed for the work of reconstruction. And manpower too would be needed—inspired leaders and courageous missionaries to take up the work of the fallen. To ensure able, consecrated leadership was a problem that he constantly pondered.

"American Lutherans have a clearer understanding of their responsibilities to fellow believers throughout the world," he said uneasily, "and the Lutheran Church is making progress toward world unity. But there still remains the problem of enlisting more *and* better-educated men for the ministry. Unless the church can provide an increasing number of outstanding pastors, men of broad sympathies and cosmopolitan minds, church statesmen at home in any country, she will be at a loss in the troubled years ahead." Through the years he himself had continued to study in the universities here and abroad, believing that culture as well as consecration are essential for an effective ministry. Muhlenberg College, Thiel College and Syracuse Uni-versity had awarded him honorary degrees. I was thinking of how exacting he was in scholarship and how many times he studied late into the night after a hard day's work, while he continued to talk . . .

"Mountains and rivers and seas are no longer of consequence in dividing nations. Ideologies are the boundaries that must be crossed. Intellectual and spiritual barriers—these are the moun-tains and seas that must be crossed in the search for peace and the struggle to preserve a free world. It is a venture of faith in which the church can and should lead the way . . . a mission that demands leaders who are citizens of the world."

"Samuel," I exclaimed, "you said that ten years ago—and long before that. You have been pleading for a better qualified, better trained, more widely informed ministry since the days of your student pastorate work in the universities and that is *thirty* years ago."

"I know," he agreed, "and I am more than ever convinced that this is vital to the future influence of the church." "And did you not plead the case for a superior ministry in a book you wrote nearly ten years ago?" He nodded. I walked over to the library shelves and took down a copy of his *Out of Thirty-Five Years.* "It was in 1936," I said, turning to the preface, "that you wrote:

The Church is facing trying conditions. In the next few years she will be tested more thoroughly than she has been tested since the days of the prophets and the martyrs. The most important link in the religious life is the minister; people will follow where they are rightly led. Because of this I have made it of first importance, both in official acts and personal contacts to strengthen the ministry of the Church. It must be more carefully selected, more thoroughly trained . . . The one method whereby the Church can meet the problems of the future is to have a superior ministry."

Samuel was compelled to smile at the ardor with which I was reading. "It was my hope," he said, "that this plea might help to focus attention on the problem." "No doubt it did," I ventured. "Think of the hundreds of letters you have received from young pastors thanking you for the inspiration and help your book has been to them and of the many letters from older churchmen commending you for your discernment and forthrightness." "Yes, yes, I remember the letters," he said. "But—"

Samuel understood the importance of graduate study, extensive travel and world-wide friendships because he knew what these advantages had meant to him during forty-five years in the ministry. He had profound convictions as to the value of the ministry in the modern world and regarded the minister of first importance in enabling the Church to meet its world problems. He believed that much greater attention should be given both to the selection and education of pastors for a more adequate fulfillment of their mission. Again and again he had pointed out that the life of the Church would be largely that of her ministers and that their preparation must not end with ordination. All agreed this was true. But the question, *What can be done?* remained unanswered. How many theological students could afford the luxury of advanced study, of travel abroad? Not many.

When we left Yugoslavia in August 1947, finding it impossible to secure a visa to enter Russia, Samuel had gone instead to Germany. With a heavy heart he had observed the toll war had again levied on the German people. Hitler was no longer shouting on the Wilhelmstrasse and the streets of Berlin, no longer decked with flags and gaudy banners, were hung with desolation. Martin Niemoeller*, his spirit undaunted by eight years in prisons and concentration camps, was again preaching at Dahlem. But the Church's struggle for survival was not over

* Today president of the Evangelical Church in Hesse.

and the clergy were in dire need of help and would be for years to come.

As soon as we arrived in the United States, glad to be home again, Samuel redoubled his efforts on behalf of Lutherans abroad. Day after day, heedless of the wear and tear on his physical resources, he addressed women's organizations, groups of businessmen, conferences of clergymen, congregations. His sense of personal responsibility toward the church made it impossible, even when the strain of the work weighed heavily upon him, to forego an opportunity to speak for her. Again in 1947 and 1948 he portrayed for American Lutherans the plight of Lutherans abroad, again pleaded for support lest the evangelical faith in Europe be engulfed by despair and godlessness. The suffering and misery of thousands of souls flowed over him. Relieved from the responsibilities of Synod, he seemed now to bear on his shoulders "the care of all the churches." And the problem of ensuring effective leadership for the church in a changing world, the urgent need to make available to young men entering the ministry, broader cultural and educational advantages continued to perturb him.

In 1948 we were in Bar Harbor, Maine, where we had spent several memorable summers together—following the course of white sails on the bright sea, watching oncoming breakers dash sparkling rainbows against the somber rocks, observing the restless gulls trace winged flight patterns against the intense blue sky, free for a time from the cares of the office.

One day we had been sitting beside the sun-lit sea for quite a while recalling the completed years and discussing the approaching fiftieth anniversary celebration of Samuel's ordination

in the ministry. Everything was golden that late August afternoon—the light of the setting sun on the summer sea, the sand
rippled by the outgoing tide, the pools of water in the hollows
of the rocks, the slender spears that crowned the dunes, a host
of small butterflies that danced above them—everything, even
the stillness.

"I have been thinking," Samuel said in his gentle voice, not
taking his eyes from the shining horizon, "that I would like to
mark my golden anniversary by making a gift to my Church.
I thought to present to our Synod my savings . . . With this
money I could initiate a fellowship that would enable young
pastors, a few at least, to avail themselves of the advantages of
graduate study and travel abroad . . . And who knows? The
fund may grow . . . What do you think of this plan, Edmund?"

"Trexler, I think it is a wonderful idea," I replied. "And I'll
tell you what I will do. I will raise additional money through
our friends. They will be happy to have a part in this fellowship—and in this way the fund will begin to grow at once!"

The sun went down as we walked home, happily tossing
plans and ideas back and forth in the golden light. Samuel's
thin face was radiant.

When Samuel revealed to President Knubel his desire to
create a fellowship in commemoration of his golden anniversary,
the proposal was warmly received. For some time the Synod
had been studying ways and means to provide financial assistance to qualified students and pastors so that they might
enhance their usefulness to their church. It was essential that
students acquire a greater appreciation of the "saving humani-
ties," that young pastors have a deeper understanding of society

as a whole, greater adaptability to a changing world. Trained men, Samuel had more than once pointed out, are not necessarily *educated* men. A progressive growth in spirit and outlook, a greater breadth of interests in the search for truth was requisite. With this point of view church leaders were agreed. They welcomed the Samuel Trexler Fellowship not only as a source of financial aid to worthy students but as an inspiration to young pastors preparing to serve the church on new Lutheran frontiers. The officers of synod were confident, as Samuel Trexler was confident, that the fund would grow.

Well do I remember the December afternoon in 1948 when Samuel handed his personal check for $10,000 (plus $7,000 which I had up to that time gathered from enthusiastic friends) to Frederick R. Knubel in the chapel of the Lutheran Church House in New York City. Staff members of the Synod and a few old-time friends witnessed the presentation, their happiness reflecting Samuel's own happiness in presenting this gift to his beloved Church.

"The press was represented by photographers and reporters," Samuel recorded, "which made it very festive." When we opened the morning newspapers, headlines announced: Samuel Trexler Founds Fellowship for Education, Culture . . . Dr. Trexler Opens Fellowship Fund . . . Lutheran Leader Makes Initial Ten Thousand Dollar Gift Toward Student Aid . . . In the *Lutheran Church Messenger* a photograph of Samuel handing his check to Dr. Knubel was captioned: "The gratification of the Heart of the Donor and the Appreciation of Dr. Knubel acting for Synod is reflected in their faces as Dr. Samuel Trexler presents his long-powered gift."

From day to day Samuel made happy entries in his diary:

"Received congratulations on every hand . . . Had cheering recognitions of my gift . . . Additional funds for the fellowship started rolling in from various and happy sources." Weaving in and out of these notations were dark strands of suffering not communicated to his well-wishers: "Consulted with my doctors . . . Rested at home . . . The severe pain let up . . . Went to see the doctors . . . Rested at home the allotted time."

Samuel was approaching journey's end. Possibly he knew this. But he did not speak of it. Between visits to the doctors and days in the hospital he attended meetings, conferences, dinners—and continued to plan, advise and work in the interests of the Lutheran Church. Like the bouquets of wild flowers he had gathered as a child for his mother, he held all the cherished hopes and dreams for his Church tightly in his hand and did not drop one on the way to his Father's house.

When he died in May 1949, Samuel left a bequest of an additional $45,000 (the greater part of his estate) to the Fellowship. At that time a further sum of $20,000 was made available through our friends and member congregations of the Synod. The principal invested (as stated in the 1953 report by Mr. Ernst S. Erickson, treasurer of the Synod) exceeds $100,000. As had been predicted, the fund continued to grow.

The bright arc of Samuel Trexler's life grows brighter. In its reflected light young men walk. Who are these men? They are men who desire to make a spiritual contribution to their generation, men who hold the ministry to be the most exciting, satisfying and rewarding career in the world. They are men who believe in God.

I have talked with two of these men—William H. Lazareth

who had studied at Tuebingen University as the first recipient of the Samuel Trexler Fellowship, and Paul E. Hoffman, son of the Reverend Paul C. Hoffman of Utica, New York, who received the award for 1952–53. Both men are graduates of the Lutheran Theological Seminary, Philadelphia. When he had returned, Mr. Lazareth called to see me. He spoke joyously of "seeing life with fresh vision and new inspiration." His introductory remarks in a report of his work in postwar Germany reflect what experience in a foreign scene can mean to a young man entering the ministry:

In the light of my experience I cannot strongly enough express my gratitude for having had this remarkable opportunity. In keeping with the spirit of Dr. Trexler's prophetic insight, it became my constant aim in Germany to receive and share in Christian love the experiences and blessings which God has graciously bestowed upon our respective churches. "You have come as a friend and are now leaving as a brother," Bishop Haug of Württemberg wrote me in a kind, farewell letter.

I am convinced that the ecumenical vision of Dr. Trexler as evidenced in his establishment of a fellowship fund will prove to be one of the most blessed of his many contributions to our Church.

I have not come back the same person from Germany, nor will my future ministry be untouched by the blessings of this experience— for all of which thanks be to God and His faithful servant, Dr. Trexler.

A few days before leaving for Europe in the summer of 1952, Paul Hoffman called at my home. He begged me to inform him further regarding the "Christian gentleman" who had founded the fellowship which it was now his good fortune to enjoy. I told him briefly of Samuel's early struggles in the ministry, of the importance he attached to education and culture and to a firsthand knowledge and understanding of the people of other lands. "I feel very humble," young Hoffman said, "and I can only hope and pray that I may become one of those whom Dr. Trexler would have deemed a pastor *qualified* to serve his church."

This is what Samuel knew, I thought. He saw it all very clearly that summer afternoon when he confided to me his intention of founding the fellowship. These young men are the first of many who will follow. The column is endless.

During the last months of his life Samuel was surrounded as he had been all through the years by devoted friends. In their presence he was happy, even gay, and pleased as a child in their plans for his golden anniversary celebration. His pleasure in the companionship of books and his enjoyment of music was undiminished, his zest for life unabated. But the marks of suffering were on his face, and as the weeks passed he spent more and more time sitting quietly in the sunshine in Central Park— watching the people. Watching the people as he had done so many years in the parks, plazas and market places of the world.

Sometimes I shared these hours in the sun with him. There were days when everything he did was misted by pain. And other days when pain left him and he would speak with eager anticipation of journeys to be made—to Rome, the Riviera, Russia, India. "It is an invitation I cannot refuse," he said one afternoon, showing me a letter from Ivan Roek, General Inspector of the Hungarian Lutheran Church in Budapest. "I can see that," I said, after glancing at the letter, in which Dr. Roek had written: "We have to embrace every opportunity to know each other better to understand each other better."

I had hoped the advent of spring would restore his vitality. Instead, as the month of May advanced, his strength declined. Returned to the hospital, his anxiety was less for himself than for the friends who were looking forward to his golden anniversary. "I must not disappoint them," he said, and by an act of will he rose from his hospital bed two days before the service and prepared to meet them. "I am not to be dissuaded," he told the doctors and nurses with a smile.

"The Order of Thanksgiving marking the Fifty Years of Service of the Reverend Samuel Trexler to our Lord and to His Church" was held on the evening of May twenty-ninth, 1949 in the Lutheran Church of the Holy Trinity, New York City. Participating in the service were the Reverend Dr. Charles B. Foelsch, pastor of the church, the Reverend Dr. Frederick R. Knubel, president of the United Lutheran Synod of New York, the Reverend Walter K. Bock, president of the New York Conference of the Synod, and Samuel's nephew, Mr. Charles D. Trexler, Jr., who was then a candidate for ordination at the Lutheran Theological Seminary in Philadelphia.

Calling upon the congregation to join in thanksgiving to God for having called Samuel Trexler to the ministry, Dr. Knubel placed a beautifully wrought gold pectoral cross and chain about his neck—a gift of love and appreciation from his friends. Devotion and deep affection were reflected in the faces of the people who had come to rejoice with Samuel in this golden hour of his life and ministry.

He stood before them, gentle and unassuming. His voice was clear but faint, his countenance pale, his dark, understanding eyes etched in violet shadows. He seemed somehow remote, apart. (He is standing near the gates of Heaven, I thought, and the gates are open wide.) He held up before the congregation a leather-bound book not much bigger than the palm of his hand. It was his diary for 1899.

"This morning," he said, turning the leaves of the little gilt-edged book, "I went in to the innermost recesses of my book shelves and brought forth my diary for the year 1899 in which on May 29, the day of my ordination in the ministry, I entered these words:

Kneeling before the altar, we made those solemn vows 'with my whole heart' and were set apart. It was the most solemn act of my life and I pray for grace to live up to my vows."

The people listened intently. "Through these fifty years," Samuel said, closing the diary, "I have striven to live up to that prayer." Then he spoke to them of the gratitude in his heart. "The deepest note in my being tonight is that of gratitude—gratitude to God our heavenly Father, the Giver of every good and perfect gift, to my sainted parents, my gentle mother and my stalwart father, to my beloved Church for permitting me to work through my entire ministry in this challenging, ever-changing metropolis, and to my friends—ministers and lay-men—who have so loyally helped me to bring into reality my dreams."

The beautiful old church was radiant with flowers and candle beams. Over all, the immortal music of Johann Sebastian Bach wove its magic spell of spiritual exaltation. Churchmen, states-men, leaders of industry, men and women from the world of arts, letters and the theater, and humble, simple people—all friends of the years—sat together in the crowded pews. Their hearts were full of gladness and of a sadness deeper than words—for they saw his frailty. They brought to him messages of good will, of love and esteem from all over the world.

No more signal honor could have been paid him than the words spoken that night by those whose lives he had touched. Words that set a golden crown on his ministry, words that transcended the brightness of the cross flashing with golden fire against his heart.

"Thanks be to God for His wonderful ministry to the Church and humanity through your talented service, your sacrifice and devotion. Blessed is the Church through such a glorious ministry as you have rendered."

"You have endeared yourself to all vitally interested in the whole program of the Church. You have also through your belief in God and your love for the Master been an example for all of us to follow. Yours has been a glorious ministry through which the Lord Jesus Christ has touched the lives of innumerable men and women. We are grateful that our lives have touched yours."

"For your life so gifted, for your life consecrated to the spiritual enrichment of mankind we thank God. You have walked in the fullness of God's light and now the golden brilliance of that light lends luster to your life as it is lifted up before your fellowmen in this jubilant hour."

They called him a true Christian, a true Shepherd, a true Prince of the Church, a true man of God. Slender and erect in his black silk robe, walking very slowly, he ascended the steps to the high altar, and lifting his hands pronounced the benediction:

The Lord bless you and keep you, the Lord make his face to shine upon you. The Lord lift up His countenance upon you and give you peace.

There was a moment of utter stillness. Then a flood of triumphant music surged across the bowed heads, and voices rang out in the stirring hymn, *A Mighty Fortress is Our Lord.*

The people followed Samuel to the vestry rooms of the church to be near him a little longer, to press his hand, to fold him in the cloak of their love. Fearful for the emotional strain he was under, I made my way through the rejoicing crowds to his side. "You are tired?" I inquired anxiously. "No, no," he replied lightly. "I am not tired." His eyes were filled with happiness. He seemed reluctant to leave. I waited, uneasy in mind, watching the people clustered about him showering him with admiration, congratulations and good wishes. For each he had a warm smile, a word of appreciation for their presence.

At last, at last, we left the church. Motoring home through Central Park with our old friend, Mr. Samuel Strauss, we settled against the dark cushions of the limousine, absorbed in our thoughts. "It is an evening never to be forgotten," Mr. Strauss said, smiling affectionately at Samuel. "What a rich and blessed ministry yours has been!" When we paused for traffic lights Samuel lifted the gold cross, holding it up and turning it in his hand to catch the rays of the street lamps. "Is it not wonderful?" he said, his eyes shining, "to have been permitted to serve one's church for fifty years?"

When we reached home we went into the living room as always, to talk over the events of the evening. It was pleasant and peaceful sitting in the old damask chairs we had enjoyed for so many years. I looked at the beautiful old desk and table, the gleaming silver, the familiar paintings, the tiers of books, the red roses in the porcelain vase we had brought from Dresden—and it seemed to me the room had never appeared so rewarding in grace and friendliness. (We have traveled all over the world, I thought, but it always has been good to come home.)

"It was a happy event," I said aloud, "but it is good to be home." "This has been the happiest day of my fifty years in the ministry," Samuel replied with a sigh and a smile. I thought then of his mother—how she had once written him: You always speak of having such happy times . . . I hope it will continue so to the end . . .

Early the next morning after glancing at the papers, I called out: "Samuel, both the *Times* and the *Tribune* have first-page stories and wonderful pictures of your golden anniversary service!" "Bring them in," he answered, "and read them to me." "How are you feeling?" I asked. "None the worse for last evening, I hope?" "I'm feeling fine," he replied. "Let me see the papers . . ."

I sat down on the edge of his bed and began to read the newspaper accounts of the momentous service. Delighted, he listened eagerly. The door bell rang and I left him for a few minutes. One of the hall boys handed me an armful of letters and telegrams. When I returned to the bedroom my heart stood still. Samuel was lying on the floor. I knelt beside him. He had gone. At the golden climax of his ministry, full of joy and happiness and love, he had gone home.

Still, I could not believe it. "Trexler," I cried, "won't you please speak to me once more!" The silence in the room was deafening. A roaring thunder raged about me. After a while the roaring ceased, and I could hear fragments of a triumphant chorus rising, surging, falling away. Was this the music that had borne Samuel Trexler heavenward? Or was it a song of salutation to the beautiful morning, a hymn of welcome to a new day that had sealed his lips with a smile when his heart had suddenly ceased to beat?

I rose to my feet and, going back to the door, called to Earl Lynde, one of the hallmen in the lobby of the apartment. He must have seen death written on my face for without a word he ran quickly to me. We lifted Samuel to the bed. Earl stood there a moment looking into the tranquil face from which all trace of pain had gone. "We were never servants to Dr. Trexler," he said brokenly. "We were his friends."

The funeral service was held on the first of June in the church where three days before Samuel Trexler's golden jubilee had been celebrated. The scene within was the same—the same clergymen in the chancel, the same congregation in the pews, the same celestial music soaring above the bowed heads. All was the same except for a casket resting in front of the chancel. At the foot of the casket stood a cross of white flowers.

His singular gifts of the spirit made Samuel Trexler's death a wide and deep sorrow. Yet his funeral service was not marked by sadness. Rather it was a service dedicated to victory over death, a drama of homage to a triumphant spirit. A people's belief rose above grief. Such was the power and the glory of their faith that sorrow was transmuted into solemn joy. The tide of life had carried one they loved to unseen and unknown shores. He had returned to his Father's house. Hearts and voices were lifted in prayers of gratitude and hymns of praise.

The music ceased. There was no sound but the beating of

hearts. Beside me sat my loved niece, Katherine McCallen, only child of my sister Charlotte, who had come from her home in Knoxville, Tennessee, to be with me in this hour of ultimate loss. She looked at me with a tender smile and pressed my hand in hers. She, too, had loved him deeply.

Samuel Trexler's service to his Church had been long and distinguished. He had served the Lord with gladness and his mission had been completed in the joy of work well done. He had prayed for grace to live up to his vows and grace had been given him. A great spirit had entered the Church Triumphant. The people mourned the passing of a gallant crusader but they did not think or speak of him as dead.

The letters that sought to comfort me in my loneliness are overwhelming testimony to the love in which this man was held by all who knew him.

"I could not feel sorrow for so glorious an ending to his earthly mission. His saintly image will forever live in my memory as an inspiring and challenging example of all things good and true and beautiful. Samuel Trexler was a great man but it was not because he was great that he meant so much to so many. It was because he was so good. He took people into his heart. He brought his congregations nearer to the vision of God. It is impossible, try as we may, to imagine him as dead . . ."

"His life was rich and beautiful and humble. We remember with joy his radiant friendliness, warm handclasp, and above all the example of Christian faith which was the foundation of his life and ministry. It is hard to become reconciled to the fact that so great and so good a man has passed from this earth. But we look upon his death as but a transition from time to eternity . . ."

"From a peaceful source to a tranquil sea how unchanging was the course of his life, devoted to Christ and His Church and to the fulfillment of the ministry to which he was called. The world is a poorer place without his abiding faith and deep understanding and sympathies, but the love and faith he kindled in the souls of his fellowmen will live on forever and ever. I think of him in terms of many small and beautiful acts. Hands were never held up to Samuel Trexler in vain. It is a wonderful thought to know that his spirit will continue to influence the lives and work of young men through the Samuel Trexler Fellowship . . ."

Among the letters was one from his nephew, Charles Daniel Trexler, Jr. It was a letter that would have brought special happiness to Samuel for he was very fond of his brother's son. Written on the evening of the golden anniversary service, it arrived, alas, by marginal moments too late.

May 29, 1949

Dear Bishop,

That was a wonderful service and I'm so proud and happy to have had a share in it!

You were magnificent. I kept thinking of that little excerpt from Percy's *Reliques* which mother sent you, by me, when you were in hospital. You certainly were "the warrior" last night, "rising up to fight again!" I also kept thinking of what may well be, in your own eyes, the least important achievement of your ministry—the fact that you have been and are so greatly instrumental in leading the Lutheran Church out of the rather dusty German corner which it had favored and bringing it to the attention of the "outside world."

God bless you and keep you always,

Charles

When the stately and solemn funeral service in Holy Trinity Lutheran Church was over, the body of Samuel Trexler was taken to the little town of Bernville, Pennsylvania, where he was born. Here in the cemetery on the hill, in the presence of those who had known him as a boy, the committal was said by his loved brother Charles, and he was laid to rest under blue skies and a blanket of flowers in the hills of home.

EPILOGUE

DRIVING SLOWLY back along familiar roads we had traveled together so many years, a flood of memories surged through my mind. Memories of all the past, all the golden years. Memories of a long, long journey, full of adventure, excitement, surprise. Memories of many cities, many people, many roads.

Steel rails . . . fir-clad hills, waterfalls . . . Inaccessible slopes, vast flights of stairs, rural lanes and ribbons of light . . . Cathedrals filled with lighted candles, coronations consummated with jeweled crowns . . . Fields blackened by battle, snow falling on barracks, protocols and prayers . . . Castles, universities, embassies, opera houses . . . The Vatican, the White House, the Riviera, the Christ of the Andes . . . Milton Street in Greenpoint . . . Streets of New York, Berlin, London, Paris, Moscow, Belgrade, Jerusalem, Valparaiso, Guayaquil . . . The sunlit peace of Bar Harbor . . . Still waters and green pastures . . . Samuel standing in the pulpit of the Church of the Messiah, Samuel kneeling in the base hospital at Savenay, Samuel at his desk charting a world course for the Lutheran Church . . . A cross of white flowers . . . A cemetery on a hill . . . The body of Samuel in the cemetery on the hill. Milestones. Memories. Memories pounding like the surf against a sea wall. Memories demanding release, utterance . . .

Soon, soon now I shall be home, I thought, alone with these memories. We were approaching the city, the light-spangled city of New York . . . Suddenly it was clear to me what I must do.

Samuel! I called, I know now what I must do. Surely you hear me, Samuel, though you answer not. I must give voice to these memories. It will take a little time. We have come a long way and there is so much to remember. But this journey from the hills of Pennsylvania to palaces, parliaments and presidencies— this story of a man who believed in God must be told. I must bind together all the golden memories of your ministry in a book. I shall call the book *Sword of the Spirit*.

INDEX

Milhollands, the, 187
Miller, Rev. C. Armand, 76
Miller, Rev. E. A., 258
Miller, Rev. Dr. E. S. Brown, 112
Miller, Jared, 33
Miller, Rev. L. R., 112
Miller, Mary, 49
Miller, Rev. Dr. W. J., 62-63, 144
Millersburg, Pa., 1, 34, 113
Minersville, Pa., 44
Ministry, better education for the, 267-69, 271-75
Mollenauer, Rev. Ernest J., quoted, 171-72
Moody, Rev. Dwight L., 28, 40-41, 180
Moore, Edward Caldwell, 92, 96, 114
Morehead, Rev. Dr. John Alfred, 148-49, 190, 201, 203-06 (quoted); S. T.'s life of, 148, 170
Morgenthaus, the Henry, 166
Mott, John R., quoted, 210
Mount Holyoke College, 91
Mt. Joy, Pa., 44-45
Muhlemberg, Henry Melchior, 21, 37, 41, 99
Muhlemberg College, 21-32, 40-41, 99, 110, 140, 267
Mussolini, Benito, 169
Myerstown, Pa., 113

Napoleon Bonaparte, refs. to, 99, 192, 223
National Lutheran Council, 105, 148
Neurath, Baron Konstantin von, 195

New England, S. T. in, 40-41. *See also* names of towns.
New York City: visits to, 30-31, 41; residence in, 90 to end
New York Herald Tribune, 280
New York Lutheran Ministers Ass'n., 153, 156
New York Ministerium, 144-45, 155; merged with Lutheran Synod into United Lutheran Synod, 156-57
New York Times, 124, 171-72, 201, 262, 280; quoted, 155, 246-47
New Yorker, 124
Newsweek, 234
Niemoeller, Rev. Dr. Martin, 191, 195-96, 202-03, 209, 269
Normann, Pastor (Norway), 206
Norris, Mrs. Susie, 27, 152
North Heidelberg, Pa., 4
Northeastern University, 106
Northfield, Mass., S. T. in, 40-41, 180
Northkill, Pa. *See* Bernville.
Norway, S. T. in, 187
Norweb, R. Henry, 215
Nussbaum, Rev. Dr. Jean, 233, 238

Oberski, Rev. Dr. Janko, 235
Orellana, Francisco de, 213, 220-21
Ostojich, Rev. Fr. Bono, 239
Oswald, Rev. F. W., 71-73
Oxford, England, S. T. in, (conferences) 169, 209

Palestine, S. T. in, 187-89